James Fraser

Parochial and Other Sermons

James Fraser

Parochial and Other Sermons

ISBN/EAN: 9783337087470

Printed in Europe, USA, Canada, Australia, Japan

Cover: Foto ©Lupo / pixelio.de

More available books at **www.hansebooks.com**

PAROCHIAL

AND OTHER

SERMONS

BY THE

RIGHT REV. JAMES FRASER, D.D.

Second Bishop of Manchester

EDITED BY

JOHN W. DIGGLE, M.A.

VICAR OF MOSSLEY HILL, LIVERPOOL.
AUTHOR OF "GODLINESS AND MANLINESS," ETC.

ΑΠΟΘΑΝΩΝ ΕΤΙ ΛΑΛΕΙΤΑΙ

London

MACMILLAN AND CO.

AND NEW YORK

1887

RICHARD CLAY AND SONS,
LONDON AND BUNGAY.

PREFACE.

MOST of the Sermons in this volume were preached while Bishop Fraser was rector of the little country village of Cholderton. A few of the Bishop's later Sermons have been added: and their character clearly shows that, as "the child is father to the man," so the Rector of Cholderton was "father" to the Bishop of Manchester. The same spirit speaks through all the Sermons: only, in later life, its voice was enlarged by the expansion of its opportunities for utterance. Bishop Fraser was a remarkable instance of a man made more outspoken, and less official, by his accession to Episcopal dignity. To him, dignity was but a high form of duty, and his Episcopate simply a splendid means of winning men to their Lord.

The first eleven Sermons in the volume follow the Course of the Christian Year: the rest are, for the most part, arranged in chronological order; and all have been selected for the sake of their simplicity, their directness, and their association of practical daily conduct with fundamental spiritual principles. The perusal of these Sermons will—it is hoped—reveal to the Christian world how *deeply* the life of one of the most popular, the most influential, the best appreciated, Bishops of the Nineteenth Century was "hid with Christ in God." May not, indeed, *the true secret* of his great influence with the masses have been just this hidden "power" of the Christian's "endless life"?

THE VICARAGE, MOSSLEY HILL, LIVERPOOL.
Michaelmas Day, September 29, 1887.

CONTENTS.

I.
ADVENT THOUGHTS . . . .   PAGE 1

II.
THE DOMINION OF THE FLESH   13

III.
THE VALUE OF THE SOUL   23

IV.
THE TEMPTATION OF OUR LORD   30

V.
THE TEARS OF JESUS OVER JERUSALEM   40

VI.
THE CROSS OF CHRIST .   49

VII.
NOTES OF A SERMON ON THE LOVE OF CHRIST   59

VIII.

	PAGE
THE ANGELS' EASTER QUESTION	64

IX.

THE POWER OF CHRIST'S RESURRECTION, ESPECIALLY AS ILLUSTRATING THE DUTIES OF MASTER AND SERVANT   74

X.

THE GIFT OF THE HOLY GHOST   88

XI.

DIVERSITIES OF GIFTS   99

XII.

THE LABOURERS IN THE VINEYARD   105

XIII.

CHRIST OUR SACRIFICE AND EXAMPLE   115

XIV.

THE LIMITS OF CHRISTIAN LIBERTY   125

XV.

BIBLE KNOWLEDGE 134

XVI.

THE CHARACTER OF JEHU   144

XVII.

OUR SUFFICIENCY OF GOD   157

CONTENTS.

XVIII.
GOD A REFUGE IN TEMPTATION 167

XIX.
THE THREE CHILDREN IN THE FURNACE 177

XX.
THE RIGHTEOUSNESS OF THE LORD 189

XXI.
STANDING ON OUR WATCH 199

XXII.
THE NEED OF CIRCUMSPECTION 208

XXIII.
THE WARNING OF DINAH 220

XXIV.
CLEANSING THE TEMPLE 230

XXV.
SPEAKING PARABLES 239

XXVI.
STANDING ON HOLY GROUND 248

XXVII.
THE POWER OF CHRIST IN HIS MINISTERS 259

XXVIII.
THE PEACE OF CHRIST 272

XXIX.
THE WORK OF THE CHRISTIAN MINISTRY 280

XXX.
THE CHRISTIAN CHURCH AND THE CHRISTIAN CREED . . 292

XXXI.
THE KEYS OF THE KINGDOM 302

XXXII.
REALITY IN RELIGION 313

XXXIII.
THE RIGHTEOUSNESS OF A NATION 321

PAROCHIAL AND OTHER SERMONS

PAROCHIAL SERMONS.

I.
ADVENT THOUGHTS.

"Take heed, brethren, lest there be in any of you an evil heart of unbelief, in departing from the living God. But exhort one another daily, while it is called To-day, lest any of you be hardened through the deceitfulness of sin."—HEB. iii. 12, 13.

THE beginning of a new twelvemonth is always a solemn season. Whether it is the anniversary of a birth or a marriage, or a death of some dear relative, or of any special providence that has happened to ourselves, its yearly recurrence awakens at least a passing thought of joy or sorrow, of satisfaction or regret, in almost every mind.

The Church has chosen for *her* New Year's Day, the dreariest, darkest period of the natural year. Not in the joyous springtide, not in the bright and golden summer, not even in early, fruitful autumn, when the fields are white for harvest, does she proclaim the message of the coming of Christ, and bid us lift up our heads with joy. No! It is just when, if we cast our eyes upon the world without, everything looks cold and drear, when days are shortest, and nights are sharpest; when trees are naked and leafless, and the sun himself, as it were, hasteth to go down, and the powers of fruitfulness in nature seem suspended, and the whole earth presents a barren, dead, cheerless landscape to the view —nay, when the influences of the season make themselves most felt upon ourselves, when we are tempted to gather round our own firesides in self-seeking after comfort; when neighbourly visitings grow few and far between; when we are always too ready to grumble and complain of the cold or the wet, or the snow, or some other of the dispensations of Providence: then it is that the Church has chosen to recall to our minds the blessings, and hopes, and privileges, and tidings, which do not change like the physical seasons; to the realisation of which she is now inviting her children for more than the eighteen-hundredth time; which have been sounded in our ears ever since we were able to hear and understand, but which to most of us hitherto have seemed but as idle tales—have created no emotions, poured no consolation into our hearts, but which, in spite of past unbelief, and past unthankfulness, are again placed within our reach, again appeal to us with an ever-increasing earnestness and solemnity, again invite us to draw near and hear what great things God has wrought for us, whereof if our hearts are still susceptible to religious impulses at all, we may indeed rejoice.

These spiritual tidings, thus ever breaking forth anew, are a kind of counterpoise to the tokens of the material world, now visibly hastening to rottenness and decay. While we see outward things thus perishing and coming to an end, the Word of the Lord endureth as steadfast as ever in heaven. When the earth is sinking into a dull, torpid, unproductive state, and vegetation ceases, and the days grow short and dim, the Christian is bidden to awake, to put on the armour of light, to behold anew the glory of God in the face of Jesus Christ, to arise and shine, for behold His light is come. If the material sun seems niggard of his beams, and they both fall more coldly and are withdrawn more speedily, it does but give an emphasis, and help us to fix our thoughts more vividly on the Sun of Righteousness who has arisen with healing on His wings, the Church's Incarnate Lord of Light and Life, to whom all that find this world cold and cheerless, the helpless, the forlorn, the poor, the disconsolate, may come and find warmth, and sustenance, and consolation.

When the old heavens and the old earth are being wrapped in their winter's mantle of cold and darkness, the Church, the faithful interpreter of the mind of God, we may even say the Holy Ghost, true to His mission as a Comforter, directs our thoughts and lifts up our eyes to the new heaven and the new earth wherein dwelleth righteousness, wherein there is no darkness nor dreariness, neither need they a candle nor the light of the sun, for the glory of God doth lighten it, and the Lamb is the light thereof. The old prophecy is ever fulfilling itself more and more as time rolls on: " Behold darkness shall cover the earth and gross darkness the people;" but for the Church's comfort it is added, " The Lord shall arise upon thee, and His glory shall be seen upon thee." This day we are bidden to think of Christ, not so much as *coming*, as *come*. He is coming indeed, though the day and hour we know not. He is coming; though to the world, and the men of the world, and the work of the world, that advent will be anything but a spring of gladness and joy. It will be a token of the final dissolution of all those things which even His elect far too eagerly pursue, though in their inmost hearts they are convinced of their vanity. Still, it is to Jesus Christ as *come* rather than as coming, to ourselves as redeemed and adopted into God's family, men who have known and seen, and believed and tasted that the Lord is gracious, (men who are already partakers of a divine nature and an eternal weight of glory) that to-day's message, as I understand the Church's deliverance of it, especially refers. It is a day for reckoning up our privileges and claiming them, and making them indeed our own, a day for kindling thoughts and affections such as must have been present to St. Paul's mind when he contrasts the hopeless portion of outcast Esau, or the awe-stricken quakings of the Israelites at Sinai, with the liberty, the blessings, the confidence, the promises, the full assurance, that are the riches of the Gospel and the birthright of the believer in Jesus Christ.

Christ *is* come to us, and we are brought nigh—very nigh—to Him. He is in the midst of us now. He makes His coming *felt* in the hearts of those whom He calls His friends, and to whom He reveals Himself while He stands hidden from the world. We are all made citizens of a city in which God dwells, not indeed visibly, but sacramentally, spiritually. The ordinances of the Church, the humble and contrite hearts of its worshippers—these are the places of His abode, the temples in which He will dwell continually and take delight therein. St. Paul tells us all this very plainly, though under highly figurative images. He does not say we are coming, but we are *come* " unto Mount Sion, and unto the city of the living God, the heavenly Jerusalem, and to an innumerable company of angels, and to the general assembly and church of the firstborn, which are written in heaven, and to God the judge of all, and to the spirits of just men made perfect, and to Jesus, the mediator of the new covenant, and to the blood of sprinkling, which speaketh better things than that of Abel" (Heb. xii. 22-24). All these things are ours—ours to appropriate, ours to claim, ours to share, ours even to make our boast of, to be the things we should talk and think about when we rise up and when we lie down, when we walk by the way and when we are standing still, *if only* we can realise them. To these things, let me repeat, we are not only coming, but *come* (προσεληλύθατε Heb. xii. 22).

They are already given to us. They are our baptismal inheritance. They are the very things for which we are called Christians, and but for which we might as well have remained heathens. It is the office of *faith* to *make* them our own in such a sense that they cannot be taken from us, that, like our natural food they become assimilated to our system and form part of it, that they do indeed minister to our strength, and growth, and perfectness, making us more and more complete in Christ and conformable to Him. To have them as dead truths, articles of a creed which we repeat, but do not understand, a way of talking that we fall into but do not realise, to treat them all as *words*, not things, —ay, and things too, with life and a power in them—is really not to have them at all. It is all very well to talk of "the blood of sprinkling," but if it does not " sprinkle our hearts from an *evil conscience*," it has no cleansing efficacy for us. It is well to believe that "the blood of Jesus speaketh better things than that of Abel;" Abel's cried from the ground for vengeance, but Jesus pleads in heaven for mercy; but there can be no comfort in that belief to those whose ungodly lives rank them among the enemies of the Cross of Christ, to those who are as truly His murderers as those who nailed Him to the cursed tree, seeing that they "crucify the Son of God afresh, and put Him to an open shame."

It is indeed a blessed thought to every regenerate and truly converted soul to be reminded this day of what Christ has wrought for the souls and bodies of His redeemed : to be told of His laying aside His glory and visiting this earth in great humility, and taking upon Him the form of a servant, and being made in the likeness of men that He might call us brethren and redeem us from all iniquity, and make us His peculiar people and sanctify us with His Spirit, and change even our vile bodies into the likeness of His glorious body according to that mighty power whereby He is able to subdue even all things unto Himself.

This is the message of every Advent season. This fills the tongue of the Church, and characterises all her services to-day. On this theme she will continue to speak, in some one or other of its manifold applications, till Christmas-tide. And yet I wonder in how many of us does it awaken a responsive note of joy? How many of our hearts has it lifted up since we heard it, to higher views of duty, to nobler aspirations after holiness? We know that Christ has come. We can count the years that have passed since He came. There have been more than eighteen hundred Advent Sundays, in fact, if not in name, since He was first born, a helpless babe, in Bethlehem. But it is with far the most of us an uninfluential knowledge. Christ is come *to us*, but we are not drawn to *Him*. We are none the better, none the stronger, none the holier, none even the wiser, for His coming. We know that He came, that where He is we might be ever also, but we say, "No, not yet. Wait a little; by and by; a little more of the world, a little more pleasure, a little more *sin* first." And so we go on, from twenty to thirty, and from thirty to fifty, and from fifty to seventy, and from seventy to our grave, unchanged, unconverted, with affections still set on things below, with our life, instead of being hid with Christ in God, eaten out and corrupted by the carnalism of the world; these eternal truths, which ministered strength and comfort and guidance to the saints of God in every age, still remaining as dead, and lifeless, and external to us, as when, as children, we first learnt them in our Catechism or repeated them mechanically in our Creed—nay, much more, for we *had* a kind of simple faith in them *then*, which a selfish and worldly way of looking at things has destroyed *now*.

Christ has indeed come to us, but we have never cared to come to Him. He has, as it were, been standing at our doors and knocking, but we have never opened them and bid Him enter. He has come to us, but He has not taken up His abode with us. As in the days of His flesh, when He entered in triumph into Jerusalem, though He received enough *lip*-welcoming, though the Hosannahs of the multitude were long and loud, yet when night came on He found none who loved Him enough to offer Him a home, and He went out to Bethany, to the house of Lazarus and his sisters, and lodged there.

The world is loud enough in its outward acknowledgments of Christ's sovereignty, but in its heart of hearts it is little disposed either to treat or serve Him as a King. And the text explains the inconsistency. It is the leaven of the Pharisees, which is hypocrisy, that is still at work. It is the evil heart of unbelief, the principle of Sadduceeism, which makes us depart from the living God. It is the deceitfulness of sin which hardens us, and stops our ears, and closes our eyes to all but earthly carnal influences, so that we cannot be converted, nor Christ heal us.

I believe there is as much Pharisaism and Sadduceeism, and unbelief, and hypocrisy, and hardness of heart in the world now as ever there was. I believe that St. John's words about Christ are as applicable to our age as they were to the first age: "He came unto His own, and His own received Him not." We do not think we should get any good by receiving Him. We judge all things by the evidence of sight. We walk by a low, unscriptural standard. We think to put off or to blind God by pretexts, and compromises, and excuses; and so we have no power given unto us to become indeed the sons of God. We are still slaves and bondmen, unable to conquer the commonest daily temptations; unsteadfast even for a week to any good resolution; unsettled in our opinions and inconsistent in our practice; as far as possible from the stature of Christian men, because we neither love the strong meat, nor the hard exercise, nor the wholesome discipline that a state of manhood requires and implies.

You cannot measure the amount of your love and faith towards Christ by any surer standard than your inclination or disinclination to that Holy Sacrament which is His own appointed memorial of the work He came upon this earth to do. Do not talk about loving Christ, or believing in Him, when you will not do this in remembrance of Him. Do not talk about His being your "life," when you are strangers, or, at best, but irregular guests, at that heavenly feast which is His own ordained channel through which that life should be conveyed. Do not boast of being Christians, while you still refuse to be communicants. By your own act and deed you give your profession the lie. Be assured of this: as many of you of full age as turn your backs on that table—who do not feel the call to come a *personal* one, who act as though it were made to others, not to you— commit an act of unbelief, depart from the living God, cast away a promise and a blessing, add one more link to that chain of carnalism and indifference which is binding you hand and foot, and from which, unless you break through it speedily, you will one day find it impossible to release yourselves.

If you regret that you have so long delayed, if you really hope and wish to be ready, begin the work of preparation this very day; make it the spiritual work of Advent-tide. Be ready by Christmas Day, when the same gracious invitation will be renewed. As the text has it, "Exhort one another daily while it is called To-day, lest any of you be hardened through the deceitfulness of sin."

You know not how few opportunities, perhaps, remain to you for fulfilling one of the most essential of those obligations which have been lying upon you ever since you were confirmed. For Christ's first coming the world was in some measure prepared. Daniel's seventy weeks had expired. The sceptre had departed from Judah. There was a general expectation of the prophet foretold by Moses when Shiloh came. But at His second advent it will be otherwise. Of that day and hour knoweth no man. He will come as a thief in the night. He cuts down men often in a moment, in the midst of their dreams of long life, and security, and ease. To scarcely any does He give a longer notice than a few weeks or days. And is it for this wretched pittance of time, when perhaps our case will be as St. Paul's once was—" without, fightings, and within, fears," a thorn in the flesh, a messenger of Satan buffeting you—is it for this that we are reserving what should have been the labour of a life, the task of our days of health and strength? It is nothing less than downright, desperate madness to act in this way. Call it what we will, it *is* plain, practical unbelief and atheism. I call atheism not the *speculative* negation of a God, but the *practical* disowning Him; the living on day after day as if there were no such being as a present Saviour, a future Judge; the cold, heartless, irreverent formalism, which wears indeed the garments of religion, and talks its language, but whose words are shams, and its clothing a disguise.

"When the Son of Man cometh, shall He find faith upon the earth?" It was our Lord's question, but He has left it to our discernment to return the answer. Let it at least be our resolve, though living in an unbelieving and irreligious age, to see that this sin of unfaithfulness, however general and subtle, shall at any rate not cleave to us, or to those over whom we have any influence. Let us exhort one another daily while it is called To-day. It is an old saying, that "to-morrow never comes." "Behold, now is the accepted time, behold, now is the day of salvation."

Surely we have all of us, as St. Peter expresses it, "wrought the will of the Gentiles" too long already. We have gone on for too many years "pleasing ourselves." Let us at length try to please Christ, to do God's will, to walk after godliness, to seek peace, to bring down our high thoughts, to keep under our bodies, to lay aside every weight, to run with patience the race that is set before us, to conform our daily lives to the Gospel pattern, to be renewed in the spirit of our minds.

Advent is perhaps the fittest season in the whole

year for entering on such altered ways. It tells us of the great High Priest in whose blood past sins may be washed out; of the mighty and triumphant King in whose strength Satan may be conquered. It warns us more emphatically than any other season, of the danger of provoking His long-suffering. It assures us that "yet a little while, and He that shall come will come and will not tarry." And finally, it reminds us that our very profession as Christians means at least as much as this, that "we are not of them who draw back unto perdition; but of them that believe to the saving of the soul."

Preached—Cholderton, Advent Sunday, 1853.

II.

THE DOMINION OF THE FLESH.

"Know ye not that they which run in a race run all, but one receiveth the prize? So run, that ye may obtain. And every man that striveth for the mastery is temperate in all things. Now they do it to obtain a corruptible crown; but we an incorruptible. I therefore so run, not as uncertainly; so fight I, not as one that beateth the air: but I keep under my body, and bring it into subjection: lest that by any means, when I have preached to others, I myself should be a castaway."—1 COR. ix. 24—27.

THE Bible, amid its manifold revelations, enlightens us very little on a subject which long has puzzled, and still is puzzling, philosophers—the mysterious law which connects together in one tabernacle our bodies and our souls. All that it concerns itself with telling us is, how both body and soul, as integral elements of our nature, are to be disciplined and fashioned and subordinated to God's glory and our own salvation. In one passage St. Paul teaches us that "the body is for the Lord;" in another, that we are to "glorify God both in our bodies and our spirits, which are His." He intimates that nothing short of this was his notion of an entire and perfect sanctification.

There were, in St. Paul's day, several speculative theories about the body, coming originally from the East, and afterwards called, when formulated, "Manicheism," which made this teaching very necessary to be borne in mind. These several theories, though speculatively the same, bore fruit in very different practical results. Starting with the maxim that all matter, by which the Manicheans meant the material substance, of which this visible world as well as the human body is made, was the work of an evil principle, itself the seat of evil, and hopelessly and radically corrupt, they taught their followers that their bodies, instead of being, as the Bible teaches us, created by God, were alien and mischievous appurtenances. They taught that the body, instead of being capable of use in the service of God, and sanctified by His Spirit, and partaker equally with the soul of the redemption which Christ has accomplished for all flesh, was a despicable and burdensome thing; a shackle and a hindrance on the nobler aspirations of the soul; a veil shutting out the light of the knowledge of God from their hearts; a vile and earthly organism in which the spirit of evil was permitted for a while to imprison man's higher nature.

The practical issue of these tenets was, in different instances, widely different. They led some—such as Tertullian and others of a somewhat morbid temperament—to a stern and gloomy asceticism such as is even now largely practised in the East, thinking to please God and overcome Satan by acts of painful, self-imposed mortification, denying themselves the most pure and innocent bodily pleasures. There was, of course, the usual reaction. Nature re-asserted herself. If they could conquer an unruly member, they failed to tame a rebellious will. In the history of many of these fanatics we find that, out of the dying embers of a carnal lust, arose the yet fiercer flame of religious intolerance or spiritual pride. Others, and those by far the larger number, the sensual part of this sect as opposed to the intellectual, found in this doctrine a most convenient outlet for every carnal desire and wanton appetite. If the body was thus vile and worthless, it mattered not how it was used, or what became of it. In yielding to the motions of sin, which dwelt in their members, they did nothing that could either taint or degrade the soul. That they had bodies was no fault of theirs. They could not help their corrupt and vicious tendencies: they were but following a law of their nature for which they were not responsible. And so deluding themselves into the notion that they could keep their souls pure while they let their bodily appetites range unrestrained, they gave themselves up recklessly to the wildest riot and most shameless licentiousness.

Now these views, monstrous and soul-destroying as they became in their development and moral results, took their rise not so much in absolute falsehood as in perversion and misapplication of the truth. Indeed, there is something in the human mind so naturally alien and abhorrent from what is false, that no system of religion or morals based on an absolute lie has ever been able to maintain or propagate itself in the world. It must have a foundation of truth, however slender, to rest upon.

These heretical teachers started with a true principle which is thus expressed by the author of the Book of Wisdom: "The corruptible body presseth down the soul, and the earthly tabernacle weigheth down the mind that museth upon many things." But they misapplied it. They borrowed St. Paul's image of "a law of sin in the members warring against the law of the mind;" but they perverted it. They were not content with saying that the body was often Satan's *instrument*, but they affirmed it was his *creation*. It was not enough to assert that in our bodies, in their unregenerate state, dwelleth no good thing, but they must further maintain that nothing good could be made to dwell there. It was the old perplexity—the origin of evil. The consciousness of concupiscence (which they could not otherwise explain than by admitting the existence of a co-ordinate evil principle in the moral and physical government of the world), led them to lose sight of, and practically to deny, those two great doctrines of the evangelical revelation—that our bodies as well as our souls are equally God's creation, and that both have been equally redeemed by His Son.

What people thought and did eighteen hundred years ago would not be of much interest to us, or at least, not of much edification, did not the same notions and practices, though under other forms and names, prevail now. Manicheism, as far as the name goes, has been dead and buried long ago, but its essential principles remain, and indeed were perhaps never more active than they are at the present time. By "its essential principle," I mean the notion that the use or abuse of the body is a thing almost entirely independent of the well- or ill-being of the soul It is a very pernicious notion, and the passage of Scripture which I have chosen for my text gives me an opportunity, which I am glad to take, of noticing it. Let me first say a few words in explanation of the *image* which St. Paul employs, for you must have perceived that his language is figurative.

He talks of a race and of striving for the mastery. Such language must have conveyed a very vivid idea to the minds of Corinthian readers, in the immediate neighbourhood of whose city one of the great national games of Greece was celebrated every fourth year. He pictures to them their foot-races and their boxing-matches, in which the noble youths of the nation strove for the mastery. He reminds them of the careful training, the strict and temperate diet, the many restraints, the painful and laborious discipline to which these ardent natures voluntarily submitted themselves. And all for the triumph of a moment, for that brief shout of applause that hailed the conqueror, for a quick fading crown of a few worthless parsley leaves! Every Greek felt his heart stir within him when he heard tell of those exciting scenes; and St. Paul, like an instructed scribe, knew well how to bring out of his treasures of earthly wisdom persuasives to a life of heavenly holiness.

It is an argument, *a fortiori*, from weaker to stronger ground, from lower motives to higher. If a meed of earthly honour could so brace men's energies and kindle their hearts, how much more an eternal recompense of reward! If a corruptible wreath could provoke such emulation, and sustain through so much self-imposed mortification, how much more a crown of glory! If the praise of their assembled friends and countrymen was so quickening and inspiring, how much more the approving voice of God and the rejoicing sympathies of the holy angels!

He calls on them all to practise the same self-discipline in their spiritual race which was allowed to be a needful preparation for a temporal. He tells them they would as much require a wary and resolute attitude in their combat with Satan, as to repel the buffetings of any fleshly adversary. He gives them the result of his own experience, the secret by which he had been himself enabled to stand his ground. He had "kept under his body and brought it into subjection." He had fixed his eye upon the mark—"the prize of his high calling in Christ Jesus"—and he suffered nothing of inferior worth to distract his gaze. He had planted his foot firmly, and dealt his blows lustily and with a definite aim. He should continue to do so till his warfare was accomplished, his victory achieved. It would be a life-long struggle, he knew. To his dying day he would still have some sinful lust to subdue, some fleshly member to mortify, some new artifice of Satan to baffle, some impatient temper of his own to reprove. His high gifts as a preacher did not exempt him from the ordinary temptations and responsibilities of a man. He might win the souls of others and lose his own. He might see others—the poor, the halt, the maimed, the blind—welcomed by Christ; and himself—the gifted, the intellectual, the master-mind—a castaway. Or, like

Demas, he might continue faithful and true for a while, but relaxing his watchfulness and self-control, the world might prove too strong for him after all.

His one security, at least the only one he mentions here, and therefore in his eyes the chiefest and most important, was the *mastery of his body*. No doubt he had—and all men have—trials of the spirit as well as temptations of the flesh. Satan surely directed his assaults against the subtler and more refined elements of his nature, as well as against the grosser and more corporeal. But he says nothing about them here. Indeed, in another very remarkable passage, where he does speak of a directly spiritual temptation, it was through an infirmity of the body that his merciful Father saw fit to open a way of escape for him. The natural tendency to spiritual pride was kept down by the presence of painful bodily suffering. It enabled him to realise his own natural helplessness. He kissed the rod that smote him: or, to use his own simple and devotional words, "he rather gloried in his infirmities that the power of Christ might rest upon him; for when he was weak then was he most truly strong."

There can be no doubt, I think, in the mind of any person who ever stops to examine the state of his own soul, that the temptations to which we are most commonly exposed, by which our faith and patience are most sorely tried, and the stoutness of our Christian armour most effectually proved, reach us through our fleshly, rather than our spiritual nature—assault the body before they hurt the soul. Where we are tempted once to a simply spiritual sin, we are drawn a dozen times into a carnal excess. Over-eating, over-drinking, over-dressing, pampering our appetites, increasing our comforts, uttering falsehoods, or propagating ill-natured stories with our tongues, these are our commonest, most easily besetting sins.

Some of you may be rather surprised to hear them called "sins" at all; you would rather term them by a softer name; but I prefer speaking of them as the Bible speaks. Nay, the more directly spiritual sins almost always wear some outward and bodily form. It is through the body that they pass from an *intention* to an *act*. Pride, selfishness, malice, hypocrisy, covetousness, always enlist the body in their service, and can seldom be gratified without its aid. It must be the nature of angels, and not of human beings constituted as we are, that can commit sin by the spirit alone.

Take that commonest and most hateful of sins, selfishness; it almost always—I may say always—has some palpable, tangible end in view. It displays itself in the wish to get more than one's fair share of the good things of this life—more money, or more comforts, or more dainty food, or more amusement. These are the things, our Blessed Lord tells us, which overcharge the heart, and make it slow to perceive, and still slower to prepare itself for the day of His coming. These are the things, St. Paul tells us, which are pursued so eagerly by the enemies of the Cross of Christ. These are the things of which St. John warns us so earnestly. "If any man love the world, the love of the Father is not in him. For all that is in the world, the lust of the flesh, the lust of the eye, and the pride of life"—all of them you will observe material objects of desire—"is not of the Father, but of the world."

The Church has wisely set apart the season of Lent to bring these things more pointedly to our remembrance. Our appetites and desires ought, of course, always to be under control, never suffered to run into excess, but at this season more especially so. The Christian feels that it is even something more. It is a preparation for Easter. It is a night of sorrow issuing into a morning of joy; a dying with Christ, enabling him to rise with Him; a condemnation of self that there may be a forgiveness by God; a putting restraint upon the body that there may be the freer scope to the energies and aspirations of the soul.

God give us all grace to spend it, not in formal abstinence, but in real self-mastery: not that we may "seem unto men to fast," but that we may humble our hearts before "Him Who seeth in secret"; not in proud contempt of a godly ordinance, but with a faithful earnestness seeking to use it to the edification of our souls.

Our Lord has told us that there are some evil spirits which go not forth "but by prayer and fasting." It were well if we looked into our hearts and saw what messenger of Satan has longest maintained his dominion there. Have we ever tried to cast him forth by these means? He has defied us hitherto. Are we content to remain in bondage to him till our dying day? Are uncleanness, and surfeiting, and drunkenness, and comfort-loving to make us their slaves without our so much as "striving for the mastery?"

Let us not be so cowardly and faithless as to think so! Let us throw the same energy into our strivings to win heaven as we so often do into our efforts to gain the world. If to win a corruptible crown can make us submit to much that would be otherwise irksome and wearying, how much more an incorruptible? If we are often content to forego immediate gratifications in the hope of future accumulated gain, how should we be encouraged to endure all things for the Gospel's sake, when we are bidden believe—and God's saints have ere now proved—that the "light affliction, which is but for a moment, worketh for us a far more exceeding and eternal weight of glory."

Preached—Cholderton, Septuagesima Sunday, Feb. 12th, 1854; and also on Feb. 5th, 1860.

III.

THE VALUE OF THE SOUL.

"What is a man profited if he shall gain the whole world and lose his own soul? or what shall a man give in exchange for his soul?"—ST. MATT. xvi. 26.

THE value of the soul is beyond the calculus of human arithmetic. We have nothing to measure it by. In a sense, it is like God Himself—immeasurable, incomprehensible, incomparable, infinite.

The soul is that which is distinguished in man from his body; it is that which constitutes his personality; that in which dwells his consciousness, the seat of his will, his conscience, his affections, his desires, his imagination, his reason, his mind. It is this of which we have to try to ascertain the value.

The difficulty is aggravated by the introduction into this sphere of thought, by Christian philosophy, of a new idea—a new word, the word *pneuma* or spirit, a metaphorical word, equivalent to breath. So St. Paul, speaking as it were philosophically, as though these three elements made up the whole man, says, "I pray God your whole spirit and soul and body be preserved blameless unto the coming of our Lord Jesus Christ."

(1 Thess. v. 23.) A very familiar distinction with St. Paul is that between the natural man (*psuchikos*) and the spiritual man (*pneumatikos*): the man with a soul, the man with a spirit. (Compare 1 Cor. ii. 14, 15, and xv. 44—46.)

Greek philosophy knew nothing of the spiritual man, because it knew nothing of the Incarnation, nothing of the work of a Divine Spirit in the world. Plato talked of man's mind and intellect, but not of his spirit. He believed in a state in which the soul, delivered from the burden of the flesh, should see God face to face. To him, as to the Christian, the value of the soul was beyond price. But the soul of the Greek philosopher's psychological system was a strange phenomenon: the home at once of noble desires, inexplicable yearnings after a beauty and a truth more than earth could offer; yet a home also, of foul lusts, loose, unbridled appetites, violent passions and desires.

In vain did Plato teach how to restrain the passions; Aristotle how to purge them; the Stoics how to extinguish them. Man remained in the hands of the philosophers an inexplicable enigma, struggling to be free, yet helplessly a slave: Godlike at once and brutish; full of the noblest thoughts, full also of the foulest, basest desires.

But the problem of man's existence was not destined to remain insoluble for ever. In the fullness of time, when the world was waiting for Him—the eager expectation of the creature waiting for the manifestation of the Son of God—Christ came, and with Him there entered a new power into the moral world. Old things passed away, all things became new.

The *psuche*, or soul, to them that are in Christ Jesus, to the children of the kingdom, to those born again, has become a new creation, a spirit, or *pneuma*. The soul is endued with new powers. Ever heir to an immortal destiny, it has become conscious of this destiny. Ever groaning under the bondage of sin, it has found a means to set itself free. Its faculties are the same, but its powers are new. It is no longer weak through the flesh, it is strong in Christ. Its vision is clearer; its horizon ampler; its hopes grander; its faith deeper; there is a transfiguring power at work within. It is in the world but not of the world; its home is elsewhere. Its joys are supernatural; the air it breathes divine.

This is the condition of the regenerate soul: a spirit, tabernacling in a body, but instinctively revolted by sin; vindicating its title to a divine origin and a divine destiny by the more than human power which, in great spiritual exigencies, it is enabled to put forth in its wrestling with the mighty powers of darkness that are arrayed against it. The true Christian saint is a man, and yet more than a man. He is a spiritualised man: a man of like passions with his fellows, but unlike them, because he is a partaker of a divine nature, endowed with a divine power.

I wish you to realise the value of this part of your complex nature by which you feel, think, reason, will, desire, act. It is the part of you which is conscious of a destiny.

The body, as such, has no destiny; at any rate no consciousness of one. It is, as has been well said, "mine, not me." We shall be judged, indeed, as we are told, "according to the deeds done in the body." But the real agent in those deeds, the responsible agent, is not the body, but the soul. The body will rise again, yet hardly the same body. "Thou sowest not that body that shall be." It will be a spiritual body, one more fitted, that is, for the abode of a glorified and transfigured spirit. But the soul that we have now is the same soul we shall have then. There will be no solution in the continuity of its existence. We shall not have a different personal identity. We shall be the same. And *we* are what our *spirits* are.

And so there is no need of taking extravagant flights of rhetoric—of saying that one single soul outweighs in value all that the earth contains besides; but at any rate, there is nothing *to you* comparable in value to the value of your soul. The eternity you dream of will be to you what your soul makes it. "The kingdom of God is within us," as Christ spake; in the sense that within us—in our souls—we are each of us building up slowly, imperceptibly, but surely, inevitably, our heaven or hell.

If you can, however inadequately, measure the relation of eternity to time—of the unknown, infinite hereafter, to the fleeting, precarious, uncertain "now," you have in the same proportion a measure of the value of the soul.

Another and hardly less important element in this value is to be found in the relation of the higher faculties of the soul—and especially of the supreme faculty, conscience—to our physical and even to the subordinate parts of our moral being. The spiritualised soul, raised above the things of sense and time, holding mysterious yet strengthening communion with God, full of yearnings "after what is good, and pure, and honest, and lovely," is, and was intended to be, the dominant element in human nature.

Bishop Butler has shown, in his philosophical sermons, that "to live according to nature" does not mean to live according to every impulse, passion, appetite that may happen to be most imperious at the moment, but to live in obedience to the conscience, the sovereign faculty of the soul. To follow every wayward passion, to be led by every earthly appetite, is the surest of all ways to degrade and brutalise the soul.

For though the soul is not of the body, it can be depraved through the body. St. Paul talks of the motions of sin working in his members, working in him all manner of concupiscence and bringing forth fruit unto death. (Rom. vii. 5-8.) Diverse as they are in their natures—the one material, the other immaterial, the one regnant, the other legitimately subordinate—there is a most mysterious connection between the body and the soul. A pampered body produces a lethargic spiritual state. Wild desires are set loose within us when we feed high, or drink deeply, or sleep in over softness, or in any other way choose for ourselves the brutish life. And so our wise Prayer-Book bids us "subdue the flesh and the spirit;" and St. Paul cries, "I keep under my body"; and the complete sanctification of which he speaks to the Thessalonians includes body, soul, and spirit.

You may, it is true, put a false measure of value on your soul. You may think it so exceeding precious to you that it shall become the only thing you care for in the world. You may become absorbed in the one work, as you phrase it, "of saving your soul." And this will make your religion selfish, narrow, idolatrous. You will reckon yourself of the elect, and look with a proud pity upon the outer world, lying dead, as you deem it, in its trespasses and sins. You will become a Pharisee, not of the narrow Jewish type, but of the equally narrow Christian type. You will count yourself to be righteous, and "despise others." You will lay down for the governance of your conduct all kinds of minute, scrupulous rules, instead of being content to be guided with a few great controlling principles.

And you will gradually lose all sympathy, all desire to share, or even to know, the struggles, the triumphs, the joys, the sorrows, of the thousands of human souls that are dear to God, possibly as dear to Him as you are. You will make no sacrifice, attempt no self-denial, practise no large-hearted beneficence, engage in no generous scheme for the melioration of the race; but will live a shrivelled, stunted, useless life, concerning yourself only with the salvation of your own soul. This is to find the soul and yet to lose it. This is, as a heathen poet phrased it, "For sake of life, to lose the very cause of living."

Friend, thou art a member of a vast body. Thou art in a Communion of Saints. Thine own salvation will be but advanced by doing something to promote the salvation of thy fellow men. If thou hast the light, it was given thee to set it in a candlestick, that others might see it too.

Christ did not take His people out of the world, but left them to fight their oft-times weary battle in it, because the world needed them. The Church is "the salt of the earth." One great element in the value of a soul is its value to the souls of other men. "When thou art converted, strengthen then thy brethren." A selfish religion can hardly have been touched by the breath of Christ. "None of us liveth unto himself," cries noble Paul, "and none of us dieth to himself. Whether we live or die, therefore, we are not our own, but the Lord's."

Preached—Lancaster, Ash Wednesday, 1872.

IV.

THE TEMPTATION OF OUR LORD.

"Then was Jesus led up of the spirit into the wilderness to be tempted of the devil."—St. Matt. iv. 1.

I cannot pretend to explain to you the whole mystery of our Blessed Lord's temptation. Why He condescended to listen to the voice, and to be assailed by the wiles of that fallen angel whose kingdom He had Himself come down from heaven to destroy, is a fact for which I could venture to give you very few reasons. We must be content to receive it as one of those mysteries which as yet we can see but as "through a glass darkly," and which wait for their fuller illumination till the day when "we shall know even as we are known."

There are some considerations, however, which may help to a partial apprehension of some of its significances.

The Son of God took upon Him the nature of man to be a kind of new root of a regenerate humanity; or, as St. Paul expresses it, "to be the first-born of every creature." He has recovered for us all that we lost in our first forefather. As Satan was the instrument of our fall, so also was he the instrument of our regeneration. As he conquered human nature in Adam, so he was conquered by human nature in Christ.

Our Blessed Lord saved men by tasting their sorrows as well as by bearing their sins. "He was tempted *in all points*," we are told, "like as we are." And so we see the temptation of our Blessed Lord was necessary:—1, To the destruction of Satan; 2, To our deliverance from bondage; and 3, For the more effectual performance of His own mediatorial work. Much of this, after all, we cannot profess to understand; and more than this, so far as I am aware, the Holy Spirit has not seen fit to reveal.

But however imperfectly we may comprehend what I will venture to call the *theology* of our Blessed Saviour's struggle with the wicked one in the wilderness of Judea—as it plainly is a matter rather for contemplative reverence than for speculative curiosity —yet the practical lessons we may draw from it are so important, though often so entirely overlooked in the presumptuous attempt to explain its mysteries, that time may be well spent in considering it under this view.

It is in this, as in so many other points of His blessed life on earth, we get out of our depth the moment we begin to speculate about Him as our *Atonement;* but we never need feel the least difficulty, if we will only take moderate pains, in gathering up the lessons of wisdom that are to be drawn from His *Example.* And the reason is obvious. The former is proposed simply to our *faith*, but the latter to our *imitation* also. We have but to believe the one; we have further to follow, to be made conformable to, the other. As St. Peter groups the two together, "Christ also suffered for us, leaving us an example that we should walk in His steps."

Let us see, then, whether the Scripture narrative of our Lord's temptation, in its *exemplary* aspect, may not be made, not only perfectly intelligible, but deeply profitable to us all.

(1) And, first, we see that no real or imaginary nearness to God, no fancies of election nor reality of personal righteousness, no earnestness of faith or long continuance in well doing, can secure us against the crafts and assaults of that ghostly enemy, who, "as a roaring lion, walketh about, seeking whom he may devour." Our Blessed Lord had just come up out of the waters of Jordan, full of the Spirit of God; had just been sealed as the beloved Son of the Father by a voice from heaven; had just by His baptism pledged Himself, as it were, " to fulfil all righteousness," " when the tempter came to Him."

And mark how the tempter began by assailing Him *through* those very spiritual prerogatives which the heavenly voice had just proclaimed to the world. " If Thou *be* the Son of God,"—if that voice spake true—if thou wouldst be received as such by men, prove it by a sign; faint not with hunger here in the wilderness, put forth thy creative power, " command that these stones be made bread." It was an artful suggestion, an appeal to a presumptuous abuse of spiritual privileges, addressing itself to the will through the selfish impulse of a bodily appetite. It was thus he had succeeded in his first machination with the mother of us all. He convinced poor foolish Eve—whose self-trustful heart was all too ready to listen to his smooth lies—that the forbidden fruit was not only good for food and pleasant to the eye, but also that it was only God's jealousy that had laid an interdict upon it, as though He wished to keep our first parents in a degraded condition, and knew that "in the day they ate thereof" their eyes should be opened, and they should "be as gods, knowing good and evil."

If there had been any pettiness, or vanity, or self-seeking in the nature of the Holy Jesus; if He had thought of Himself and His own glory, instead of being absorbed by the purpose to do His Father's will; if He had been impatient to be acknowledged as the "Son of God with power," and had snatched eagerly at the Crown before He had taken up the Cross, He too might perchance have yielded to the enemy of souls, and by prematurely grasping at a title which as yet the world in general were not prepared to own, but the confession of which His obedience and sufferings would ere long extort from the reluctant lips even of those who shed His blood,—He might have marred and hindered, if not have entirely frustrated, the work that His Heavenly Father had given Him to do.

At least, humanly speaking, such a result is plainly supposable. The whole narrative implies that it was a real *temptation;* and if so, then, addressed to a human nature which, as it was in all things like to ours, must also have been open to the *possibility* of a fall. What sustained Him, both now and through His whole aftercourse of suffering, was that Spirit—that Indwelling Consubstantial Divinity—of which we are told that it was given Him by His Father, "not by measure," but in all its fullness.

But the point for us to notice is that the very richness and plenitude of our privileges may become an instrument of our temptation. If Satan can only persuade us to think that because we are the sons of God there shall no harm happen unto us, "that He has given His angels charge over us," and so we need exercise no forethought, no watchfulness of our own; if he can puff us up with spiritual conceit, get us to talk of our being "children of the light, and all the world around us lying in wickedness,"—statements in all of which there is a certain mixture of truth, and which thus become the more dangerous and delusive,—his victory is won; he claims us for his own both in body and soul.

Have you never heard people talk in this way whose daily lives give every word they utter the lie? Have you never heard persons boasting of their faith, though they gave no proof of it by their works; relating their experience of conversion, though the grace that has wrought such wonders has not been sufficient to cast out the spirit of uncleanness or pride or selfishness from their hearts; lamenting the darkness and rebellion of others, while the most careless stander-by can see that they themselves are walking quite uncertainly, often stumbling very grievously in the way?

Such forms of spiritual self-delusion are rife on all sides of us. There are thousands who make their boast very loudly of Christ now, whom I fear, at the great day when He comes as Judge, He will never own; thousands who say, " Lord, Lord," " who shall never enter into the kingdom of heaven." It is in these dreams of security that the greatest dangers lie. It is when men say " peace and all things are safe, that sudden destruction cometh upon them, and they cannot escape." It was when he was dreaming of ease and comfort for many years that the soul of that rich man in the parable was " required " of him. It was when David had, as he thought, gotten him the victory over all his enemies round about him and was sitting at peace in his own house at Jerusalem that he fell into that deadly sin that destroyed all his bright visions of happiness, and though on his true repentance he was forgiven as to the eternal consequences of his sin, yet as a warning to them " who afterwards should live ungodly," the effects of the sin brought down his gray hairs with sorrow to the grave. And so each of us has great need to remember St. Paul's wise caution, if haply we see a brother fall, while we by God's mercy are enabled to stand our ground, " Be not high-minded, but fear." Let the sight of human frailty in others only make us the more apprehensive and mistrustful of our own.

(2) The story of our Blessed Lord's temptation shows us, further, what weapons we must use if we too would conquer Satan. Jesus Christ overcame by a faith anchored on God's Word. It was by Scripture rightly

understood and rightly applied that He baffled the sophisms of the Wicked One. St. Paul bids us take "the sword of the Spirit, which is the word of God." But "the word of God" only becomes "the sword of the Spirit" in the hands of a soldier who can wield it skilfully. Satan could quote Scripture for his purpose. St. Peter tells us of some, the like of whom have been found in every age, who "wrest the Scriptures to their own destruction." Hence the frequent admonitions of Holy Writ "to rightly divide the word of truth"; to "prophesy according to the proportion of faith"; to "compare spiritual things with spiritual." Otherwise our Bibles may easily become a snare to us. If we read them for any other purpose than that of godly edifying in the faith, they *will* become a snare to us. They will fill us with a thousand fancies that are merely the offspring of our foolish prejudices or diseased imaginations.

It is indeed sad to see that Blessed Book appealed to, as it so often is, simply to furnish weapons for controversy; to strengthen men in their uncharitable judgment of their neighbours, to bind them only the more strongly to error; to encourage them in their courses of self-pleasing and self-will. It was put into our hands by God's providence for far other ends than these,—to teach us to know ourselves; to make us feel our weakness; to lead us to look to God for strength; to open our eyes to the duties that lie at our feet; to enable us to walk, not, as the Gentiles walk, " in the vanity of their mind," but soberly, righteously, and godly in this present world; and so to enlighten us about God's purposes concerning us, as under all circumstances never to leave us in doubt for a moment as to what He would have us to do.

(3) Another noticeable fact in our Saviour's temptation is one related by St. Luke, though not mentioned by St. Matthew, that "when the devil had ended all the temptation he departed from Him *for a season.*" We know when it was that he returned to renew his malignant purpose of frustrating man's salvation, for Christ Himself intimated it to His disciples. While sitting with the twelve in that upper chamber at Jerusalem, on the night of His betrayal, He said, "Hereafter I will not talk much with you, for the prince of this world cometh, and hath nothing in Me." He was coming to more than one on that memorable night. He had already entered into one heart—that of the traitor Judas—and filled it full of all iniquity. He was even now desiring to have the bold but unstable Peter, that he might "sift him as wheat." He was already spurring on the emissaries of the chief priests and scribes to their dastardly and vindictive purpose. To all these he came, and not in vain. He found in one some sin, in another some infirmity, to lay hold of and use for his ends. On the Lord Jesus alone—He who was still learning "obedience by the things which He suffered"; He in whose will there was the same strong conflict manifested in Gethsemane that always takes place when the path of duty seems hard, and our indolent, ease-loving natures instinctively shrink from it—did Satan spend every weapon of his fiendish armoury in vain. There were the great drops of sweat,

as of blood, bearing witness to the throes of that struggle, the tremendous issues of that agony. But there was nothing in that pure and guileless and loving heart on which temptation could fasten or where Satan could find a home. There was the resistance unto blood in the strife against sin. This is the part of our Blessed Lord's example that St. Paul especially bids us contemplate. We may have beaten off Satan once, ay, twice and oftener, but he is not one to be easily dismayed. Like all who play a desperate game, he will return to what is to him the business of his life again and again.

You know the story of the unclean spirit cast out of his house, yet anon finding means to enter again with "seven other spirits more wicked than himself," and dwelling there with sevenfold more than his former tyranny. He is always spoken of throughout the Bible as a "*strong* man." St. Paul, as it were, exhausts the resources of language to make us feel the fearfulness of the strife in which we are for life engaged. "We wrestle not," he says, "against flesh and blood, but against principalities, against powers, against the rulers of the darkness of this world, against spiritual wickedness in high places."

Good need have we, therefore, to take unto us "the whole armour of God"—prayer, and fasting, and Holy Scripture, and continual circumspection—that we may be proof against devices which it is impossible wholly to avoid. Be assured that in no other way is an escape open to us. The careless, the prayerless, the selfish, the unwise are overcome of Satan as often as he thinks it worth his while to bind them in his chains. The slightest temptation is enough to unsettle their steadfastness and to draw them from the path of duty. The Lord Jesus has taught us, by the manner in which He met His temptation, how, and how only, Satan may be conquered. When, therefore, you are tempted, resist the temptation in Christ's strength and in Christ's way, ever remembering that "to him that overcometh will He grant to sit with Him on His throne, even as He also overcame, and is set down with His Father on His throne."

Preached—Cholderton, First Sunday in Lent, March 5th, 1854.

V.

THE TEARS OF JESUS OVER JERUSALEM.

"And when He was come near, He beheld the city, and wept over it, saying, If thou hadst known, even thou, at least in this thy day, the things which belong unto thy peace! but now they are hid from thine eyes."—St. Luke xix. 41, 42.

THE last Sunday in Lent is often called Palm Sunday, because it is believed to have been the day in which the lifelong earthly sorrows and humiliations of our Blessed Lord were relieved by one brief hour of glory and triumph—when, fulfilling the inspired vision of Zechariah, the King of Zion entered His city, "just, and having salvation: lowly and riding upon an ass, and upon a colt, the foal of an ass," while the air was rent by the hosannas of assembled thousands, who spread their garments under His feet (as was the custom of welcoming home some mighty conqueror) or cut down branches from the palm trees that lined the roadside, and "strewed them in the way." For a moment it seemed as though the picture that was ever in the disciples' hearts was on the eve of being realised; as though He who was thus hailed as the Son of David was indeed at this time about "to restore the Kingdom unto Israel;" as though His sceptre was about to be set up visibly upon earth, and those who had forsaken all and followed Him were presently to enter into His joy, and at length be satisfied with the promised thrones. Some such thoughts may have occurred to St. James and St. John and some others among His followers whose minds had not yet been taught by the Holy Ghost to apprehend the spiritual character of His service, and who, in spite of their Master's express warning, still seemed to look for the Kingdom of God " to come with observation."

If so, what followed must have been a sad casting down of soaring hopes. We can easily understand "what manner of communications" they must have been which the two disciples " had one with another as they walked towards Emmaus and were sad." The Agony, the Betrayal, the Arraignment, the Condemnation, the Mockery, the Scourging, and last and sorest trial of all, the Cross and Passion, must all have been as so many irons entering their soul. He whom they thought should have redeemed Israel thus taken from them, and themselves left, forlorn and without a friend, to bear a name and sustain a cause which had already brought Him in Whom they trusted to what they deemed an untimely and dishonoured grave.

It is thus that the Gospel and the Cross always look to those who have not yet learnt to raise their eyes above this lower world and to realise and dwell with the unseen. The whole picture seems sad and gloomy and cheerless; nothing to compensate for what we are called upon to forego; the sacrifices immediate and the reward remote; life a scene of mourning and self-denial and repentance, instead of a place for taking our ease, eating, drinking, and making merry. Such is the view which thousands take of the Gospel, and so they have no heart for it, and put it away from them, at any rate for the present, as an irksome and distasteful thing.

And, indeed, if the hopes of the Christian rise no higher than this; if he thinks that, for his individual benefit, the kingdom of Christ shall immediately appear; if he looks for some direct, tangible compensation for taking up the Cross and following Christ; if he has not faith enough to wait yet for a little season, and thus be a partaker with those who inherit the promises, he is "of all men the most miserable." He seems to be renouncing the world without winning heaven; he knows not the pleasures of sin (if, indeed, those wretched gratifications deserve to be called pleasures at all), but neither has he tasted of that "peace which passeth understanding."

Living thus, as we do, in the midst of such imperfect notions of the spiritual nature of Christ's kingdom, it will not be unprofitable if we dwell on some of the circumstances which marked this day, and made it stand out in such broad contrast with every other day of our Divine Saviour's brief sojourning upon earth.

It was His only day of *earthly* triumph. His Transfiguration was *un*earthly — a sort of intermediate transaction between earth and heaven; a drawing aside as for a moment of a curtain, and showing us some of the mysteries of the world of spirits. But His triumphant entry into Jerusalem was such as might have marked the progress of a mere earthly conqueror. It showed itself in the usual demonstrations of joy and shouting and excited crowds. And yet even *it* was wonderfully of a piece with that portion of meekness and humiliation which our glorious Redeemer, in the days of His flesh, chose for His own.

In the midst of all this enthusiasm and rejoicing, He still remained " a man of sorrows." " As He drew near the city "—whose whole population came pouring out of its gates to welcome Him—the thoughts of the past and of the future came rushing on His mind,—the foresight of its impending desolation; the memory of His own unheeded warnings; the voices which now uttered their " Hosannas, Blessed be the King that cometh," so soon to change into malignant yells, calling for His blood and "requiring that He might be crucified " ; the fatal Calvary, even now visible " from the descent of the Mount of Olives," on which He stood. All this must have produced an overpowering conflict of painful sensations ; and as once before at the grave of Lazarus, so now He found relief from the thoughts of which His mind was full in a flood of tears: " When He was come near He beheld the city, and wept over it."

It was not for Himself that He wept, but for them. No word or action of His life was selfish. His whole care was for others—their bodies and souls. Even in Gethsemane—though a veil rests upon much that must have passed there—we can well believe that it was our impenitence and obstinacy in sin, our still continued refusal to wash ourselves in the fountain for uncleanness which He was about to open, and not His own sufferings or sorrows, that formed the bitterest element of that cup which it was the Father's will that He should drink even to the dregs. This was the thought that rent His heart and moistened His cheek with tears as He gazed upon the city—*the doom of impenitent sinners.* He could die Himself without a murmur. What gave the sting to death was that even the spectacle of His Cross, the merits of His sufferings, would be insufficient to reclaim a lost and perishing world, or to save more than an elect soul here and there, even as a "brand plucked from the burning." It is not that God's arm is shortened, but that we *will* not be saved.

As the offer of salvation is universal, so is it God's wish that it should be universally accepted. It is we who are too slothful, or too worldly, or too hardened by the deceitfulness of sin, manfully and persistently to take God's side. We love our gains and our pleasures more than Christ; or even if we think it better to accept the invitation and profess to be thankful for it, we will not be at the pains to make preparation; we venture into the King's presence without a wedding garment; we come to church without reverence and remain there without devotion; we leave it without having derived one particle of spiritual strength from what might have been, if we had used it rightly, an opportunity of communion with Christ—a draught of that living water which He has to give to quench all thirst, and to be in us a "well of water, springing up into everlasting life."

Yes, so it is. Christ has shed His blood, and the

great majority of those for whom He poured it forth are none the better for it—no nearer heaven, no safer from hell. Nay, our godless, carnal lives do but "crucify the Son of God afresh," and involve us in their fearful doom who with their own lips called down the vengeance for His blood upon themselves and on their children. There are many of us for whom Christ perhaps weeps now as mournfully as once He wept over outcast and impenitent Jerusalem. If He can be touched with the feeling of our *infirmities*, be sure He can be touched also with sorrow for our *sins*. He is the same merciful High Priest that He ever was. He is still the Good Shepherd, and it cannot but be pain and grief to Him to see sheep for whom He laid down His life refusing to hear His voice and follow Him.

Oh, my friends, have you ever really considered with yourselves what a solemn, awful thing it is to be a Christian? to be one of those redeemed by the Blood of the Lamb? one of God's children, privileged to have access by the Spirit to the Father? what kind of life it requires to answer to all this at our hands? how watchful, how prayerful, how pure, how sober, how full of love and earnestness? Can you think that coming to church once a day, or hardly that, the reading of a chapter in the Bible, the saying a few set prayers as a matter of form—anything, indeed, merely outward and formal—is all the acknowledgment Almighty God asks for, is all that the Scriptures mean when they tell us of faith and holiness and obedience?

Do not read your Bibles with such self-deceiving hearts, with such one-sided views. Believe that he who would follow Christ here and be owned of Christ hereafter must do what the Bible bids him—keep under his body, and set a watch at the door of his lips, and "let no filthy communication proceed out of his mouth," and "do justice, and love mercy, and walk humbly," and "abstain from all appearance of evil," and "walk circumspectly," and "have no fellowship with the unfruitful works of darkness," and "speak truth with his neighbour," and "study to be quiet and do his own business," and "flee youthful lusts," and "follow after righteousness, faith, charity, peace, with them that call on the Lord out of a pure heart."

It is a fearful text for us all to think upon, that "*without holiness no man shall see the Lord.*" Decency, honesty, diligence, by themselves, will never bring a man to heaven: they are found to answer in a worldly point of view, and are often practised on worldly motives. But holiness is something greater and nobler. It is God's gift and not our own creation; and yet a gift not arbitrarily bestowed on a chosen few, but to be won by all who will seek for it by earnest prayer. It is, indeed, seldom gained, because it is seldom sought for. Men keep putting off the search because it is troublesome and encroaches upon their worldly engagements and amusements, and would require the surrender of many things that they cannot yet prevail on themselves to resign.

Alas! that so few of us ever seem "to know the things that belong unto our peace until they are hid from our eyes." We go on to the last hardened, blinded, reprobate; always promising ourselves a day when we will repent, but as often putting it off again when it arrives. What fearful words are these which Wisdom uttereth in the streets: " Because I have called, and ye refused, I have stretched out my hand, and no man regarded; but ye have set at nought all my counsel and would none of my reproof: I also will laugh at your calamity; I will mock when your fear cometh."

With such unmistakable plainness does the Word of God speak to us all. If words mean anything, they tell us this, that every day we put off the work of repentance and conversion makes it less likely and, indeed, less possible that we should ever repent and be converted at all. Death-bed repentances—true saving conversions at the eleventh hour—are the rarest things in the world. I speak the words of soberness when I say that I do not believe one sick bed in a hundred witnesses that blessed change of a soul—a whole lifetime wedded to the world in those few last distracted days softened and "turned as it were from idols to serve the living God."

And yet I can see that many—must I not say *most* among you?—are waiting for this which you fondly deem a "more convenient season." How is it else that so many of you, not only young people, but those well grown in years—though the young have no surer hold on life than the old—are such rare frequenters of God's house, entire strangers to Christ's Table, so weak in grace that you cannot resist the devil when he assails you, but are overcome by the least temptation to wrath or quarrelling, or swearing, or drunkenness. Alas! again I say, that we should not know "the time of our visitation"; alas! that instead of "pressing towards the mark of our high calling in Christ Jesus," we should rather be of those who draw back unto perdition; alas! that neither the tears of Christ nor the wrath of God should awaken us from the slumber of death!

O Blessed Saviour, Who wouldest so often have gathered us together unto Thee, "even as a hen gathereth her chickens under her wing," oh! call us unto Thee yet again by such constraining tones, either of love or fear, that we cannot choose but *hear*, and that before "our house is left unto us desolate" our unloving hearts and wayward wills may be strengthened to adore Thee and obey!

Preached—Cholderton, Palm Sunday, March 20th, 1853.

VI.

THE CROSS OF CHRIST.

(A Good Friday Sermon.)

"Looking unto Jesus the Author and Finisher of our faith: Who for the joy that was set before Him endured the cross, despising the shame, and is set down at the right hand of the throne of God."—HEB. xii. 2.

ON Good Friday we are bidden to look to the Cross of Christ. Though it is a thought that should never, even for a single day, be absent from our minds; though in every sermon the preacher of the gospel must determine to know nothing else amongst his hearers "but Jesus Christ, and Him Crucified"; yet, upon this day, it is a subject that is more emphatically brought before us. On Good Friday the preacher's tongue should savour more strongly of it; to-day above all other days of the year, the devout Christian, walking in the steps of saints that have gone before, will endeavour to "lay aside every weight, and the sin which doth so easily beset him, and run with patience the race that is set before him, *looking unto Jesus, the Author and Finisher of his faith.*"

For to-day it was, more than 1800 years ago, from nine o'clock in the morning till three o'clock in the afternoon, that the Cross of Christ was seen set up on Calvary; the fulfilment of types and prophecies which had gone on pointing to it for full four thousand years; the anchor of the hopes, the emblem of the faith, of all generations to the end of time. The Lamb, slain in the eternal counsels of the Father "before the foundations of the world," was then offered up, an atoning sacrifice for the sins of the world, in very deed. It was the same Lamb that God had promised Abraham that He would provide in the place of Isaac, his only son. It was the same Lamb, the efficacy of whose sprinkled blood had arrested the hand of the destroying angel in Egypt, and saved His chosen people from the plague. It was the same Lamb that St. John the Baptist indicated, when with more than a prophet's distinctness he showed Him to the gazing multitude, as the "Lamb of God Which taketh away the sins of the world." It was the same Lamb Which the rapt seer beheld in his apocalyptic vision, when he saw the throne of God in heaven, "and in the midst of the throne, and of the four beasts and the twenty-four elders"—the four evangelists, and the glorious company of the apostles, and the goodly fellowship of the prophets (as some have read these numbers)—"there stood a Lamb as it had been slain."

Oh! what a moving and unspeakable sight it must have been, which, on this day, must have riveted many an eye in Jerusalem. Outside the city gate, on the brow of a low, sloping hill, stand three crosses. On them hang three human forms for six long hours; their hands and their feet pierced, and men standing and looking on them. They are called "malefactors" (it was part of the prophecies which had to be accomplished, that He of whom we speak "should be numbered with the transgressors"), and so indeed two of them are; suffering, as they themselves confessed, "justly" for their sins.

But Who is He in the midst? and of what is He accused? What fault found they in Him that they have condemned Him to die the painfullest death that human cruelty can devise — the death which they inflicted on none but the vilest criminals and slaves? The scroll written over His head tells us something of Him: "This is Jesus, the King of the Jews." There is something in His face that speaks of agony and suffering unutterable, something worse than the pains of death, bitter and sharp though these be. And the words that He utters from time to time, how strange they sound: "*Eli, Eli, lama sabachthani*"—"My God, My God, why hast thou forsaken Me?" Surely He must be a righteous and God-fearing man! And then again, presently to a weeping woman who stood nigh, "Woman, behold thy son"; and to a man who has seemingly known Him,—"Behold thy mother." Surely He must be tender-hearted and pitiful thus to think of others' woes in the midst of His own deep agony. Presently we again hear His voice, waxed faint and feeble now, "I thirst"; and then again, as the rude passers-by shoot out their lips and wag their heads, mocking what they deemed His vain and impotent pretensions, we hear Him pray, "Father, forgive them, for they know not what they do." Surely it must be some angel's spirit, and not one of us rude and violent and revengeful men, that can thus pray for His murderers and bear their insults meekly.

And once more, the sad tragedy now drawing to its close, we hear two more strange and awful utterances— "It is finished"—"Father, into Thy hands I commend my spirit." And now all is over. The spirit has returned to the God who gave it—it is but a lifeless, earthy corpse that hangs there. And yet no: methinks the day grows dull, and there is a noise of rending heard, and a trembling of the solid ground. It is even so. For three hours there has been darkness over the land, though the sun is still only in his mid-course through the sky. And now the veil of the temple is rent in twain from the top to the bottom, and the earth quakes, and the rocks are rent, and the graves are opened and give forth their dead, and all the people that have come together to see this sight, "beholding the things which are done, smite their breasts and return" with downcast eyes and musing hearts to their homes: one only, and he a poor uninstructed Roman soldier, is moved to give utterance to his feelings in words, than which none were ever more truly spoken. Lifting up his eyes he glorifies God, and says, "Certainly this was a righteous man; truly this was the Son of God."

That rude and untaught soldier read the signs of that day aright. He had not stood, keeping watch at the foot of the Cross, in vain. Whether he fully fathomed the depth of his own words or not—whether they were an involuntary ejaculation or a deliberate confession—an angel from heaven could not have told us more. He Who had been hanging for six weary hours on that accursed tree, He on Whom men had spat, Whom the very thieves in the same condemnation had reviled, He though suffering the death of a sinner and a slave, "crucified," as St. Paul says, through "weakness," was a righteous man : " He was the son of God."

Yes, my friends, you and I have reason to thank God that it was so: that they were not His own sins for which He was punished, that He was no fellow-mortal of ours who endured such things. In the beautiful words of the prophet, " Surely He hath borne our griefs and carried our sorrows." " Neither," as St. Peter tells us, " is there salvation in any other; for there is none other name under heaven, given among men, whereby we must be saved."

Not only upon this day, but every day of our lives, are we bidden by the apostle to " look unto Jesus, the Author and Finisher of our faith." Gaze on Him "enduring the Cross, despising the shame "; follow Him with the eye of faith to where, with the marks of His sufferings still upon Him, He is now " set down at the right hand of the throne of God." The print of the nails may still be seen in those hands and feet; the side is still gashed by the wound, where entered the savage Roman's spear. For even at the last day, when He shall again be visible to the eye, they that pierced Him shall behold their handiwork. " I saw in the midst of the throne *a Lamb as it had been slain.*"

"Of course," you will say to me, "we must look to Christ. We do look to Him. We are continually thinking about Him and talking about Him. We are here now to show that we are looking to Him. We call ourselves Christians, and the name would have no meaning did we not believe the doctrine of the Atonement. You are only preaching to us about a duty that we have always acknowledged and are perfectly familiar with."

It may be so, my brethren, and I trust that it is so. But I cannot conceal from myself, or from you, that there are many "who call themselves Christians," who talk glibly about religious feelings and religious subjects, who are still no better than those whom St. Paul describes as "enemies of the Cross of Christ, crucifying the Son of God afresh, and putting Him to an open shame; whose end is destruction, whose God is their belly, whose glory is in their shame, who mind earthly things." Every drunkard is one of these; every whoremonger; every profane swearer; every Sabbath-breaker; every liar; every scoffer at holy things; every hard-hearted man; the selfish, the envious, the wrathful, the proud, the covetous, the prayerless. Every one is an enemy of the Cross of Christ who does not help, like Simon of Cyrene, to bear the Cross of Christ. In this case, he that is not with Jesus is against Him. He that loves any earthly thing better than the Lord Who redeemed him, who sets gain before godliness, pleasure before duty, comfort before self-denial, acts of self-indulgence before acts of mercy, cannot be His disciple. Jesus Christ knows nothing of him, be he young or old, rich or poor, who lives only for amusement, or for covetousness, or for ease—in a word, for self.

All I say is, beware of *unreality;* beware of *professing* to know God, but in works denying Him; beware of cant; of words that mean nothing as you use them; of feelings that are unfruitful. Still "look unto Jesus, the Author and Finisher of our faith," but look *practically*, look *earnestly*, look *humbly*. Look till you feel within you some holy influence issuing from that bruised and pierced body, some secret power derived from that mystical Cross, making you have fellowship with those sufferings, conforming you to that death. Look till you feel a desire to take up your own cross too. Look till you have learnt what faith, and patience, and humility, and resignation, and contentment mean. Look till you become a Christian in *deed;* thyself crucified, and dead to the world; "always bearing about in the body the dying of the Lord Jesus, that the life also of Jesus may be made manifest in thy body."

And there is one lesson especially that we cannot afford to lose sight of, in presence of the Cross. The world worships success; and, dazzled by its brilliancy, we are too apt to forget that disappointment and failure would be to many, perhaps to most men, the more wholesome discipline. I am sure that for ministers of the Gospel what is called "success," as the world measures it at least, is a most perilous trial. Better a thousand times to fail, and *know* that we have failed. We shall then go forth again to the battle with more trust in God, and less confidence in ourselves.

In every department of human activity, the men, I take it, whose names now stand highest on the roll of fame are those who have *succeeded by failure;* men whom disappointment has crossed, but whom it has not turned aside; whom truth has baffled, but by whom she has at last been won; whom, beaten in many battles, the world has been forced to own as conquerors after all.

And the same law holds in spiritual things. "Tribulation worketh patience, and patience experience, and experience hope." To have failed is no sign that we are forsaken of God. "The gifts and calling of God are without repentance." The promise stands sure and steadfast, "I will never leave thee nor forsake thee." Only let us banish two things—banish vain regrets, and banish guilty despair. The past is irrevocable, but the present and the future are our own. To have failed before is no ground, to any but a superstitious man, for the fear that he must fail again, or always fail. It is simply a motive to greater watchfulness and more earnest faith. God hath called us to salvation. "We can do all things through Christ which strengtheneth us." The Holy Ghost's heart-cheering call is, "Work out your salvation while it is called to-day." Whatever may be our condition in life, or the circumstances of our trial, or the lamentableness of our past failures, the Cross of Christ is what we may always look to for strength and instruction, and enduring hope. Though a single fact, it is pregnant with manifold influences. Not only in saving *efficacy*, but also in sanctifying *example*, "He tasted death for every man."

Look to it then in the time of trouble, when distress and anguish come upon you, when you are out of work, or things turn out ill for you, or you are slandered and evil spoken of—look to the Cross of Christ, and draw from it a lesson of patience and confidence. Look, then, thou forlorn one, who hast no friends, on whom the world gazes coldly, and who seest "no man" to pity thee; look to the Cross of Christ and see there Him Who in His own deep sufferings still thought of finding a home for His weeping mother, and believe thou hast a place in His heart and that He careth for thee! Look there, thou penitent, who, like the sad prodigal, findest that thou hast sinned very grievously, and would fain return to thy father's home, but fearest lest thou shouldest be refused admission and disowned: look to the Cross of Christ, and see there One whose blood, if thou hast faith, can wash out thy deepest stains, and present thee faultless before the throne with exceeding joy. Above all—for it is a picture that has two sides—look to the Cross of Christ thou who art in prosperity; thou who callest thyself "a happy man"; thou with whom "to-day is as yesterday, yea, and much more abundant"; thou of whom all men speak well, who hast no cares, no discomforts, no privations; "who canst take thine ease, eat, drink, and be merry"—look thou, above all, to the Cross of Christ, and see that thou hast fellowship with it. Remember that faithful saying, "If we *suffer*, we shall also reign with Him," *but surely not otherwise*. "For *all* that will live godly in Christ Jesus shall suffer persecution." "We must, *through much tribulation* enter into the kingdom of God." It is the *law* of the

Gospel, the portion of God's elect. It must then, in some sense, be *our* portion. Let us look about us and see whether, if we know it not and cannot realise it, it is because we are giving up ourselves too entirely to the world, and the things of the world. If we look for the Cross we shall soon find it. We shall see what it is that Christ would have us take and bear after Him. We shall discover some work of God lying before our feet—as masters or servants, or fathers, or children, or ministers, or people—which we have not done yet, and which we had better do while it is still day. "For the grace of God that bringeth salvation, hath appeared unto all men, teaching us that, denying ungodliness and worldly lusts, we should live soberly, righteously, and godly in this present world; looking for that blessed hope and the glorious appearing of the great God and our Saviour Jesus Christ, who gave Himself for us, that He might redeem us from all iniquity and purify unto Himself a peculiar people zealous of good works."

Preached—Cholderton, Good Friday, March 25th, 1853 ; April 10th, 1857 ; April 6th, 1860 ; Kersal, Manchester, Good Friday, April 15th, 1870.

VII.

NOTES OF A SERMON
ON
THE LOVE OF CHRIST.

"The love of Christ constraineth us . . . . ."—
2 CORINTHIANS, v. 14.

WHAT is it that draws our thoughts to the Cross with so strong a fascination? It is the ineffable thought of God's love thus, there, manifested.

The spectacle in itself, whether we gaze on it in pictures, or raise it before our minds by an act of imagination, is horrible, piteous, agonising. Yet on that scene have been fixed the highest, tenderest, holiest thoughts of men for nineteen centuries. It filled St. Paul's heart, and formed his life, and sustained as well as constrained him.

It is strange that it should be so hard for the heart of men to realise this love of God. Yet plainly it is hard. Till Christ came, men feared God rather than loved Him. Even in the evangelical prophecies of Isaiah there is the deep undertone of a solemn fear. The powers of Nature, man feels, cannot proclaim God's love. Earthquakes only make men doubt and tremble. John Stuart Mill could discern in the physical, and even in the moral world, no token of God's benevolence, or at best only of a limited benevolence. The poet has spoken of "nature, red in both tooth and claw"; and of her seeming carefulness of the type alone, careless meanwhile of single lives.

And so the better, fuller revelation — the better covenant established on better premises—the bringing in of the better hope, came. It was needed, and it came. The Cross of Christ proclaimed it. "God so loved the world that He gave His only-begotten Son"; "He spared not His own Son, but delivered Him up for us all"; "For when we were yet without strength, in due time Christ died for the ungodly." "God commendeth His love toward us, in that while we were yet sinners Christ died for us."

We may not understand the exact method of the Atonement, and I do not pretend to be able to explain it. I have no theories wherewith to reconcile it with our abstract theories of justice or wisdom. Others—the great Bishop Butler for instance—have attempted this with more or less success. I approach the subject, as it is best approached, not from the high *à priori* road, but from the ground of Christian faith and experience. I see what it has done for humanity. I recognise the power of such a statement as this: "Seeing then that we have a great High Priest, that is passed into the heavens, Jesus, the Son of God, let us hold fast our profession. For we have not a High Priest which cannot be touched with the feeling of our infirmities, but was in all points tempted like as we are, yet without sin. Let us therefore come boldly unto the throne of grace, that we may obtain mercy, and find grace to help in time of need." I know what it has done to sweeten and sanctify beds of sickness, hours of suffering, which before, at least, were only endured with a kind of stoical apathy or despair. I contrast even the patience of Job with the patience of St. Paul, and I see the difference—the higher level to which the human heart, at once so weak and so strong, has, by virtue of this great sustaining belief, attained.

No wonder that symbols of the Cross meet us everywhere — in our churchyards, in the shape of our churches, even in our women's ornaments; for it is the symbol of the love of God, His last, best revelation of Himself and of His character to the heart of man.

And it is the heart rather than the intellect which has embraced it. The inte'lect has raised difficulties which the heart has had to remove. The "I know," "I am persuaded," of St. Paul were conclusions not of his reason, but of his faith—of his heart, that is, rather than of his head. When we talk of " love," we are talking of a passion of the soul, not of an inference of the understanding.

Does this "love of Christ" draw out any corresponding affection in our souls? Indeed, the phrase—the love of Christ—is doubtful. Does it mean *my* love towards Christ, or *Christ's* love towards me? The two indeed act and react. "We love Him because He first loved us." And though the first spring comes from the thought of God's love to us yet this thought branches out into a thousand forms. "In this was manifested the love of God towards us, because that God sent His only-begotten Son into the world that we might live through Him. Herein is love, not that we loved God but that He loved us, and sent His Son to be the propitiation for our sins." Beloved, if God so loved us we ought also to love one another. If we love one another, God dwelleth in us, and His love is perfected in us.

Cold, careless, selfish hearts can hardly be objects of God's love. Christ showed love that He might win love. He drew us "with cords as of a man, with bands of love." In it we may bask as in the sunshine, till its warmth has penetrated our whole nature.

And yet perhaps this is not a happy metaphor. For nothing is less like basking in the sunshine than the energy of faith—faith which worketh by love; or rather perhaps, faith energised by love, of which love is the moving and sustaining power. No! the *Aprici senes* of the past are hardly types of Christian manhood, or even of Christian old age.

I don't like to talk—sweet as the book is which bears that title—of "the Shadow of the Cross." True, its shadow fell darkly on Him who bore it, and I cannot penetrate the mystery of that suffering; but to me, to you, it has made the whole world full of light No shadow of it fell on the great heart of St. Paul—"Yea, God forbid that I should glory save in the Cross of our Lord Jesus Christ."

We should be strong indeed if we could lay hold of this Cross with equal faith and firmness.

Some there are who in their worship almost degrade, certainly unspiritualise, the power of this Cross, by attempting to associate it with all the emblems and accessories of a sensuous and almost physical worship. How the poor weak human heart, unable to reach the higher is always falling back upon the lower! It must have something outside itself to rest upon, and it is so much easier to fall back upon what is carnal than to rise to what is spiritual. A repeated sacrifice upon the altar—to use a phraseology which, however unscriptural, is in vogue—seems so much easier to conceive than the finished sacrifice on Calvary and the new and risen life with Christ in heaven. It is easier to gaze upon, if that is all that is aimed at: but is it more helpful to sustain? How is it that men, like the Galatians, having begun in the spirit, are made perfect —or think they are—by the flesh?

Oh friends, rise higher in your conception of this great mystery! Let these words help you: " Yea, though we have known Christ after the flesh, yet now henceforth know we Him no more. All things are of God, who hath reconciled us to Himself by Jesus Christ, and hath given to us the ministry of reconciliation; to wit that God was in Christ reconciling the world unto Himself, not imputing their trespasses unto them. For He hath made Him to be sin for us who knew no sin, that we might be made the righteousness of God in Him." Yes, this is the love of God in its fullness and in its power.

Preached—Kersal Moor, Manchester, Good Friday morning, 1884.

VIII.

THE ANGELS' EASTER QUESTION.

"Why seek ye the living among the dead?"—St. Luke xxiv. 5.

Such was the angels' address to the holy women of Galilee, who had come from Jerusalem to the sepulchre, where the body of their Lord had been laid, "on the first day of the week very early in the morning," bringing with them "spices which they had prepared," to anoint His body for the burying.

There had not been time to do this perfectly on the Friday evening when He was slain. The next day was the Sabbath of more than usual solemnity (a "high day" as it is called), and the bodies had to be taken down from the cross and laid with as much decency as haste allowed in the nearest tomb. The last offices to the lifeless corpse were performed by Joseph of Arimathea and Nicodemus, both members of that Jewish council which had condemned to death the Lord of life; both disciples of Jesus, "but secretly, for fear of the Jews." The one brought the linen clothes and spices, a mixture of myrrh and aloes about one hundred pounds weight, "as the manner of the Jews is to bury"; the

THE ANGELS' EASTER QUESTION.

other lent his new sepulchre in the garden, wherein was never yet man laid. "There laid they Jesus therefore, because of the Jews' preparation day: for the sepulchre was nigh at hand."

And now the Sabbath, with its appointed rest from labour, was past and gone. The sun had scarce shown himself in the east on the morning of the first day of the week when "Mary Magdalene, and Joanna, and Mary the mother of James, and certain others with them," issued on their errand of love and duty from the well-warded gates of Jerusalem. Their hearts were sad within them, and they journeyed musing on many things. They questioned one another, perhaps, whether the rude soldiers who watched the tomb would suffer them to perform their last office of affection to Him they loved. They thought, too, of the difficulty which their weak women's hands would find in rolling away the stone.

Nor, may we be sure, was their perplexity lessened when, on drawing near, they found the stone rolled away from the sepulchre, and, entering in, "they saw not the body of the Lord Jesus"; for as yet, like the Apostles themselves, "they knew not the scripture, that He must rise again from the dead." "And it came to pass, as they were much perplexed thereabout, behold, two men stood by them in shining garments. And as they were afraid, and bowed down their faces to the earth"—conscious that they were in the presence of messengers from heaven—"they said unto them, Why seek ye the living among the dead? He is not here, but is risen. Remember how He spake unto you when

He was yet in Galilee"—words which they had never rightly understood till now—" saying, The Son of Man must be delivered into the hands of sinful men, and be crucified, and the third day rise again? And they remembered His words."

This then explained the mystery. He whom they sought—the Saviour of the world—was risen. He was not there. They had been looking for the living among the dead. The days of familiar intercourse, "the speaking face to face as a man speaketh to his friend," the strength, and the weakness also, of an abiding presence in *the body* are passed way; " behold, all things are become new." Death was now robbed of its sting ; the grave of its victory; Satan of his power. The Messiah's personal sufferings were finished ; the Kingdom of His glory was begun. " They that had known Christ Jesus after the flesh were henceforth to know Him as such no more." In one word, sight gave place to faith. From this time the blessing was for those " who had not seen, but yet had believed." Mary Magdalene, forbidden to touch Him with a fleshy embrace, was told of a spiritual contact by which she might still apprehend Him, when He should have ascended to " her Father and His Father, her God and His God."

Everything pointed the same way. His forty days sojourning upon earth after His resurrection was but a condescension to His disciples' infirmity. He would not have His leave-taking too abrupt, lest their weak faith should be shocked and overpowered. He prepared them for the new state of things—the ministration of His kingdom henceforth to be carried on by the Holy

Spirit, tenderly and gradually; herein, as in so many other things, showing Himself that merciful High Priest, who can be touched with a feeling of our infirmities; who will not try us beyond what our strength is able to bear.

Accordingly St. Paul uses this new feature of the Gospel dispensation—I mean its purely spiritual character—as the most constraining motive to heavenly-mindedness: "If ye be risen with Christ, seek those things which are above, where Christ sitteth on the right hand of God. Set your affection on things above, not on things on the earth, for ye are dead, and your life is hid with Christ in God."

As in His Passion, so also in His Resurrection, Jesus has left us an example. As we must be "crucified with Him" and "buried with Him," so we must "rise with Him"—rise from the grave of corrupt affections and carnal lusts and earth-bound thoughts to high and heavenly things; to an appreciation of our birthright, to a sense of our calling, to self-renouncement, to newness of life. "He was delivered," we are told, "for our offences: He was raised for our justification." His Resurrection was the earnest and pledge of that train of glorious privileges which His death purchased for them that believe—predestination, election, justification, glory—privileges which will run their appointed course and issue in their preordained consequences in all who do not themselves "frustrate the grace of God" by their own carnal and ungodly lives. They are as a strong cable, bearing up and sustaining all who will lay hold on it, through the storms and waves of time, to the safe waters and peaceful haven of eternity. "Who shall lay anything to the charge of God's elect? It is God that justifieth. Who is he that condemneth? It is Christ that died, *yea, rather that is risen again,* Who is ever at the right hand of God, Who also maketh intercession for us." Nothing, indeed, "can separate us from the love of Christ" but our own cold hearts and feeble faith. Satan has no longer power against us except we give him leave. The commandment is no more "found to be unto death," because, by the help of grace, it can be fulfilled, as it is wrtiten, "Sin shall have no more dominion over you, for ye are not under the Law."

If all this be true—and that it is true we have the sure warrant of God's most Holy Word—one cannot help asking, How then is it that this fair picture of a Christian's condition in the Kingdom of God is so seldom realised? How is it that Satan is still unbound, and "walketh about as a roaring lion seeking whom he may devour"? that sin is still fulfilled in the lusts thereof? that men, though redeemed and born again of grace, are either unable or unwilling to "stand fast in the liberty wherewith Christ has made them free"? The answer may be given in the language of the text. It is because "they seek the living among the dead." It is because they busy themselves about things which perish in the using, fashions that pass away, objects that can neither profit nor deliver, instead of rising with Christ, "and forgetting the things that are behind," and throwing all their care upon God, and living as men "who have here no continuing city, but who seek one to come."

Look at the world and see what it is doing. Take nine men out of ten and see what they are doing. Are they labouring "for the meat that perisheth, or for that which shall endure unto life eternal"? Are they "making provision" for the flesh, or for the spirit? Are they "crucifying" the old man, or pampering him? Are they counting gain godliness, or "godliness with contentment" gain? Are they professing to serve God, or in works denying Him? Are they walking by faith or by sight? Are they ready to spend and be spent for their brethren or for themselves? Do they rise early and late take rest, and eat the bread of carefulness, that they may have to give to him that needeth, or that they may "buy and sell and get gain"?

The Scriptures paint both pictures. Which is the one we see most frequently exhibited before our eyes? There cannot be a moment's doubt. The world is still carnal; and so far as it is so, "Christ is dead in vain." Its works are dead; its faith is dead: and yet it still looks, or professes to look, to be saved by Him "that liveth." The thing cannot be. It is impossible. It is a simple perversion of the doctrines of grace. We must seek Christ where He is, "at the right hand of God." We must "know the power of His resurrection" to transform us "in the spirit of our mind." We must "purify ourselves even as He is pure." We must walk as "partakers of a heavenly calling" here, if we are ever to reign with Christ in heaven hereafter. We are called to be saints; we must be saintly.

Now we can never do this unless we live by rule. No man ever went to sleep a sinner and woke up and found himself a saint. The great change of heart which is commonly expressed by the term "conversion" is no sudden impulse, perfect from the very outset, but the gradual and often slow result of pain and discipline and watchfulness. The man who seeks to turn with his whole heart to God, "sets a watch at the door of his lips," and "makes a covenant with his eyes," and "takes heed what he hears," and "keeps his foot," not only when he "goes to the house of the Lord," but at other times also, and has his "loins girt about and his light burning." He puts on that attitude of watchfulness and self-control which his own reason, no less than the Bible, tells him is alone safe and prudent for his soul. It is as unreasonable as it is unscriptural to expect to have all done for us and nothing left to be wrought for and by ourselves. We have "to work out our own salvation," and that "with fear and trembling."

This can only be done by living by rule; by setting before our eyes a standard and trying to live up to it; by acting upon principle, not upon passion; from a sense of duty and not merely as suits our convenience. This is the only way to make progress, to grow in grace. It is the only thing that can give us consistency. Men are irregular and make mistakes and contradict themselves, because they have no settled rule within themselves to determine questions by. They act right to-day and wrong to-morrow. They spend the morning of Sunday at church and the evening at a public-house. Out of the same mouth will proceed blessing and cursing on the same day. Or again, the law is kept in some points, but broken in others. A man is sober, but he is also covetous; or generous-hearted, but also profligate; or honest, but cross and peevish; or honourable, but vain and proud. Here still the secret history of his heart is, he lives by no rule. He puts himself under no constraint. He cannot bear to be crossed in an inclination. There is no "patient waiting" for grace.

I am describing a spiritual state that is more or less true of us all. None of us, it is to be feared, makes it as much a matter of conscience "to live godly in Christ Jesus" as he might do. None of us perhaps takes all the pains he might to "to mortify his members upon the earth." None of us resists with his whole energy "the motions of sin." Some probably do not even try to do so at all. It is mere chance work whether they are conquerors or conquered in any conflict with the wicked one. No one can tell beforehand how they will behave. They never stop to calculate consequences or think where roads must lead; but "do even what they list," and walk on heedlessly, just where the mood takes them. Now surely this cannot be the Christian race. This is not the way to win the "incorruptible crown." "He that striveth for the mastery is temperate in all things," that is, puts a bridle on his appetite and lives by rule. So must we. We must "bring every thought into captivity unto the obedience of Christ." At least this is what the Bible says, and he is hardly wise who disregards it.

It is nothing better than "seeking the living among the dead" to think that we shall find Christ, or rather be found of Him, while our affections are wholly buried in these earthly things. We must set them, we are taught, "on things above." It was while men ate and drank, and bought and sold, and builded and planted, that the Flood came and destroyed them all. Even so shall it be in the day in which the Son of man is revealed. He will come upon those men whose hearts are taken up with the care of this world and the deceitfulness of riches, *unawares*.

Let the day of His Resurrection remind us of the day of His Judgment. As St. Paul warned the Athenians on Mars' Hill, God "hath appointed a day in the which He will judge the world in righteousness by that man whom He hath ordained; whereof He hath given assurance unto all men, in that He hath raised Him from the dead." Oh! let us seek Him where and while He may be found; "for in the great water floods they who have never begun to seek Him till then shall not come nigh Him." Let us seek Him by a "new and living way"; by the renewing of our minds; by the putting off the body of the sins of the flesh; by a faith which worketh by love. Let us seek Him in those living channels of grace which He hath opened in His Church—the new Jerusalem—as fountains to cleanse from sin and from uncleanness. Let us seek Him in private prayer, in common worship, in Holy Communion. The two disciples with whom He supped at Emmaus knew Him not till "He had taken bread, and blessed it, and brake, and gave to them." Then, we are told, were their eyes opened, and they knew Him. Their hearts, indeed, had "burned within them" before, as He opened to them the Scriptures; but now, by a

Sacramental illumination, they knew Him to be indeed the Christ, the Saviour of the world. Let us seek to know Him in the same way. His Table is spread, and all things are ready, and the Master of the house is waiting for His guests. He bids us come, and shall we ungratefully turn our backs and go away?

Come, then, in your wedding garments—not the putting on of gold or apparel, the only way that *some* have of keeping their Eastertide, but "with the ornament of a meek and quiet spirit," "with your hearts sprinkled from an evil conscience and your bodies washed with pure water." In one sense it is indeed still true that "He is not here; He is risen." It is a spiritual presence that we must realise in the heavenly feast: His dwelling in our hearts is by faith. And this *is* to be realised sacramentally. We have His own word for it: "He that eateth My flesh and drinketh My blood dwelleth in Me, and I in him." Let us believe that what He hath promised He is able also to perform. Let us pray God to strengthen us "with might by His Spirit in the inner man," that so our dull hearts may be quickened, and our cold affections kindled to know the love of Christ which "passeth knowledge," and "to ascend in heart and mind to whither our Saviour Christ is gone before," and "is now seated at the right hand of the Throne of God."

Preached—Cholderton, Easter Sunday, April 11th, 1852.

IX.

THE POWER OF CHRIST'S RESURRECTION,
ESPECIALLY AS ILLUSTRATING
THE DUTIES OF MASTER AND SERVANT.

"For as yet they knew not the scripture, that He must rise again from the dead.—St. John xx. 9.

THE text gives us the explanation of a phenomenon that, without it, would be somewhat perplexing—viz. the incredulity and slowness of heart with which the disciples received Mary Magdalene's and the other women's news, that the tomb in the garden was tenantless and the body of the Lord Jesus had disappeared. Instead of "remembering the words that He had spoken to them in Galilee," and instantly welcoming the fact as a sure token of His resurrection, they knew not what to make of it; "their words seemed to them as idle tales, and they believed them not."

So opposed do the tidings appear to have been, not only to all their experience but even to their expectations, that, like Thomas himself, they were indisposed to accept any evidence short of personal sight and actual handling. Mary Magdalene was the first to announce to them both that the sepulchre was empty and, soon afterwards, that He Whom they had laid there "was risen indeed." And they, when they had heard that He was alive and had been seen of her, *believed not*. After that He appeared in another form—a significant fact, and very much of a piece with the changed and mysterious character of the intercourse which He held with His followers *after* His resurrection —unto two of them, Cleopas and his companion, on their way to Emmaus. And they went and told it unto the residue : " neither believed they them."

Indeed, so entirely was their usually simple and teachable faith overpowered by the suggestions either of a carnal doubt or fear, as to require, not only the actual assurance of their senses, but a formal Scriptural proof, and even some asperity of rebuke, before they were in a condition to be witnesses of a fact, much less preachers of a doctrine founded upon a fact, which as yet troubled instead of comforting them, and caused " thoughts to rise in their hearts," instead of restoring them at once to confidence and joy.

He appeared, we are told, to the eleven " as they sat at meat, and *upbraided* them with their unbelief and hardness of heart," because they believed not them which had seen Him after He was risen. Then opened He their understanding that they might understand the Scriptures, and said unto them : " Thus it is written, and thus it behoved Christ to suffer and to rise from the dead the third day. And that repentance and remission of sins should be preached in His Name among all nations, beginning at Jerusalem. And ye are witnesses of these things."

The text explains this phenomenon and accounts for this seemingly strange and obstinate scepticism. It appears to have been a fact, for which they were absolutely unprepared, and which, therefore, when it was presented to them, in the cogency of all but physical demonstration, their minds refused to realize. "As yet they knew not the scripture, that He must rise again from the dead."

Yet their ignorance is as marvellous as their incredulity. If they knew not the scripture, it was not for want of having had it brought before them. While they abode still in Galilee, Jesus had said unto them, "The Son of Man shall be betrayed into the hands of men, and they shall kill Him, and the third day He shall be raised again." They certainly understood the outward meaning of the words, for it is added, "And they were exceeding sorry." And again, as they were on this very last journey to Jerusalem which issued in such memorable circumstances, scarce ten days perhaps before, Jesus had taken them apart in the way and said unto them, "Behold, we go up to Jerusalem, and the Son of Man shall be betrayed unto the chief priests and scribes, and they shall condemn Him to death, and shall deliver Him to the Gentiles to mock, and to scourge, and to crucify Him; and the third day He shall rise again." Here we have every event detailed exactly in its historical sequence, no longer under the sign of the prophet Jonah or the parable of a destroyed and rebuilt temple, but in the plainest and most unambiguous language; and yet, though they had drunk them in with their ears, the words had never settled in

their hearts; had not even *enlightened*, still less
consoled or guided or strengthened them.

Of course, in estimating such a state of mind as this,
we must not forget to take into account the moral and
spiritual disadvantages under which, as compared with
ourselves, the disciples laboured. He Who had been
their constant strength and stay, Who, they had trusted,
"would have redeemed Israel," at Whose either hand
they had hoped to sit on thrones in all the pomp of
earthly sovereignty, was suddenly taken away; and the
"other Comforter," Who was "to guide them into all
truth, and bring all things to their remembrance that
Jesus had said unto them," was not yet sent from the
Father to supply the void.

Christ's death and resurrection and ascension; the
spiritual nature of His Kingdom and its propagation by
the force of inward influences, and not by the more
imposing power of observation and outward show—
truths which are now familiar even to the children of
our village schools—were dark mysteries or disappoint-
ing revelations *to them*. From the strength of national
prejudices or the dreams of personal ambition, their
notion of the new dispensation was simply secular.
They had thought of a Redeemer of Israel from the
Roman bondage, not a Ransomer of mankind from the
yoke of sin; of a triumphant Conqueror, not of a dying
Saviour; of a literal fulfilment of Jeremiah's words,
" Kings and princes entering into Jerusalem, and
sitting on the throne of David, and riding in chariots
and on horses, and the city itself remaining for ever,"
not of One Who, by washing us in His blood, should

make "us kings and priests unto His Father," or of a "Jerusalem which is above, and is free, and the mother of us all."

And so what they beheld on Calvary had completely unmanned them, had shipwrecked their faith by violently severing it from the anchor of their hopes. A great mental "tempest lay upon them"; they saw no haven to flee unto, and their hearts not unnaturally sank in the depths of perplexity and fearfulness and despair. It is a moral phenomenon analogous to what we sometimes witness physically—a strong constitution breaking down all at once; a general derangement resulting to the system from the inroads of disease at a single point. So here, a fervent faith and an enthusiasm that had never yet stopped to count the cost, was suddenly checked by an unforeseen disappointment; and as a consequence the whole current of the disciples' being was thrown out of its channel, to burst the banks by which hitherto it had, for the most part mechanically, been confined.

We do not speedily recover from any crushing blow. They to whom the Cross had been so painful a stumbling-block were not likely to be in a mood to understand the mystery or appreciate the comfort of the Resurrection. Memory is but a weak help in such emergencies. If we have ever experienced or can imagine the force of any strong reaction, we shall perhaps cease to wonder that the eleven poor, friendless Galileans, in spite of all they had been told beforehand, "as yet knew not the scripture, that He must rise again from the dead."

Let us see whether the text does not convey some practical instruction and warning to ourselves. Do we as yet know the scripture that He Whom we call our Lord has risen again from the dead? No doubt we accept the fact historically. We are satisfied that " the proofs" were "infallible" by which He " showed Himself alive to the Apostles after His passion." We do not question the testimony of Peter and James and John and the rest who tell us that they "ate and drank with Him after that He rose from the dead."

But this is very different from the "excellency of the knowledge of Christ Jesus our Lord" of which St. Paul speaks, and which it was the aim and object of his life to attain, " that he might know Him and the *power of His resurrection*, and the fellowship of His sufferings, being made conformable unto His death, if by any means he might attain unto the resurrection of the dead." We may be fully conversant with the *fact* without being in the smallest degree, or at least only very imperfectly, penetrated by its power. Without this, however great our biblical or theological attainments, we " as yet know nothing as we ought to know."

The great truths of the Gospel, the stories of the Evangelists, are not a mere collection of unproductive facts, to be stored in the memory, or paraded in controversy, or taught in a catechism, or squared to a system; but they are the basis of a Christian faith, the pattern of a Christian life, at once effectual and exemplary; mighty, living influences, welcomed and cherished and felt in every renewed and converted soul; for indeed they are the secret springs of its renewal and conversion. It is the resurrection of Christ in the teaching of St. Peter that makes Baptism a saving ordinance and inspires the regenerate with "a lively hope" of an incorruptible inheritance. Take away this doctrine from the Creed, and St. Paul tells us that "faith is vain," sin unforgiven, joy impossible. It is not only the motive, the pattern, but the enabling principle, the effectuating source of "the death unto sin and the life unto righteousness." At least this is how the Bible speaks of it. If it has not been so to us, it must be because we have only known it historically, not realized it spiritually.

It is indeed difficult to speak of so high and transcendent a doctrine, even though one use the very words of inspiration, without one's language seeming to savour of dreaminess and unreality. It is not easy to translate the mysteries of the faith into phrases intelligible to common minds. I am afraid that some of the most striking passages in St. Paul's writings in connection with this doctrine sound very much like mysticism to most of you. We can hardly enter into those deep feelings and that earnest faith and those kindled hopes which saw in the single article of the Resurrection of Christ, as in a germ, the whole scheme of Redemption, the entire mystery of godliness. Who can thoroughly comprehend what it is "to be dead, and have his life hid with Christ in God"? what it is to be "quickened together with Christ, and made to sit with Him in heavenly places"? what it is to "have the Spirit of Him that raised up Jesus from the dead" dwelling in us? what it is to be delivered from condemnation through Him who died for us, yea rather that is risen again?

And yet I fear St. Paul would have replied to us that we were but babes and unskillful in the word of righteousness, if we had told him that such language as this conveyed no distinct ideas, no guidance, no strength, no consolation to our minds. We are become such "as have need of milk, and not of strong meat." Our worldly, self-indulgent lives, our low notions of the sinfulness of sin, our self-complacency, our waywardness, our reluctance to acknowedge that we stand in need of a teacher; all help to make us "dull of hearing," and slow to believe, and slower still to act upon those "principles of the doctrine of Christ" which, in a moral aspect, alone distinguish the Gospel from a mere philosophy; and which appeal for acceptance rather to the teachable temper of a little child than to the shrewd discernment of the man of the world, or the inquiring spirit of the man of science.

Thus, to take a single instance, the precept, "Mortify your members which are upon the earth," would be congenial with the philosophies either of the Academy or of the Porch. Plato would say, "Do it, that you may have your soul freer for its proper function of speculative contemplation"; Zeno, "that you may be indifferent to carnal gratifications, and be the better able to realise the highest good, and supreme perfection of man." Contrast these motives but for one moment with that inculcated by St. Paul. With them the precept is but a rule of prudence, grounded on nothing better than a psychological theory; with him it is a moral duty, issuing at once from the relation in which we stand to Him upon Whom our whole spiritual life depends. "Set your affections on things above, not on things on the earth. For ye are dead, and your life is hid with Christ in God; when Christ Who is our life shall appear then shall we also appear with Him in glory."

The Bible is never satisfied unless it runs up even the meanest duties to the highest principles. We are to pay taxes for *conscience' sake.* If we esteem one day above another it is on the principle of "*regarding it to the Lord.*" The thought that we may perchance destroy with our meat one for whom Christ died, is to determine both the quantity and quality of our food. We are to let no corrupt communication proceed out of our mouth lest we should "*grieve the Holy Spirit of God.*" We are to submit ourselves to the laws of the land—to every ordinance of man—"*for the Lord's sake.*" We are to love the brethren because "*we are born of God.*"

Who will say that these are obvious or *naturally* influential motives? What disputer of this world would have ever thought of them? Even now, what Christian adequately comprehends, or consistently acts upon them? To the natural man they still are "foolishness." The schools of the day ignore them. The princes of this world repudiate them. But "God hath revealed them unto us by His Spirit," and "he that is spiritual," feels their force; and though "through the weakness of the flesh" often serving "the law of sin," yet he acknowledges "with the mind" the obligation and supremacy of the law of God.

It is what God has done and is still doing for us, that determines all our duties both towards one another and to Him. His acts to us *all* seem to *centre* in the Resurrection of His Blessed Son. It is, as it were, a focus, which first collects and then transmits, both the light and warmth of the Divine Love. As by it, more emphatically than by anything else, Jesus was " declared to be the Son of God with power," so St. Paul tells us, it is the " power of His Resurrection " above all other articles of the faith that we must make it our chief business to know.

By way of illustration how the doctrine may be brought to bear on every point of Christian duty, and every variety of individual condition, I will endeavour to apply it to the circumstances of a portion of this congregation, that is, *college servants;* to whom, from the peculiar difficulties of their trial, spiritual counsel should be specially profitable, as it is unhappily, specially necessary.

You, my friends, are placed by the Providence of God in the condition of servants, a state of life which—whatever to a worldly eye may be its temporal disadvantages —can never be regarded without deep interest and sympathy by a religious mind, as being that which our Blessed Saviour, when " He took upon Him our flesh," chose as His own. He " made himself of no reputation, and took upon Him *the form of a servant*, and was made in the likeness of men." If it is the state of life which Providence has marked out for us, no true follower of the Cross will repine at it, or envy others who are differently situated, or think that he is unfavourably placed for forming Christian habits, or carrying out Christian principles. If it was Christ's lot it may well be ours.

St. Paul, having laid down the general rule that "every man should abide in the same calling wherein he is called," at once applies it to such a case as yours. "Art thou called," he asks, "being a servant? care not for it; but if thou mayest be made free, use it"—that is thy servitude—"rather." "He that is called in the Lord, being a servant, is the Lord's freeman: likewise also he that is called, being free, is Christ's servant. Ye are bought with a price; be not ye the servants of men."

Oh, how blessed to spiritual ends might be the relation of master and servant, if it were always under the influence of these two great constraining principles! The servant remembering that he is the "Lord's freeman," and the master not forgetting that he is "Christ's servant." What honest self-respect and independence on one side, "with good will doing service as unto the Lord, and not unto men": what considerateness and forbearance on the other, as "knowing that there is a Master also in heaven, neither is there respect of persons with Him." You see at once that the thought of the Risen, Ever-Living Lord, of Him Who was once Himself a servant but in Whom now every believer is made free, is the true Scriptural foundation of the relative duties of either party. The forgetfulness of it is the real cause of all that domestic discomfort of which any one who chooses may hear complaints made every day. We have eye service instead of fidelity on one side; and oppression and imperiousness instead of justice and gentleness on the other. Servants complain of their masters as harsh, and exacting and suspicious: and masters speak of their servants as thankless, and evasive, and untrustworthy. I fear that this state of things prevails even more extensively in colleges than in private households—at least I know it used to do. I would fain hope that a better spirit towards one another is rising up amongst us all.

Your masters are mostly young men, and it is unhappily too common with young men to be insolent towards those whom they deem inferiors, careless of the trouble they cause, expecting orders to be executed without ever stopping to consider whether they are proper or even possible. And the peculiar difficulty of your position is that you are *always* serving such masters. One generation succeeds another with pretty much the same tempers, and tastes and habits. You have continually to deal with young men, in the first flush of imaginary independence, with very little self-control, surrounded by temptations to frivolity, and extravagance, if not to vice. You have to minister to their whims, to bear their humours; often I am afraid to connive at their delinquencies, perhaps even asked to aid them in what both you and they know to be wrong.

It is a hard trial, and Satan will make the most of his opportunity. He will always be pointing out to you indirect ways of advancing your worldly interests by taking advantage of the extravagance or inexperience of your masters. He will whisper to you that you are but a servant, and have no business to ask questions; and that if a service involve a wrong, the blame will fall, not on those who execute it, but on those who enforce it.

How shall you escape, but by never letting slip from your thoughts even for a single moment the Apostle's words, that "though called to be a servant, you are the Lord's freeman." *He* bought you with His blood: *He* rose from the dead to set you free: *He* is your true Master which is in heaven. "He that doeth wrong, shall receive for the wrong which he hath done; and there is no respect of persons." On the other hand, "Whatsoever *good* thing any man doeth, the same shall he receive of the Lord, whether he be bond or free."

Your trial may be, and is, hard. You are subjected to influences that make a conscientious conformity to the law of God difficult, but not impossible. "As your day is so shall your strength be." Our Lord has said "My grace is sufficient for thee: for my strength is made perfect in weakness." In the living strength of the prevailing Advocate and Intercessor, your temptations may be avoided, or overcome. But you must seek that Intercession and have faith in that Advocacy. Be sure that your cry if earnest, if springing from a sense of spiritual need, will at length enter into the ears of the Lord of Sabaoth. He will show you how to walk and please Him. He will teach you the narrow path of duty, even towards unbelieving masters. He will make you know the power of His Resurrection. He will claim you as His own servants, in Whom alone you can have perfect freedom.

And may we, who are masters, have grace also to remember our own grave responsibilities. The capital sin that drew down God's judgment upon the inhabitants of Jerusalem, in the days of Jeremiah, was because they "dealt harshly and untruly with their servants." If we occupy different positions in the kingdom of God's Providence, yet in the Kingdom of His grace "we are in no wise better than they." What law determines the appointments of Providence we do not know; but it is no fighting against God to endeavour by gentleness, and forbearance, and brotherly kindness, to mitigate, as far as we can, their seeming inequality. In Christ Jesus all these distinctions cease and are done away. In Him "is neither Jew nor Greek, bond nor free, male nor female." We are "all one" in Christ Jesus. As brethren together in Christ are we baptised: as brethren, we approach the Table of the Lord, there, in faith and charity to receive those tokens of His sustaining love and care, which testify now as freshly as they did in the cottage at Emmaus, that He liveth; and because He liveth, "we shall live also."

Preached—Oriel College Chapel, March 27, 1853.

X.

THE GIFT OF THE HOLY GHOST.

(A Sermon for Whit Sunday.)

"For as many as are led by the Spirit of God they are the sons of God ; for ye have not received the spirit of bondage again to fear ; but ye have received the spirit of adoption, whereby we cry, Abba, Father ! The Spirit itself beareth witness with our spirit that we are the children of God : and if children, then heirs, heirs of God and joint heirs with Christ ; if so be that we suffer with Him, that we may be also glorified together."—ROM. viii. 14-17.

WHITSUNTIDE is one of those great Christian festivals on which the preacher need have the tongue of an angel, and use words that burn like living fire, to deliver his message of great joy, and raise every hearer's heart to an adequate sense of the blessed privileges that he may call his own.

There is perhaps no festival of the Church that is more peculiarly and emphatically Christian than this. It marks and commemorates a gift that is the special heritage of the Church, the distinctive privilege of the baptised, *the* gift without which all that Christ wrought, and spoke, and suffered for man would have been insufficient to achieve the salvation of a single soul. For it is the Spirit of God—the third person in the Blessed and Undivided Trinity, the Comforter Who

proceeds from the Father and the Son, Who spake by
the prophets and sanctifies the elect—He it is who alone
enables God's people to do unto Him "a true and
laudable service." He it is Who inspires us to accept,
and appropriate, and realise, the Redemption wrought
out upon the Cross. He it is Who teaches us the depth
of our spiritual need, and sends us to Jesus as alone
able to stand between our sins and God's consuming
fire. He it is Who enables us to say, with any vital
meaning in our words, "that Jesus Christ is Lord," and
brings us "boldly to the throne of grace," and lifts up
our voice in confident, but not presumptuous, utterance,
to cry "Abba, Father."

Indeed, it is because this gift of the Holy Ghost, to be
with us and dwell in us, is the property in common of
the whole Church, and specially of every Christian, that
we do not estimate the blessedness of enjoying it so
fully as we should do if to some of us it were given and
to others denied. If we had living by our side men
sunk in the hopeless darkness of heathenism, bowing
down to images of wood and stone, human beings
degraded almost to the level of the beasts that perish,
and that not only in their spiritual but also in their
moral nature; we should then be in a better position
to judge what a blessed thing it is to "have the mind of
Christ," and to be taught by the Spirit of truth; to see
the end of our being, and to be able to unlock the
mystery of this puzzling world; to hear of "a shedding
of blood" that *can* take away sin; of a "house not
made with hands eternal in the heavens"; of a God
that is "very pitiful and of a tender mercy" and of

things passing the power of man to conceive " which He has prepared for them that love Him."

Though I do not mean to say that all who have heard of these things, and are ready enough to talk about them, have received their knowledge by direct communication from the Spirit of God—though I know that all men, even in a Christian land and with Divine ordinances lying as it were before their feet " have not the Spirit," and when they talk about religion only do it in an unreal way, at second-hand, in phrases that they borrow from the religious world, but which their own experience does not verify, and which their lives belie—still it remains true all the same that the Holy Ghost is the fount and spring of this knowledge. It is He Who first taught Christians those truths and that language which many who are not Christians, save in name, venture to use. If He had never been sent by Christ from the Father, no living man would have " known the mind of the Lord," or been able to speak of the things which are freely given unto us of God.

Accordingly, St. Paul represents the whole visible creation, both men and beasts, as " groaning and travailing in pain together until now "; as possessed by an inexplicable yearning for something they feel they want but cannot express; as living in "earnest expectation, waiting for the manifestation of the sons of God." And each Christian though himself, too, groaning inwardly, and " waiting for the adoption, to wit, the redemption, of his body," and " knowing not what he should pray for as he ought," feeling that he is not yet fully delivered from "the bondage of corruption into the glorious liberty of the children of God," "having a heavenly treasure in earthly vessels"—still feels also that he *has* a heavenly treasure, *has* the first-fruits of the Spirit, "the earnest of his inheritance"; feels "the Spirit helping his infirmities" and sustaining him by hope; has a witness within him of his adoption as God's child, and so has a living faith that "all things work together for good" unto one that loves God and is called according to His purpose.

This is the Christian's privilege; the advantage of the spiritual over the natural man—to feel that God is his Father, and that He is enabling him, it may be slowly, but on the whole surely, to overcome the world, by that renewing influence of the Holy Ghost which He has shed on him abundantly in Jesus Christ our Lord. The worldling may use the same language; he may talk of the "consolation in Christ," "the comfort of love," the "fellowship of the Spirit," the "bowels of mercies"; but he uses words without meaning. In his mouth they are not realities; they neither guide nor strengthen him. He is "intruding into things which he has not seen, vainly puffed up by his fleshly mind." St. Paul, when he speaks of "spiritual gifts," is describing the state, not of the nominal Christian, but of the earnest believer; of *his* comforts, and supports, and hopes, and confidences; how *he* may speak and what he may trust: in a word, what God's faithful servants have gained by that Gospel "which is preached with the Holy Ghost sent down from heaven."

And of these, of God's faithful servants, of the earnest believers in Christ, it is written that they have "received the Spirit of adoption," and have "the Spirit itself bearing witness with their spirit that they are the children of God." The very purpose of the mission of the Holy Ghost was to make us *feel*, with an experimental sense, what we have won in Christ; in what respect the Christian is better than the Jew; what is the profit of that title of access to the Father which our regeneration invested us withal. He was sent that we might " know the things that are freely given unto us of God." He came to write the law of Christ not in tables of stone, but " in the fleshly tables of the heart." It is His work to make God's strength " perfect in our weakness " ; to make us feel that out of our lowest estate and most embarrassing circumstances we can rise " more than conquerors through Him Who loved us ;" to build us up together, not singly but collectively in a Church, " for an habitation of God "; " to set us free from the law of sin and of death "; to make obedience possible ; " to strengthen us with might in the inner man " ; to assure us, with all the power of a living conviction, of the riches of our inheritance. So long as we abide faithful, doing God's work diligently " in the calling wherewith we are called," there is nothing—so says the Spirit— either in earth or heaven, " neither death, nor life, nor things present, nor things to come, which shall be able to separate us from the love of God, which is in Christ Jesus our Lord."

This is what the Bible tells us of the work and office of that Blessed Spirit of Promise, for Which our Divine Lord bade the Apostles tarry in Jerusalem till they had received it; Which, as on this day of Pentecost, came from heaven " with a sound as of a rushing mighty wind," "and in the likeness of cloven tongues of fire"; Which enabled those poor ignorant fishermen and tradesmen of Galilee to go forth boldly and powerfully, and " preach the Gospel to every creature"; Which we are taught to believe dwells in each of us who has been baptised, making our bodies His Temple, and through Whom Christ verifies still the last words He spoke on earth, " Lo! I am with you always, even unto the end of the world."

All these are burning words, too high and excellent, it would seem, for sinful, earthly creatures to use, and yet such as the Bible plainly puts into the mouth of every Christian, and bids him utter them fearlessly. Observe! I say, "into the mouth of every *Christian*"; for here lies the point of the whole matter. The inspired writers of the New Testament, when addressing us on the subject of our common salvation, plainly suppose that they are speaking to, and of, persons who see a value in Christianity, who would be thankful to be told what things God has done for their souls; who would prize the hope of their calling, and do all that lay in their power to make it "sure"; who would seek grace in every channel in which it was ordained to flow; who, in St, Paul's comprehensive phrase, "knowing that their bodies are temples of the Holy Ghost which is in them," and that they "are not their own, but bought with a price," would recognise in such acts of Divine Love manifested towards them a plain and constraining obligation to "glorify God both in their bodies and their spirits, which are God's."

But whatever might have been the influence of the

Gospel upon men's hearts in the Apostolic times, it plainly is not of this transforming and renewing power now. Not that the power of the Gospel itself is less, but that our hearts seem harder and our ears more dull of hearing. We listen to the same unchanging message of God's love to fallen man, of the method of redemption and the means of grace, of the nature of faith and the duties of the believer, but it makes no impression upon us. It sounds like "an idle tale," or at best but a pretty picture. It does not stir up the ground of our hearts, or awaken us to a sense of our own danger, or determine us to any real effort after godliness, or bring home that solemn question to our fears which brought the trembling jailer at Philippi on his knees before Paul and Silas, saying, "Sirs, what must I do to be saved?"

If this be the amount of our spiritual discernment, this the measure of our religious life; if, though baptised and born again in Christ, and pledged thereby to a life of faith and holiness, though once enlightened and made partakers of the Holy Ghost, we have not led the rest of our life "answerably to this beginning"; "have counted the blood of the covenant, wherewith we were sanctified, an unholy thing"; "have put Christ to an open shame, and done despite unto the Spirit of grace," it would be the madness of presumption to apply to ourselves that blessed language in which St. Paul and St. John describe the strength of the believer, the privileges of the regenerate, the comforts of the justified, the liberty of the redeemed, the assurance of the elect.

The text only speaks of those "who are led by the Spirit of God." The burden of the whole chapter from

THE GIFT OF THE HOLY GHOST.

which it is taken is that "to be carnally minded is death; but to be spiritually minded is life and peace." Can a man be "led" by the Spirit of God who is a Sabbath-breaker, a drunkard, a profane swearer? who has an evil eye at his neighbour's prosperity? who is only hasting to get rich? who is proud or imperious, or selfish and impatient? who turns his back on God's ordinances, and, as the prophet speaks, "snuffs at the table of the Lord"? who thinks he is good enough and all safe, instead of "forgetting the things which are behind and reaching forward unto the things which are before"? who never sacrifices any whim or humour or inclination for the sake of duty, and so is a stranger to all the exemplary teaching of the Cross? who takes no pains to conquer bad habits and unruly tempers? who is rude and coarse in his language, careless of his company, negligent of his duties as a father or a husband, and in no part of his conduct keeping the fear of God, as an abiding restraint, before his eyes?

Some parts of this description, I fear, will apply to every one of us—to some, perhaps, a good deal. There are some who go to church and who, I am afraid, get little good by going: upon whom the words spoken, the invitations to the Holy Table, the voice of prayer and thanksgiving, the blessed opportunities of public worship, produce no visible effect, operate no perceptible change: who, instead of living by faith and growing spiritually wiser and stronger, seem to be standing still, if not positively drawing back—strangers, I am sure, to all the true comforts of the Spirit, because they are not yet delivered from the bondage of the world.

The Holy Spirit will not dwell in a defiled or a neglected temple. He will go and seek another home if He be not welcomed in ours; He will only abide in a holy place, "with him also that is of a contrite and humble spirit, to revive the spirit of the humble, and to revive the heart of the contrite ones." He cannot put up with "proud looks and high stomachs, which say, We are they which ought to speak: who is Lord over us?" He has no good news to tell, no comfortable hope of acceptance to offer, the formalist, the lip-server, the covetous, the dishonest, the slothful, the filthy. It must be a pure and upright heart for Him to place His habitation in; a heart weaned from the world, and with "affections set on things above"; a heart "risen with Christ," and seeking to taste of the fulness of that joy which no human potentate can either give or take away. Like some rich and fertilising manure cast upon a barren and unkindly soil, His presence is revealed by its fruits. They are fruits which, if we are not bringing forth ourselves, we can at least recognise and appreciate in others. Every one in his conscience bears witness to the beauty of such graces as "Love, peace, long-suffering, gentleness, goodness, faith, meekness, temperance." "Against these there is no law"; for indeed they render all law superfluous. Their animating motive is not *fear*, but *love;* the love of Him "Who first loved us," not the dread of a Being Who cannot be touched with a feeling of our infirmities; it is an obedience issuing from the pure devotion of the heart to a kind Benefactor, not from slavish bondage to a hard task-master.

These fruits must be manifested in each one of us. "We have received the Spirit of adoption," been made sons of God, been chosen out of the world for this very end, that we should "show forth the praises of Him who hath called us out of darkness into His marvellous light," that we should be "a kind of first-fruits of His creatures." We have no right to speak of ourselves as "free," except so far as we have refused to make ourselves the slaves of sin.

Oh! pray the Father of Mercies, the God of all Comfort, to make you feel the strength and privilege of this adoption; to break Satan's yoke from off your neck; to make you "free indeed;" free from carnal appetites and selfish tempers, free from covetousness and worldly lusts, free from a cold and fashionable formalism, free from the tyranny of confirmed but unchristian habits. Pray to God the Son that He would keep His word to you individually, that He would send unto you "the promise from the Father," that He would endue you "with power from on high," that He would enable you to realise the "expediency" of His going away by an experimental conviction that a mightier Comforter— mightier because more abiding—is dwelling in your souls. Pray, too, to that Comforter that He would teach and enlighten you, and bring Christ's "words to remembrance," and show you the breadth of the commandment, and bruise Satan under your feet, and spiritualise your affections, and help your prayers, and take away whatever veil is upon your hearts, and enable you "with open face to behold as in a glass the glory of the Lord."

Be sure if His light is not burning in your souls it *ought* to be. If you have never found Him "a very present help in time of trouble," it is because you have sought after other comforters. If you find your way dark and difficult, it is because you have never asked Him to make it plain. If He bears not "His witness with our spirit that we are the children of God," it is because a life of worldliness and disobedience has made us strangers to the feeling, as well as forfeited the title, of "sons."

Preached – Cholderton, Whitsunday, June 5, 1854 ; May 23, 1858.

XI.

DIVERSITIES OF GIFTS.

"There are diversities of gifts ; but the same Spirit."
—1 Cor. xii. 4.

THERE is an ordinary theological distinction of the manifestation of the Holy Ghost, into "gifts" and "graces." I do not know that the distinction rests on any ground of Scripture, or is worth much in itself. At the most I presume it to mean that when the Holy Ghost manifests His presence in a man's moral or spiritual nature we call the result a "grace;" and when the epiphany is in his intellectual or mental nature we call it a "gift." Thus, we should call eloquence, poetic genius, musical talent, philosophical power, "gifts;" and gentleness, patience, chastity, truthfulness, "graces." If the distinction is helpful to us, we may of course retain and use it : but I am afraid that it has sometimes exercised a prejudicial and narrowing influence upon the conception we form of the work of the Holy Ghost in the new creation. For though we have been ready enough to recognise the presence of the Holy Ghost in the graces of the saints, we have been much slower of heart to believe that He is equally manifest in the intellectual gifts of man.

And yet, mark the gifts which the Apostle distinctly enumerates as tokens of the manifestation of the Spirit: not as though they had not existed before in what might be called the dispensation of nature, but as though now, in the dispensation of grace, their authorship and divine original were unequivocally recognised. "To one is given by the Spirit the word of wisdom: to another the word of knowledge by the same Spirit; to another faith; to another the gifts of healing; to another the working of miracles; to another, prophecy"—*i.e.* the power of preaching in demonstration of the Spirit and of power; "to another discerning of spirits," winnowing false doctrine from true; "to another divers kinds of tongues; to another the interpretation of tongues."

Though these gifts have ceased in these latter days—for some inscrutable purpose of the divine counsel—to be *miraculous*, they still exist, *every one of them*, as the fruit of labour and reward of toil; tokens of a great and blessed law, the necessity of man's co-operation with God, as in his spiritual, so in his intellectual development; tokens of the Holy Spirit's continued presence with the Church, and that the promise of the Lord Jesus has been abundantly fulfilled.

To some persons, whose notions have been formed upon a narrow, and, as it seems to me, untenable theory, this language will appear overstrained and extravagant. They will say "Do you mean to assert that these gifts of which the Apostle speaks can really be claimed for men and women now?" I do mean it, and that in very truth and soberness. I do not wish to put forth a paradox, but to proclaim what I believe to be a real doctrine of the Gospel. The power to heal; the power to prophesy; the power to discern between the spirit of truth and the spirit of falsehood; the power to interpret tongues, are gifts that are actually enjoyed and exercised by living men.

Surely Mezzofanti, with his knowledge of thirty-seven languages, had the gift of "divers kinds of tongues"! Surely they who, with such wonderful ingenuity, deciphered the hieroglyphics of Egypt, or the cuneiform inscriptions of Assyria, had the gift of the "interpretation of tongues." Are the things less "gifts" because they are not instantaneously acquired? Are they less worthy tokens of the Spirit because He thus sees fit to reward patient diligence, and to verify in every department of human nature the Lord's word "Ask, and ye shall have; seek, and ye shall find."

If you still think that at any rate the faith which could remove mountains and which wrought miracles is at least an extinct gift, I would only ask you to read the story of George Müller, of Bristol, who feeds, clothes, and educates I know not how many hundreds of orphan children *simply in faith;* dispensing with the usual eleemosynary machinery, not knowing what each day may bring forth, but finding himself, as he would say, "miraculously" sustained and encouraged and provided for—mountains removed and his way made plain.

We often raise unnecessary difficulties about this word "miracle;" and yet religious philosophy has taught us that it does not mean a *violation* of one of Nature's laws—which, remember, are God's laws—but simply a result which the mind of man, with its imperfect apprehension of the scope and range of those laws, could not have foreseen or calculated. It is not necessary that a miracle should be something sudden, instantaneous, effectual in an instant. The man to whom our Lord restored the gift of vision, saw "men as trees walking," before the film cleared utterly away from his eyes. The sustentation of the Israelites in the wilderness was a standing miracle for forty years. In nearly the same sense the history of George Müller is a standing miracle—a miracle too rewarding faith: a result, if not contrary to experience, at least outrunning all the ordinary laws of probability and reasonable anticipation.

I say this, not to degrade our notions of a miracle—God forbid!—but to raise and enlarge our notions of the works of God.

In the popular theology of the day, large departments of human life are cut off utterly from the domain of God's administration. Philosophical discovery, literature, the mechanical arts and trades, political systems, are spoken of as though they lived by an inherent power of their own, and were, in fact, influences independent of, and extraneous to, the kingdom of God. Such a system of theology will hardly square with the express language of the Bible. "For His God doth instruct him to discretion, and doth teach him," says the prophet Isaiah, speaking of the ploughman and his labour. And if the simple skill of the husbandman is thus distinctly ascribed to the teaching of God, shall we not in all the mighty inventions of Watt, and Arkwright, and

Stephenson, which have revolutionised the world, and are exerting such an incalculable influence on the condition and destinies of the race, shall we not in these too trace the finger of God—the gifts of the Spirit—and say, "This also cometh from the Lord of Hosts, which is wonderful in counsel and excellent in working!"

These conclusions, if true, have some important practical bearings :—

1. How they ennoble every man's calling! It is a "gift" of God. It is the sphere in which God means him to work out his salvation.

2. How they extend the range of faith! It becomes —at least it ought to become—the animating principle of all I do. Believing that it is God that worketh in me, I am supplied with an inexhaustible resource of elasticity and energy, and power. "Genius," said Buffon, "is patience." Newton and Stephenson, and all men of true genius have been emphatically men of faith, content to "bide" their time. If the vision tarried, they waited for it, and at length it came.

3. What a wider domain is thus thrown open to the power of prayer! What a privilege to feel that we may safely ask God to bless the work of our hands! What a check upon undertaking anything which our consciences tell us we dare not pray God to approve!

4. And, lastly, how clearly in the power of this conviction do we perceive that all things work together for good to them that love God! The poet Wordsworth, says:

"I could wish my days to be
Bound each to each by natural piety."

Here is God's own provision for realising the wish. For thus everything is brought under the influence of religion. Thus, the whole of life, so to speak, would be saturated with the Gospel. Thus, the Spirit of God penetrates every part of our complete nature, and consecrates, sanctifies, elevates the whole.

Wherefore, brethren, "covet earnestly the best gifts;" the best bodily gifts, the best intellectual gifts, the best spiritual gifts. And if you covet them labour to win them. And if you win them, see to it how you use them. For each gift carries with it a proportionate responsibility. It is to be turned to account in promoting the glory of God and the happiness of man. It must not be wrapped up in a napkin. It is not given to advance mere selfish ends. "The manifestation of the Spirit is given to every man *to profit withal.*" And again another scripture: "As every man hath received the gift, even so minister the same *one to another*, as good stewards of the *manifold* grace of God."

Preached—Salisbury Cathedral, Thursday in Whitsun Week, 1860; St. John's, Broughton, II. after Epiphany, January 15, 1871.

XII.

THE LABOURERS IN THE VINEYARD.

"So the last shall be first, and the first last: for many be called, but few chosen."—ST. MATTHEW xx. 16.

ST. PETER tells us that there are many things in the Bible "hard to be understood," which "they that are unlearned and unstable wrest to their own destruction." I am afraid that the parable of the labourers in the vineyard has been one of "these things," that it has often had directly the opposite effect to that which it was intended to have, and which, if rightly weighed and compared with other Scriptures, it *would* have had. It has encouraged sloth, and fanaticism, and presumption, instead of begetting earnestness, diligence, and lowliness of mind. This has been because people will not be at the pains to ascertain what its lesson really is, or how far it may be explained by the other passages in connection with which it is found.

The parable occurs in the course of a continuous conversation which Jesus had with His disciples; and we cannot rightly understand the parable unless we take the whole of the conversation into account. A young man, it seems, came to our Lord with a good deal of confidence and pretension, asking "What good thing he was to do, that he might inherit eternal life." He appears to have entertained no doubt that he *should* finally be saved. He had found no difficulty, he said, in keeping the Commandments; and perhaps he had not, *in his way* of keeping them. He was very decent, very respectable, very wealthy, very self-satisfied; and when Jesus quietly referred him to the two great principles of love towards God and man, as the sum and the substance of religious duty, it is in a tone of triumphant self-complacency that he replies—as though tired of hearing the familiar words—"All these things have I kept from my youth up; what lack I yet?" Poor young man! He little thought how soon his vain confidence and self-righteousness were to be dashed to the ground. He who reads the heart knew, that in the midst of a formal profession and outward respectability, there had never been any real sacrifice, or a single moment's true self-denial. Mammon had more of his heart than God; though till now he knew it not. When he heard of "selling what he had, and giving to the poor," of "laying up treasure in heaven and following Christ," he "went away sorrowful: for he had great possessions."

Our Lord was thus naturally led to speak of the exceeding danger of earthly riches, when they enslave the heart, and dull the spiritual perception, to the extent they had done in this young man. "It is easier for a camel to go through the eye of a needle than for a rich man"—one, that is, who *trusts* in riches—"to enter the kingdom of God." Then answered Peter—his thoughts naturally led to dwell upon the difference between his own case and his fellow-disciples' and that of this rich young man—and said unto His Master, " Behold we have forsaken all and followed Thee : what shall we have therefore ? " And Jesus said unto him, " Verily I say unto you, that ye which have followed me, in the regeneration when the Son of Man shall sit on the throne of His glory, ye also shall sit upon twelve thrones, judging the twelve tribes of Israel. And every one that hath forsaken houses, or brethren, or sisters, or father, or mother, or wife, or children, or lands for my name's sake, shall receive an hundred fold, and shall inherit everlasting life. But many that are first "—the case of this young man again perhaps coming across His mind, so wealthy, surrounded with so many advantages of rank and fortune, and yet unhappily with his heart so far from God—" many, therefore, that are first shall be last, and the last first."

And then, according to His wont, illustrating this solemn truth by a familiar and homely example, showing that the method of God's government, far from being harsh or unfair, is the very best principle upon which, under similar circumstances, we should act in the world, He introduces this parable of the labourers in the vineyard, which ends, as in the text, with the same weighty saying with which it begins—" So the last shall be first, and the first last; for many are called, but few are chosen."

The details of the parable must be familiar to all. It is the picture of a farmer going out at different hours in the day, hiring such labourers as he found unemployed, and when the evening was come, paying them all the same wages. Those who had borne the burthen and heat of the day would doubtless have been quite content with what they got—it was indeed the rate at which they had agreed to work—if they had not seen others, who had worked fewer hours, receiving the same. They did not complain that they were underpaid; but they felt aggrieved that the last should be put upon an equality with themselves. They forgot that their complaint really amounted to this—a restriction upon their employer, who was behaving with perfect fairness to *them*, from doing in the case of others as he chose with his own.

Now the dangerous practical perversion to which the parable is liable is twofold. As I have said, it may be made to foster either sloth or presumption. People may say, "Oh! I must wait till I am called before I set to work at all. I am idle because no man hath hired me. When God wants me He will let me know, and come and look after me." Or on the other hand, they may fancy that they have plenty of time before them, and that they will fare just as well at the great payment of wages if they begin to work at the eleventh hour as if they spend their lives in God's service, or, in the language of the parable, "bear the burthen and heat of the day."

It is impossible to conceive anything more unreasonable or more unscriptural than either of these notions. I would ask in all soberness is there any one, from the merest child who has learnt to discern good from evil, to the hoariest head, who can either say or think that God has not called him: that God has given him nothing to do—left him without work—permitted him to be idle? Every baptised Christian "as soon as he knows to refuse the evil and to choose the good," is reckoned by God among His "called." At our baptism God took us into His service; told us what He required us to do; promised us our wages; and we undertook the work and bound ourselves to execute it under the most solemn vows. In our families, in our households, in our business, as husbands, as wives, as masters, as servants, as employers, as labourers, as tradesmen, as customers, as neighbours, as parents, as children, as teachers, as learners—there lies the sphere of our duties: within those limits we have to serve God, and "make our calling and election sure."

If you will follow out the exhortation of the Apostle "to walk worthy of the vocation wherewith ye are called," into the practical rules by which he explains his meaning, you will find they relate almost exclusively to duties of this kind. By courtesy, by forbearance, by truth-speaking, by honesty, by purity of thought and word, by sobriety, by attention to family duties —husbands loving their wives, children obeying their parents, householders bringing up their families in the nurture and admonition of the Lord, servants doing their master's work in singleness of heart as unto Christ—by this daily course of watchfulness and circumspection, the Christian's calling is fulfilled, and he himself grows up more and more "unto a perfect man, unto the measure of the stature of the fulness of Christ."

After this, how can anybody say that God has not given him enough to do? God has called us one and all to "holiness." He has put His Spirit upon us for no other end. Our duties lie under our feet. They awake with us every morning. They go forth with us every time we leave our door. In our homes, at our shopboard, behind our plough, in the sheepfold, in the stable, on a journey, on an errand, in household work, in professional employment, there they are, and there they must be discharged. Alas! that in a Christian land any should be so blind and slow of heart as to suppose that God has excepted him from the universal law of labour, has sent him into this world without giving him any duty to do! It is the peculiar prerogative of the Christian not only that all his duties rest on spiritual motives and bear a religious aspect, but that he has supernatural power vouchsafed to him also to enable him to perform them. What St. Paul says of himself is true, according to his measure, of every member of Christ. "He can do all things through Christ who strengtheneth him." God's strength is "made perfect in our weakness." If the poor heathen African stands idle, living only to himself, doing nothing to God's glory; or if the thousands in the dark lanes and by-places of our great cities, still living in the shadow of death though in a land where light has sprung up, whose ears the message of the Gospel has never reached, among whom —to our shame be it spoken—the ministrations of our Church are not known — if these stand idle *they* have much to plead in their excuse, they may well think that "no man hath hired them." They belong to those of whom it is written, "they shall be beaten with *few* stripes," because they knew not what the will of their Lord was. If, haply, one of these is by God's converting grace brought to a knowledge of the truth, and turns from his evil ways, and brings forth the fruits of righteousness, in him we see one of those labourers hired at the eleventh hour, and yet who shall receive at his heavenly Master's hand as much as those who have borne the burthen and heat of the day.

God measures our claims upon His favour by our *earnestness* and by our *opportunities*. He will not ask us *how long* we have known His will, but whether, since we have known it, we have done it. There is not a single individual among ourselves who can lay the blame either of ignorance or lack of opportunity at God's door. We are all within the reach of the means of grace and instruction if only we cared to use them. There are few families without a Bible. The Church is free to all. You may all partake of that enlightening grace that flows through her sacraments. Be assured God marks your advantages even if you do not. Every Lord's Day, according as it is spent, is one of these precious opportunities either treasured or cast away. Every Lord's Supper is another. Every sermon is another. The very fabric of the Church, pointing heavenwards, is a witness of our duties and of the purpose for which we came into the world.

Of course, if we please, we can disregard all these things. We can spend our Sabbath evenings in an alehouse. We can turn our backs on the Lord's Table. We can sleep through a sermon. We can think as little of God in His church as in our own homes. But do not let us say, as an excuse, that we do not know any better, and that we cannot help bad habits or bad thoughts coming into our minds. We *do* know better, and we *can* conquer bad thoughts and bad actions; the indulgence in which forms bad habits. When I say *we* can conquer, I mean that Christians can conquer, for Christians have the Holy Ghost given to them for this very purpose. St. Paul tells us that in "all these things they may be *more* than conquerors through Christ who loved them." The very object of our Lord's ascension was "to receive gifts for us," that we too might be enabled to ascend with Him. If our affections are still set on the earth, it is because we have never tried to raise them. God waits to be gracious; and we have only to ask for the Spirit in order to receive Him.

I have dwelt at such length upon the necessity of religious earnestness and religious diligence as the two grand elements of that judgment of God which will determine our positions in the future world, that I can do no more than barely notice other points in the parable which are well worthy of an attentive consideration. I could have wished to say something on that jealousy, which seems to be the last infirmity, even of spiritual minds; which we see to be at the bottom of the complaint of the labourers who were first called; and which is also illustrated in so striking a manner in the behaviour of the elder brother in the beautiful parable of the prodigal son. I suppose it will be the element of the old Adam that will stick longest by us—that grudging spirit of envy which always thinks its own claims superior to its neighbours', and feels aggrieved at others being admitted to advantages which we have been in the habit of considering exclusively our own. I would gladly also have endeavoured to show you in what sense God has an undoubted right "to do what He wills with His own;" because in so dispensing His favours, He follows no arbitrary whim or caprice, but a just and unchangeable law—the law of measuring men's work by their motives and judging every man by his opportunities.

In conclusion I would only press one warning upon you. As I have cautioned you to beware of thinking that you may stand all the day idle because God has given you no work to do; so beware no less carefully of another, and not less fatal delusion—the delusion of supposing that you have done your work and may pass the rest of your time in ease. God's days are of different lengths. Twenty-four hours for one purpose make a day. In another sense we are told "a thousand years are a day" also. In spiritual things a day is a *lifetime*. As long as we are in the world God's work is still before us to do. On this side of the grave it is all *work*; on the other, it will be all *rest*.

Oh! thrice blessed are they who enter into that rest with "their works following them"! Rest remaineth only for them that have laboured. The idle, unprofitable servant shall not taste of it. It is not for those who ran well, but only for a time. It is for the faithful, the earnest, the humble, the persevering. It is for those who ran "with patience" their race, "looking unto Jesus, the Author and Finisher of their faith." It is for Paul and not for Demas; for those who have fought their fight out, not for those who, after a while, grew weary of well-doing. It is for you and me in proportion as we realise that blessed promise, " Be thou faithful unto death, and I will give thee a crown of life." In the beautiful words of the Christian poet :—

> " The gray-haired saint may fail at last,
> The surest guide a wanderer prove :
> Death only binds us fast
> To the bright shore of love."

Preached — Cholderton, Septuagesima Sunday, January 23, 1853 ; January 31, 1858 ; Third after Epiphany, January 22, 1860.

XIII.

CHRIST OUR SACRIFICE AND EXAMPLE.

"Christ also suffered for us, leaving us an example."—
I. PET. ii. 21.

THE death of Jesus was at once vicarious and exemplary; a propitiation and a pattern: an inestimable benefit and a perfect model: a "sacrifice for sin," and also an "example of godly life." To look at the Cross under any one of these points of view taken alone is to miss half the lesson it was intended to teach us. It leads to false faith and corrupt practice.

The Antinomian, the man who thinks that all religion is centred in the single grace of faith, looks at Christ as his Saviour, but forgets that He is also his Example. The Socinian professes to follow Jesus as an Example, but rejects Him as a Saviour. The Bible-taught Christian unites these two opposite systems into one. Confessing with St. Peter that "there is none other Name under heaven given among men, whereby we must be saved," he also allows with St. Paul that he who would taste of this salvation must "so walk as He walked." In the simple and unmistakable language of the text, believing with all his heart that "Christ suffered for him," he has an equally deep conviction that He has "left us an example that we should follow His steps."

Without the Atonement there would have been little use of the Example. Moses is an example, and Abraham, and Joseph, and David, and every holy man or woman that ever lived—many in our own times and neighbourhood, whom we may ourselves have known. St. Paul, who was the last person in the world to speak presumptuously or vain-gloriously, exhorts the Philippians to "be followers together of him, and to mark those who walked so as they had him for an ensample."

And yet in another epistle, after calling his readers' attention to the great cloud of witnesses with whom they were encompassed, all of them "examples" of patience, faith, and other heavenly graces, he does not suffer their thoughts to rest there, or on any merely human object, but carries them on with him still further, even to the foot of the Cross, there bidding them "look to Jesus, the Author and Finisher of their faith, Who for the joy that was set before Him endured the Cross, despising the shame, and was now set down at the right hand of God."

He wished them to feel that there was something about the life and death of Christ which placed it quite above the level of other men's lives or deaths, and invested it with an awfulness, and value, and interest all its own. Jesus was no mere "Martyr for truth," as some have represented Him, but He was made unto us of God "wisdom and righteousness and sanctification and redemption." He "gave Himself a ransom for all." "By

CHRIST OUR SACRIFICE AND EXAMPLE. 117

His stripes we are healed." He was "the reconciliation of the world." In Him sinners have hope of pardon. He is "our righteousness." "In Him, whosoever believeth shall never die." As the doctrine is all summed up in one verse, "He was once offered to bear the sins of many, and unto them that look for Him shall He appear again the second time without sin unto salvation." His is that "blood of sprinkling which speaketh better things than that of Abel." Abel was a righteous man, but nothing more. He had sins of his own to answer for, and "could make no agreement with God" for the iniquities of others. His "blood cried" unto God "from the ground" for vengeance upon his murderer. It spoke not a syllable of peace, or propitiation, or cleansing, or redemption. Of One, and of One only, is it written, that "His blood cleanseth us from all sin." In One, and One only, "being justified by faith," can we have "peace with God," and not peace only, but joy.

It was the mystery of the *Incarnation* that gave this efficacy to the mystery of the *Atonement*. It was because "He was found in fashion as a man, and became obedient unto death," being also the Eternal, Only-begotten Son of God, that that death became fruitful of such precious and everlasting consequences. Though we do not pretend to be able either to explain or understand so deep a revelation, though the fact of salvation will remain a mystery to the end of time, yet all who have any serious concern for their souls must feel their need of a Saviour. Weak, helpless, sin-stained as we are in ourselves, we could never endure the judgment, or venture to appear in the presence of God. If "in His sight the very heavens are not clean, and He charges even His angels with folly," what must man be, "who is a worm, and the son of man, who is a worm"?

The very heathen acknowledged, with tears and groans, their need of a redemption, though they had never heard the name of their Redeemer. Ignorant of the true propitiation, they went about to devise all sorts of sacrifices—many of them monstrous and horrible in the extreme—to stand between themselves and the sentence of divine wrath under which they felt they lay. In Christ crucified we behold, in the prophet's striking words, "the desire of all nations"; "a light to lighten the Gentiles," as well as "the glory of His people Israel."

The doctrine of the Atonement, then, is this: that we who were by nature "afar off from God," in Christ are "brought nigh": that God, for His sake, "hath blotted out our trespasses," "and our sins and iniquities will He remember no more": that He gives "the water of life," to all that will take it, freely: that we are not, and cannot be, saved by our own righteousness: that God's purpose towards us is full of mercy and tenderness in His Blessed Son: that "He willeth not that any should perish, but that all should come to repentance": that those will be saved who, renouncing their own merits and all carnal titles to God's favour, look for salvation only through the blood of Christ; who come unto Him that they may have life; who appropriate the benefits of His sacrifice by personal faith, confessing that "they are

CHRIST OUR SACRIFICE AND EXAMPLE.

bought with a price," and feeling that "he who glorieth must glory in the Lord."

It is a blessed and comfortable doctrine! the anchor of our hopes as well as the object of our faith; the only sure ground of peace, and confidence, and joy; not only enabling but impelling us to "come boldly to the throne of grace that we may obtain mercy and find grace to help in time of need." It has bridged over the wide gulf that lay betwixt ourselves and God; and shows even to the most obdurate sinner, if he will only follow it, a way by which he may yet hear of joy and gladness; and to the heaviest-laden a place where they may find rest unto their souls." "God hath made Him to be sin for us, Who knew no sin, that we might be made the righteousness of God in Him."

If I stopped here, comfortable and consolatory, and cheering as these truths are, I should only have given you a one-sided, and therefore a dangerous view of them. I have been talking of Christ's death only as a *Sacrifice;* I have said nothing about it as an *Example.* I have spoken of *faith;* I have not as yet mentioned *obedience.* I have bidden you take comfort in the thought of Christ having suffered for you; but I have yet to speak of the duty of following His steps.

There is a reciprocal feeling of love and interest between Christ and His redeemed; or as it is figuratively expressed in the Gospel, between the Good Shepherd and His sheep. "I know My sheep and am known of Mine." "My sheep hear My voice, and I know them and they follow Me." "He that loveth me I will love." "He that loveth Me not keepeth not My sayings."

There is an awful verity contained in those few pregnant words of Our Divine Saviour, "Many are called, but *few* are chosen"; or in the kindred, and not less fearful, saying, that "Strait is the gate and narrow the way that leadeth unto life; and *few* there be that find it." Many ill-instructed and ill-read persons— who read their Bible by patches and not as a whole, picking out favourite texts and building up one-sided views upon them—when they hear of the doctrine of Christ having made upon the Cross "a full, perfect and sufficient sacrifice for the sins of the whole world," immediately, and without any serious thought, appropriate the blessed tidings to themselves, say consciously, or else unconsciously, "Oh, then, I am safe! My sins are blotted out: God has forgiven me." They feel quite easy about themselves. They know nothing of that "fear" which St. Paul sets off as the proper corrective of high-mindedness. They talk of other people, who seem to them to have a less vivid apprehension of the doctrine, as "lying in darkness and the shadow of death," and claim for themselves all the high and glorious privileges which the Bible enumerates as the inheritance of God's elect.

I am not describing a fanciful creation of my own mind, but a living existent phase of the popular religion of the day. There is scarcely perhaps a parish in the land in which you will not find half-a-dozen people who think and talk in this way. I believe these to be most dangerous and unscriptural delusions; mere presumptuous handlings of Gospel truth; as much *perversions* of "the doctrine which is according to godliness" as anything can be conceived to be. They not only assert that Christ has done everything for us, which in one sense is true, but they also assert that we have nothing to do for ourselves beyond a mere inactive acceptance, which is the very reverse of truth.

Great as may be the theoretical difficulty of reconciling the sufficiency of Christ's sacrifice with the necessity of our co-operation — just as there is a theoretical difficulty in reconciling the sentence of Divine Predestination with our own consciousness of Free-Will— yet I am sure that no simple, earnest-hearted Christian ever found any *practical* incongruity between them. He can accept unquestioningly both parts of the Apostle's sayings, and find no clashing or jarring between them.

He can "*work out his own salvation* with fear and trembling," at the same time that he is the first to confess, with humility and thankfulness, that it is " God who worketh in him, both to will and to do."

Exactly in the same spirit he accepts such Scriptures as the text. He feels not only that " Christ suffered for him," but that " He left him an example." Nay; he feels more than this! His conscience tells him that these two statements are only true when they are *held together*. They cannot be separated. They are eternally indissoluble. As the mere *Example* would have been worthless, or at any rate ineffectual, without the *Sufferings;* so are the *Sufferings* of no saving import to those who are strangers to the power of the *Example*. I do not remember that our Lord ever said, " Look at my Cross and you shall be saved " ; but He did say more than once, " Take up thine own Cross, and follow Me."

It is indeed nothing better than madness, as St. Paul says, " to profess to know God, but in works deny Him "; to think that we are "in Christ" while we are not "new creatures." The old Adam must be "crucified" *in* us as the New Adam was crucified *for* us. The Apostle teaches that we are to "put off all these; anger, wrath, malice, blasphemy, filthy communication out of our mouth;" some of them subtle and stealthy sins that lie hid in the self-complacent Christian's heart without his knowing of them; others open and profane sins, "going," as it were, "beforehand unto judgment." "Put them all off," says he, and "put on" in their stead "as the elect of God," " bowels of mercies, kindness, humbleness of mind, meekness, long-suffering" —those patient, homely, modest graces which, though the world mark them not, form the true garniture of a converted soul; " the ornament," as St. Peter calls them, "of a meek and quiet spirit, which in the sight of God is of great price."

If then we would be saved *by* Christ we must be followers of Christ. We must not think that faith is the barren acceptance of any external doctrines, or the indolent play of any internal feelings. It is neither mere belief nor mere excitement. It consists not in utterances of the mouth, or in emotions of the breast. It is a living principle of conformity to Christ: a "growing up unto Him in all things, Who is our Head:" "a continual looking on the things that are not seen:" "a patient waiting upon God:" a cheerful contentment with our lot: "a victory that overcometh the world."

Of such a principle and of no other it is written, "Whatsoever is not of faith is sin." We cannot rise above the corrupt influences that surround us, we cannot conquer the thousand temptations that beset us, without it. "Repentance towards God, and faith towards our Lord Jesus Christ"; there you have, in St. Paul's words the sum and substance of religion, the beginning and end of the Gospel. They are the twin elements of that renewal of the heart which the Scriptures mean when they speak of that "holiness, without which no man shall see the Lord." To be perfectly holy, without spot or blemish is for flesh and blood, impossible, But we must be continually "reaching after" it, and mourning that we cannot attain it, and sighing over our shortcomings, and trying to recover our backslidings; and so, in spite of many lets and hindrances, advancing on the whole, "bringing forth more fruit in our age," and the shorter the time is the more carefully gathering together "the fragments of it that remain that nothing be lost."

For a man to say "I have done my work: I am safe: I may fold my hands, and lay aside my armour, and rest my weary limbs a while, and wait at ease for my Master's summons," is the language either of the grossest ignorance or of the most fearful presumption. The Master whom we serve has "given every man his work," and commanded all "to watch." He has warned us of the danger of His coming "suddenly and finding us sleeping." Patience must have her "perfect work," even unto the coming of the Lord.

But to those alone will that coming bring comfort and joy who, like holy David, have looked for Christ's presence *in righteousness;* who have not only embraced the Cross, but helped to bear it; who, if in a momentary weakness, like Peter, have been ashamed of their Master, and taken the world's side instead, have also, like Peter, wiped out their disloyalty with their tears; have, like David, "hated the sin of unfaithfulness"; and like the woman that was a sinner, who anointed the feet of Jesus, as they were the more *forgiven*, have *loved* also the more.

Have you understood these things? If you have, happy are ye if ye do them. It is, in my conscience I believe, the only true view of our duties and privileges, of the work and of the reward of faith. "This is the will of God, to believe on Him whom He hath sent;" a belief not of the head, but of the heart, of the life; a beholding, "as in a glass the glory of the Lord," transfiguring us into the same image; a continual *apprehension* of Christ in the literal sense of that word; "a death unto sin and a birth unto righteousness," the one work which we pledged ourselves to achieve in our baptism, and which we must be accomplishing more and more perfectly unto our dying day. Thus in our generation shall we have held forth the word of life, and find for ourselves, to our unspeakable joy and triumph, " in the day of Christ," that "we have neither run in vain nor laboured in vain."

Preached—Cholderton, Second Sunday after Easter, April 10, 1853; April 29, 1854; April 26, 1857.

XIV.

THE LIMITS OF CHRISTIAN LIBERTY.

"For so is the will of God, that with well-doing ye may put to silence the ignorance of foolish men: as free, and not using your liberty for a cloke of maliciousness, but as the servants of God."—I. PET. ii. 15, 16.

IF there is one prerogative of our regeneration more emphatically dwelt on in the Bible than another, it is our moral and spiritual freedom; our deliverance from the bondage, not only of sin and Satan, but of opinion, of fashion, of worldly maxims, of customs, of prejudices.

The Christian is free to act independently; according to his own judgment; as his conscience directs him; as "he is fully persuaded in his own mind." He is not bound to pause every moment before he acts, and ask himself, "Does the world sanction this?" "Shall I be justified in the eyes of men?" "Is this usual, customary?" and so forth. In a certain sense every Christian is "a law unto himself." He carries a standard of what is right and becoming within him. He "needs not that any should testify of him." He is satisfied with the approval of his own conscience. He has confidence in his own discernment. He refuses to acknowledge the self-constituted tribunal of fashion, or honour, or custom, or whatever else the world sets up and worships in the place of God. He feels that this is not the judge before whom he shall have to give "an account of his works;" and therefore looks upon the censures which mere worldly people may pass upon his conduct with proportionate indifference and unconcern. He realises the force, and acts upon the principle of the Apostle's maxim, "Ye are bought with a price: be not the servants of men."

Now such a view of the Christian's spiritual condition, if carelessly taken up, or indiscriminately applied, is plainly liable to a very dangerous perversion. It may engender conceit, and pride, and an overbearing and self-complacent temper, and an insufferable self-confidence, and a contempt for lawfully constituted authority, and a presumptuous defiance of all the restraints of custom or law. A man may say, "I will call no man my master upon earth; I will recognise no supremacy but that of my own conscience; I will not be brought into bondage to any set of opinions; I will follow the light that the Holy Spirit gives me, because it is written, 'Where the Spirit of the Lord is, there is liberty.'"

If such a person could prove to us that he was "led by the Spirit of God," we could have nothing to say against him. We should have to allow that he was right and we were wrong. But unhappily there is room for great delusion here. "All men have not" the Spirit who *think* they have. We are bid to judge everything "by its fruits": and the fruits of the Spirit, we are told, are "kindness, gentleness, humbleness of mind, meekness, long-suffering." And therefore if we saw any man professing to be guided by the Spirit of God, but at the same times "covetous, proud, unthankful, incontinent, fierce, a despiser of them that are good, heady, high-minded, having the form of godliness, but denying its power," we should say that he was only deluding himself or others. We should call him a hypocrite, or a self-deceiver, should be slow to allow his claim to superior discernment, and should question the right he had to set himself up as a "guide to the blind or an instructor of the foolish," when he had plainly made such little progress in the education and mastery of himself.

Indeed, so far is this doctrine of individual Christian liberty, which the New Testament evidently inculcated as the great prerogative of the Gospel dispensation, from having a natural tendency to beget conceit or foster pride, that its legitimate influence on the truly spiritualised character should be directly of the contrary effect. For the freer we are, the more responsible we become. The higher we rise above the state of a servant, the more we have to answer for, both towards God and man. When our Blessed Saviour would impress the obligations of obedience with greatest emphasis upon His disciples, it is by addressing them as His personal *friends*. "Ye are my friends," He says, "if ye do whatsoever I command you. Henceforth I call you not servants, for the servant knoweth not what his lord doeth: but I have called you *friends*, for all things that I have heard of my Father I have made known unto you."

The fulness and freeness of His communication demanded a corresponding willingness and frowardness of obedience in return. A slave has no responsibility. He is the mere creature of his owner's will. He has simply to do what he is bid, and need not trouble himself with questions of fitness, and expediency, and duty. Christ by His death—by laying down His life for His friends—has ransomed us from this slavery, has made us free, has delivered us, in St. Paul's glowing language, "from the bondage of corruption into the glorious liberty of the children of God."

It is indeed this very thought that is the strongest check to prevent this imagined privilege of liberty from becoming an abuse and a snare and a delusion to our souls. "He that is called, being free, is Christ's servant." Because we are bought with a price, St. Paul tells us *not* to become "servants of *men*," but for the self-same reason we *are* "servants of *God*." God's law is still supreme over us, though man's opinion is not. The unchangeable Word is to be our guide, though the shifting code of fashion or of honour must not. While "we are not careful to answer" any self-constituted human questioner about the reasons of our conduct, or the ground of our hopes, we must remember that "we must all stand before the judgment seat of God to give an account" of every thought we have entertained, every word we have spoken, every deed we have done.

The Bible puts forth two great counterpoises, or checks to the doctrine of Christian liberty, lest it should degenerate into licentiousness. The first I have mentioned—the recollection of our duty of obedience to

God: the second, not perhaps so fundamental, but hardly less extensive, a regard to the consciences of weaker brethren. Before engaging in any matter, or gratifying himself with any indulgence, he that has "the mind of Christ" will ask himself not only whether it is consistent with conformity to God's law, but also whether it is conducive to his "neighbour's edification." St. Paul is very strong on this point. "If meat," he says, "make my brother to offend, I will eat no flesh while the world standeth lest I make my brother to offend." It is in this sense that he is to be understood when he says, "All things are lawful for me, but all things are not expedient: all things are lawful for me, but all things edify not. Let no man seek his own, but every man another's wealth."

It is easy to see the application of such a rule. For instance, there are many worldly amusements which may be innocent within due limits in the case of others, but which I should consider unseemly in myself, as a clergyman, however fond I might naturally be of them; because if I indulged in them I might "give offence to the Church of God," or cause my own office to fall into disrepute, or afford a handle for the enemies of religion to blaspheme. Again, my position as a master of a family, a father, a husband, an employer, requires at my hand a stricter and more circumspect conversation than if I had no one depending upon me upon whom my example and influence might tell. It would be an abuse of my liberty to set at nought all these restraints; to "look only on my own things"; to be indifferent to the duty of "pleasing my neighbour for his good to edification." The stronger we are in ourselves, the greater obligation lies on us "to bear the infirmities of the weak." Of Christ, our Great Example, it is specially recorded that He "pleased not Himself." The motive of all He did was not what He liked himself—else He would have put from Him the cup of suffering, and prayed to His Father for the twelve legions of angels—but what might best set forward the salvation of men, and the glory of Him who had sent Him into the world.

It is only in proportion as we recognise these obligations that we taste any real or genuine freedom. Of the spurious allurements of the world we may truly say with St. Peter, "while they promise us liberty, they themselves are the servants of corruption: for of whom a man is overcome of the same he is brought in bondage." It is only *Christ's* yoke that is "easy": *God's* service that is "perfect freedom." As the world's *sorrow* worketh death, so its so-called liberty forges chains for the soul. It is really slavery to some corrupt inclination, some carnal infirmity, some besetting sin. Look at the drunkard's liberty. Every public-house he passes is his master. He is the slave of every coarse boon-companion that "puts his bottle to him," or, as it is called, "offers him a drink." "He suffers," to use St. Paul's language, "if a man bring him into bondage, if a man devour him, if a man take of him, if a man exalt himself, if a man smite him on the face." He reaches his home at last, degraded in point of intelligence—for I say nothing about religion: the drunkard has no true religion, it is merely a *form* to him, not a *power*—below the level of the very beasts that perish, a laughing-stock to the ungodly and careless; to his own household, and to all who remember that man was created in the image of God, a source of sorrow, and regret, and shame.

Alas, that any among us should be found to rejoice in such a liberty! a liberty to work wickedness and to cast God's laws behind us: a liberty of following our own pernicious ways and selling ourselves to Satan, both body and soul! "All such rejoicing is evil." It is only "glorying in our shame." He only is truly free who "has power over his own will"; who can check wrong inclinations; who has learnt the lesson of self-denial; who can forego gain that he may ensue godliness: who can "cast down imaginations, and every high thing that exalteth itself against the knowledge of God, and bring into captivity every thought unto the obedience of Christ."

It is one of the many paradoxes, or seeming contradictions, of the Gospel, "Christ's servant is the only freeman." As He Himself told the Jews, "If ye continue in my word, then are ye my disciples indeed. And ye shall know the truth, and the truth shall make you free. They answered Him, We be Abraham's seed and were never in bondage to any man." They were quite indignant at any imputation being cast, even by implication, either on their personal or national freedom. "How sayest Thou then," they continued, "ye shall be made free? Jesus answered them, Verily, verily, I say unto you, he that committeth sin is the servant of sin. And the servant abideth not in the house for ever: but the Son abideth ever. If the Son therefore shall make you free, ye shall be free indeed."

And yet we boast of our freedom, and talk proudly of the liberties of Englishmen. We pique ourselves as much on our "glorious constitution" as the Jews did on their being "Abraham's seed." And yet these very liberties are only used by many of us as a "cloke of maliciousness." As long as we keep out of the reach of the law we think we may do what we please; and we forget or disown that higher law, the Word of God, which is "quick and powerful, and sharper than any two-edged sword, piercing even to the dividing asunder of soul and spirit, and of the joints and marrow, and is a discerner of the thoughts and intents of the heart: neither is there any creature that is not manifest in His sight, but all things are naked and opened unto the eyes of Him with whom we have to do."

What the maxims of the world allow us, or the example of others justifies us in doing, is of little consequence. We have to satisfy the searching scrutiny of One by Whom actions and the secrets of the heart are "weighed." He has set before us life and death, good and evil, and has left us free to choose. And yet He has guided our choice. "He left not Himself without witness." He hath said, "Choose life, that thou and thy seed may live, and that thou mayest love the Lord thy God, and mayest obey His voice and cleave unto Him: for He is thy life and the length of thy days."

It is a poor bargain that "gains the whole world," and "loses" a man's own "soul." And yet it is a bargain that thousands upon thousands all round us are making, and flattering themselves that they are great gainers by the trade. So they seem to the eye that judges by the outward appearance : that knows nothing of those unspeakable, unconceivable joys that "God has prepared for them that love Him." May ours be a better wisdom than theirs! May one of the things we learn by coming into the sanctuary of the Lord be "the end of such men." May we be taught more and more "to cast all our care" upon One who has told us that "He careth for us." While "we stand fast in our liberty," "let us not use it for an occasion to the flesh," "but in love serve one another." Let us cherish a tender conscience and a genuine humility, and a deep thankfulness, and an unstinted charity." Let us be among those "who use this world, as not abusing it, for the fashion of this world passeth away."

Preached—Cholderton, Third Sunday after Easter, April 17th, 1853 ; May 15, 1859.

XV.

BIBLE KNOWLEDGE.

"If they hear not Moses and the prophets, neither will they be persuaded though one rose from the dead."—St. Luke xvi. 31.

Most persons are familar with the very solemn warning which the story, in connection with which these words occur, contains: of the portion that is in store for all those, whether rich or poor, who have abused their opportunities of usefulness, and lived in this world only to please and indulge themselves, instead of seeing how far they could be of service to others.

It would be a great mistake to suppose that it is a lesson only needed by, or applicable to, rich men; though to rich men it is especially applicable, because of the greater extent of responsibility of their stewardship. A poor man may be just as selfish, just as regardless of the wants and feelings of others, just as hard-hearted, just as thoughtless and reckless of a future world, just as much occupied with the cares and vanities of this world, as was this rich Israelite, who shut his heart, no less than his doors, against the wretched Lazarus.

However small our share of this world's goods, it is always in our power to lend a helping hand to a neighbour's need. It is not the amount of the aid, but the spirit and motive of it, that God regards. I am not speaking of cases of distress produced by a person's own recklessness or dishonest conduct—which are to be regarded as punishments on such ways, and contribute no claim for assistance, and where indeed assistance would do more harm than good by encouraging, instead of checking, a continuance in the same courses—but I refer to such cases as this of Lazarus: cases of sickness, poverty, friendlessness, bodily infirmity, old age; cases in which no man in whose heart the love of God is shed abroad can pass by without interest and concern.

But I pass on to draw out the particular teaching of the text, and endeavour to apply it in a practical way to our own circumstances.

The rich man in torment, finding no way of procuring relief for himself, bethought him of "five brethren" whom he had left living at home—living very likely in the same selfish, godless manner that he had lived himself—and he could not help feeling the natural concern of a kinsman for what he *now* saw was a situation of exceeding peril to them.

How easy this is—to talk and express concern for others, while we do not mind our own way! St. Paul was aware of the danger when he tells us what pains he took to avoid it. It is a danger to which all those who have to watch over others as they that must give an account—pastors, school-teachers, fathers of families, employers, householders—are peculiarly exposed: the danger, in their carefulness for others, of forgetting themselves.

And so this rich man, who had never, so far as we know, shown one spark of concern for his own spiritual welfare and future destiny, now that he is in the torment of hell (now that he finds out by a bitter, but too late, experience, what a fearful thing it is for an impenitent sinner to fall into the hands of the living God), is filled not so much with remorse and compunction for himself, which he saw was unavailing, as with fear and concern for his five brethren. He remembered they had all lived together in the same jovial, self-indulgent, God-forgetting way, and he had no doubt too good reason to be afraid "lest they also should come to that place of torment." He felt convinced that "if one went unto them from the dead they would repent." It was his prayer, therefore, that Lazarus might be sent to "testify unto them." He was sure they could not resist such a solemn testimony. They must be persuaded and converted, and God would heal and spare them.

So he reasoned, and who shall say unnaturally? It needed One "Who knows what is in man"—what a world not only of iniquity but of self-deceit the heart is; what an impossibility it is, even by a miracle, to change the heart of one who has set his face like a flint and will not be turned—One who knew us better than we know ourselves to teach us this salutary lesson—that it is "an evil and adulterous generation that seeketh after a sign": that men who have their Bibles in their hands and the Gospel sounded into their ears, and still remain deaf of ear and hard of heart, are incapable of being influenced by anything simply supernatural. As it is written, "neither will they be persuaded though one rose from the dead."

We shall never know again, till the day when every secret of the heart is revealed, how men who are gone, like the traitor Judas, " to their own place," look back upon their past lives. We shall never be told by anybody besides this rich man how he would give the whole world, all the riches this earth contains, for the hopeless permission of living his life over again, retracing his ways, undoing his evil deeds, abhorring his iniquities, his drunkennesses and uncleannesses and oaths and lies, and making him a new heart, so that, through God's mercy, he might escape coming to that "place of torment."

This is the only place of Scripture where the veil is for a moment lifted up, and we are permitted to catch a glimpse of the awful realities of the unseen world—the torments of the cursed side by side with the rest of them that die in the Lord. If one did rise from the dead he could tell us no more, he could speak no plainer. We know now the end of all these ungodly, carnal, self-seeking schemes, with which the minds of so many men of business and of every man of the world are wholly occupied, just as well as though we could " raise spirits from the vasty deep " to relate to us their experiences. If this parable has not taught us, depend on it nothing will. "If we hear not Moses and the prophets, neither should we be persuaded though one rose from the dead."

I think it will be well not to evade the conclusions to which this will lead us. That is a dangerous and fatal habit into which we are all so ready to fall, of deceiving our own souls and lulling to sleep our own consciences, or prophesying smooth things to ourselves, and saying peace where there is no peace. What a folly it is thus to play the hypocrite with ourselves! to wish to seem better than we are, not so much to the world around us as to the *judge within* when he would take account of our lives. Do not, then, let us try to escape the conclusion of this story, even though it tell against ourselves. It is far better to be too strict with ourselves than too lenient. For if we would judge ourselves we should not be judged. "But when we are judged we are chastened of the Lord, that we should not be condemned with the world."

The standard by which we are to judge ourselves—by which we are to ascertain our present state and future destiny—is *God's Word*. It is not fashion, or other people's opinion, or any private impressions and fancies, which are all shifting and uncertain, and often contradictory, but it is the unchangeable, living, eternal Word, manifested in an Incarnate Saviour, enshrined in an inspired Book, witnessed to and preached by a visible Church, in which is no "variableness, neither shadow of turning."

It has indeed its mysteries, its dark places, its hard passages; and therefore I have spoken of the teaching of the Church as a divinely ordained instrument for the right understanding of it. But no one who is familiar with his Bible will say that these dark places make up the bulk of it. It was expressly written for the "wayfaring men, though fools"; and it is writ so plain upon tables that "he that runs may read." The merest child, who has just begun to frame letters into words, can go to that Book and learn something. He can read the Sermon on the Mount, and imbibe the spirit of Christianity. He can study the parable of the Ten Virgins, or the Servants with the Talents, or the Prodigal Son, or the Good Samaritan, and gain an insight into Christian faith and duty.

Even if he cannot understand the first eleven chapters of the Epistle to the Romans, he can hardly fail to gather instruction from the last five. Or of the Epistle to the Ephesians, if the first half be dark and difficult, the latter half, at any rate, is clear and plain. No man can miss the path of salvation if he look for it in earnest. It may be narrow, but it is not hidden. The gate may be strait, but it is open. Even if we are overtaken for a moment by any perplexity—if a case occurs in which we are doubtful how we ought to act—even then an earnest prayer for the enlightening help of the Spirit of God, a committing of our way unto Him as unto a faithful Creator, an ear listening keenly to catch the tones of the guiding voice within, will probably clear up the difficulty, and cause the light of undoubting assurance to shine upon our way.

The misfortune is that though we have Bibles we do not use them. We may use them for curiosity, from habit, for show, but not for "reproof, for correction, for instruction in righteousness." Even to those who profess to set most store by their Bible it is often a sealed book, a mere lifeless idol before which they bow their heads with unmeaning homage, but not their hearts with a living obedience.

And yet it is the Book which God has given us to be

the rule of life. Do you suppose it has been treasured in the Church with so much care, and so wonderfully multiplied by the discovery of the art of printing, and so diligently distributed by Societies, and reduced to so low a cost as to be within the reach of the poorest man or woman that can read—do you suppose that God has taken all this care for this Book over all other books in the world, that we should merely go to it to pick out entertaining stories, to have a string of texts running glibly off our tongue, to dabble in mysterious surmises about predestination, election, justification, and so forth, instead of learning practical lessons, daily duties, a personal faith, a saving wisdom? Alas! that the most precious gift of God in the whole world should be so abused, so misapplied: that the very thing that should have been for our good, should be to so many an occasion of falling: that the Bible should, in so many cases, darken men's eyes instead of enlightening them, or set them upon judging others, while they would be better employed in considering themselves.

And so, the sum of the whole matter is that we are not to be looking for signs, and wonders, and mysteries. and revelations, and prophecies, but for plain instruction in home duties; for knowledge of the way in which the temptations which meet us in our daily employments may be overcome; that, as St. Paul says, "the man of God may be perfect, throughly furnished unto all *good works.*" Other enquiries may be curious, interesting, instructive; but it is this only which is edifying. Be sure of this, except so far as we read the Word of God for *guidance,* for clearing up the difficulties that beset our path, for self-knowledge, for ability to discharge the duties of our station, it is but labour in vain. God's purpose in putting that Book into our hands was to counterbalance the knowledge of evil—the inheritance of our fall—by the knowledge of good. It is the work of the Holy Spirit striving against the wiles of the evil spirit. It is the Divine stamp upon what is righteous, and seemly, and true.

Of course we can follow other guides, or profess to be waiting for fuller revelations. We shall never have them. The Gospel is the final manifestation of the Divine Will to the world. Nay, One *has* risen from the dead, even the Lord Jesus Christ; not, however, to contradict the testimony of Moses and the prophets, but to set His seal upon it. All He did, we are told, was "to open their understanding, that they might understand the Scriptures." This is what we must daily pray Him to do for ourselves—not to send to us one from the dead, or break through the ordinary laws of nature— but that He would grant us, according to the riches of His glory, " to be strengthened with might by His Spirit in the inner man, that Christ may dwell in our hearts by faith, that we being rooted and grounded in love may be able to comprehend with all saints, what is the breadth and length and depth and height of the love of Christ, which passeth knowledge, that we may be filled with all the fulness of God."

It is only thus that the curse of knowledge can be averted. There is no spiritual state more sad, more hopeless, than that of those who " are ever learning, yet never come to the knowledge of the truth." The home of our knowledge must be the heart, not the head. It must make us wise unto salvation, not armed for controversy. It must humble us with the sense of our shortcomings, not lift us up with a conceit of our attainments. Above all, we must remember that *obedience* is the condition, as of spiritual *power*, so also of spiritual *discernment*. "He that will do God's will shall know of the doctrine." If we only take up our Bibles for a serious, practical purpose—for instruction in righteousness—we shall find them not only throw light upon our paths, but speak peace unto our souls.

And remember further, that the Bible is the only revelation of God's will to which we must look, and by which we must be guided, as the ultimate standard and determiner of all that relates to the lines of our duty or the state of our souls. It is there—and not by any fancied secret whisperings—that God is calling us to Himself: bidding us repent and be converted, and become as little children, and take up our Cross, and follow the example of our Saviour. We can cast those words behind us if we please, but we shall find no other teacher to supply us with better or wiser ones.

O that we all would read our Bible with more teachable hearts; with more determined will to find out what it has to say to us about our calling here, our destiny hereafter! that we would store up its *precepts* in our memory, to be our strength in the moment of sudden temptation: its *examples* in our imagination, to be the pattern and model of our daily lives! Do not think that having a Bible, or reading a Bible, is any good, except so far as we live by the Bible. It is the rule of *life* as well as of *faith* : of what we are to *do*, as well as of what we are to *believe*. We know from a beautiful parable that it is a seed which, though scattered on all sides, only takes root and bears fruit in the soil of " an honest and good and patient heart."

Pray God to give you this. Pray Jesus Christ, the great Prophet of the Church, to strengthen you to walk in the path which He has marked out, both by His teaching and His example, for the journey of every Christian. Pray the Holy Ghost, the Giver of all truth, to keep you from the many deceitful dealings with this Blessed Book, which abound in these latter days. So shall it be indeed to you a Book of life, making your way plain before your face, teaching you how to walk and please God ever more and more ; and preparing you, slowly it may be, but surely, for that fulness of Divine knowledge when the Elect shall see God face to face, and know all things perfectly, " even as they are known."

Preached—Cholderton, First Sunday after Trinity, May 29, 1853; May 25, 1856; June 6, 1858.

XVI.

THE CHARACTER OF JEHU.

"So the young man, even the young man the prophet, went to Ramoth-Gilead. And when he came, behold, the captains of the host were sitting: and he said, I have an errand to thee, O captain. And Jehu said, Unto which of all us? And he said, To thee, O captain. And he arose, and went into the house: and he poured the oil on his head, and said unto him, Thus saith the Lord God of Israel, I have anointed thee king over the people of the Lord, even over Israel. And thou shalt smite the house of Ahab thy master, that I may avenge the blood of my servants the prophets, and the blood of all the servants of the Lord, at the hand of Jezebel."—II. KINGS ix. 4-7.

THESE verses contain the account of the anointing and mission of Jehu; and the rest of the chapter, together with the following one, informs us how he accomplished it.

I will make a general observation at the outset. Scripture-Biography, the study of the sayings and doings of the men and women whose names catch our eye on the sacred page, is perhaps one of the most *profitable*, as it certainly is the most interesting, method of instruction in Divine things, if it be pursued in a proper spirit and a right way.

But it may, at the same time, be most hazardous and deceiving. If we bring our own prejudices and prepossessions to interpret the simple letter of the story, if we fix our thoughts on one or two striking incidents in the life of a man, instead of gathering together the scattered notices that constitute the whole ; if we add an unauthorised fancy of our own here, or shut our eyes to an actually recorded fact there—because *without* the one or *with* the other we cannot fit the man to the character which beforehand we have made up our minds he must have been—this is " wresting Scripture " and, it may be, " to our own destruction," from its fair and legitimate teaching, just as much as building up a theory of doctrine upon one or two isolated texts can be.

For instance, if we took by itself, and were much struck, as we could hardly help being, with the narrative of the affecting interview between Nathan—at once the messenger of God's displeasure and of His forgiveness, on the one hand—and David, so suddenly changed from a self-complacent sinner to a self-condemning penitent, on the other ; without stopping to read the history of those after years, in which he seems hardly to have known a day of peace and comfort—all traceable to this single sin and its manifold consequences—without calling to mind those psalms of exquisite heartrending agony, in which the still accusing voice of conscience seems ever to make him doubt whether the Lord could indeed forgive the exceeding wickedness of his sin—if, forgetting or not knowing all this, we should conclude that all the Lord requires of a sinner to say is, " I have sinned," and that he who says so will immediately hear those words of peace and comfort, " The Lord also hath put away thy sin," and were thereupon to set up a theory of our own about the instantaneousness of conversion and the fulness of God's mercy, we should be plainly doing no less violence to the very facts of the history than to the sober doctrines of the Gospel. We should be weaving a most entangling net of error against our own souls.

Or again, a man who only thinks of Judas Iscariot as the traitor who sold his Master for thirty pieces of silver, without having watched how Satan had been laying snares for him in this very way all along; how he had always had thievish thoughts in his heart; how his very position—"he bare the bag"—was turned against him, and became an instrument in his ruin; how all the good advice and warning words he must have been continually hearing from that Master's tongue were so much wasted breath, pearls thrown before swine, insufficient to open his eyes and show him the pit on the edge of which he was even then standing—to miss all these little points, which do not lie together, but are only to be picked up by careful pondering here and there, but which are absolutely necessary, not only to profit by the *example* but even to understand the *character*, is a way of reading Scripture which most people think sufficient for its comprehension, but which robs it of all that power "for reproof, for correction, for instruction in righteousness which may make the man of God perfect, and throughly furnish him unto all good works."

This caution is even more necessary in reading the account of those *mixed* characters, like Jehu, which form the staple of the Bible-story, just as they are what constitute the mass of everyday society. It can never be too carefully remembered that the Bible is not a history of heroes or saints—of moral and spiritual giants—far beyond our compass, or of sinners whom we are not likely to imitate. We are told again and again that Abraham and Moses, and David, and Elijah, and Paul, on the one hand, and Esau, and Korah, and Saul, and Jeroboam, and Gehazi on the other, were *simple men*—men of like passions with ourselves, tempted as we are, strengthened as we must be. They were not exceptions to the average, but examples to all, which they could not be if their trials had been different, or their spiritual experiences different, from those by which *our* characters are formed, and the steadfastness of *our* faith tried.

We miss the whole point of the *exemplary* teaching of the Bible when we read it in this way. There is not a man or woman whose character is drawn in the Old Testament, not even of those who served God *most* faithfully, of whom not only we may be sure that they fell into some sin, but of whom some sin is not actually recorded. Noah, Abraham, Lot, Moses, David, were none of them perfect, and the Scripture does not conceal their imperfections. There is only one perfect example—that of our Blessed Saviour. The rest, though saints, still were men, and were tempted as men, and sometimes sinned as men.

You do not suppose that Abraham, that great pattern of faith, when he denied his wife in Egypt, was acting faithfully. You must surely see that this was one of those moments of weakness—to which we are all liable as often as we forget that our strength is not in ourselves —when Satan had him at advantage, and betrayed him into an act the very contrary of his general character— an act of faithlessness and mistrust in God. The Bible never says he did right in thus equivocating. If we were to say so because we have a general notion that Abraham was " a friend of God," and that everything he did must therefore have been inspired, we should not only be adopting a view that has no Scriptural warrant, but should be confounding those eternal distinctions of right and wrong which God has planted to be unerring guides in every soul. There is no reason in the world, except in our own sloth and carnalism, why every one of us should not be as much God's friend as Abraham was. We are living in far fuller light, and under, as St. Paul tells us, " a far better covenant founded upon better promises." It was " by the grace of God " that he was what he was, and the same grace is even more plenteously offered to *us* than to *him*.

If you have followed me in what I have said, you will be in no danger of making the mistake of supposing, because you are told that " the Lord God of Israel anointed Jehu to be king over the people of the Lord," and sent him to smite Ahab and avenge the blood of His servants the prophets slain at the hand of Jezebel, that, therefore, he was an approved or righteous man. You will look at his *whole* history before you draw a conclusion as to his *character*. You would no more feel sure that he was actuated by a right spirit when he bade the eunuchs throw Jezebel out of the window than Samson was when he sent the foxes to burn up the

THE CHARACTER OF JEHU.

Philistines' corn; or Jael, when she drove the nail into Sisera's temples.

Indeed, I think, if you make up your mind at starting that whatever Jehu does will be right, you will be sorely perplexed and startled before you get to the end of his history. Even when engaged on God's errand of smiting Ahab's house, and taking vengeance on Jezebel, and destroying the worshippers of Baal, he does it all in such a bloodthirsty, and withal in such a calculating and even deceitful way, that we could not but be most miserably puzzled if we were as sure that God approved or suggested the *means*, as we are that He willed and fore-ordained the *end*. Jehu was simply *an instrument*, like Jeroboam, of a Divine purpose, and that a purpose of visiting a house and a nation for their sins. A *fitter* instrument for the purpose could hardly be conceived. A soldier by profession, and familiarised with scenes of blood, he seems to have possessed just that bold, adventurous, fearless character which was necessary to play the part that was assigned to him. He took his own way of fulfilling his mission: whether by craft or open violence was all one to him. Though a minister of Divine vengeance, all he did was coloured by his own strong passions; just like that brutal judge, Lord Jeffreys, with whose name every reader of English history is familiar, who, even in passing legal sentences upon unhappy criminals, made the very standers-by shudder at the inhuman and fiendish vehemence with which he seemed to thirst for blood.

The character of Jehu, regarded as a whole, seems to be as nearly as possible the opposite of that of Jehoshaphat. Jehoshaphat, you will remember, was a man whose general *rectitude* of conduct was marred by a single *infirmity*. Jehu, on the other hand, was one who was only redeemed from utter godlessness by a single course of obedience to God's command. The one, in St. James's words, "kept the whole law, but offended in one point": the other kept his *one* point, but if he did not break, at any rate disregarded, all the rest of the *whole* law. Jehoshaphat was God-fearing, just, gentle, anxious for his people's welfare, zealous against idolatry, but he had one weakness. He did not take pains enough to avoid the company of sinners, to make a stand against the lax morality of the fashionable world. Jehu was selfish, artful, bloodthirsty, cruel. He could go quietly in, and eat his meal, while the dogs were mangling the unburied corpse of Jezebel outside his door. But what God bade him do he did, I will not say in God's *spirit*, but at any rate with a right good will.

For, indeed, it was a mission that just jumped with his own humour. His work was after his own heart. To shed blood, and to get a kingdom, were just the things that the bold-hearted soldier was most ready to do. He smote Jehoram with his bow, and trode Jezebel under foot, and slew the worshippers of Baal with the edge of the sword. But in all that he did I fail to discover one token of a high or holy motive; one sign of a hatred of sin, or a love for righteousness, or a zeal for God's true honour, or a heart purposing to keep His commandments. Compare him with Josiah, who had the like work given him to do in rooting out idolatry from Judah, and you will recognise at once the difference in their characters. Of Josiah it is particularly said that "his heart was tender, and that he humbled himself before the Lord"; from which anything more remote than Jehu's temper it is impossible to conceive.

Still Jehu did his work, though with a rough hand, and so he received his reward, though the reward sets no stamp of approval upon his conduct, nor indeed reached beyond this present world. Because he had executed what was right in God's eyes upon the house of Ahab, "his children of the fourth generation were to sit on the throne of Israel." And yet, as though to show us that this reward is very far from being intended to make us fancy that Jehu's general character is one of which God approves; in the very next verse, side by side with this qualified commendation, we are expressly told that "Jehu took no heed to walk in the law of the Lord God of Israel *with all his heart;* for he departed not from the sins of Jeroboam, which made Israel to sin." As far as he had served God he found his account in it. All obedience has its reward, though it be a partial and imperfect one. But for his failures of duty he found that God had scourges ready for *him*, as well as for Ahab and Jezebel. "In those days," the historian tells us, "the Lord began to cut Israel short; and Hazael smote them in all their coasts." As God had sent Jehu from Ramoth-Gilead to slay Ahaziah, so now He bade Hazael go forth from Damascus to smite and distress *him*. Each was an instrument in God's hand, though permitted to do their work in their own way.

Mysterious, and in this life, inexplicable problem! How God can accomplish His foretold purposes, and we, His creatures, still continue *free*. How *we*, the instruments, may be self-seeking and defiled, and *He*, the Ordainer, remain Holy, and Just, and True! Yet, that *so it is*, we need no other proof than the history of Jehu to be assured.

How often do we meet characters like his! Men with a bold hand, or a free heart, or a high spirit, or generous impulses; capable of great things, and perhaps achieving them, whom after all we cannot pronounce to be "men of God," with no token of saintliness about them : who, we are sure, cannot on the whole please God, though to some extent, and in temporal things, they may be blessed by Him! Jehu had all those moral qualities that might have made a David, or an Elijah, or a Paul. He was brave, and bold, and zealous, and high-spirited. No danger daunted him; nothing that God set him to do was more than he dared venture on. But it was a temper wholly savouring of the old Adam; never chastened by suffering or disciplined by self-contol; and so, without the least regard for the feelings of others, under the guidance of no principle, at the mercy of circumstances, wrong in spirit, even when it was right in deed.

There is no temper that more needs to be brought under the discipline of the Cross of Christ than this. If you will think what St. Paul was when he persecuted the Church, and was puffed up with the conceit of his own righteousness in the Law, and compare him with what he became when, like his Divine Master, "he had learnt obedience by the things which he suffered," and "determined to know nothing else but Jesus Christ and Him crucified"—compare, I mean, Saul the persecutor with Paul the Apostle; Saul breathing out threatenings and slaughter against the disciples of the Lord, with Paul at Thessalonica, "gentle among them even as a nurse cherisheth her children"—and you will understand that what I mean, when I speak of the need of discipline for such tempers, is the converting influence, without which they are just as likely to be weapons in the hands of Satan as instruments in the hands of God.

Perhaps you still have a difficulty in accepting this account of Jehu, because you see that he actually *did* receive a blessing from God. *For what he did,* he is told that "his children of the fourth generation should sit on the throne of Israel." No family, as yet, had sat so long on that apostate throne. Jeroboam's son had been slain by Baasha: Baasha's by Zimri. Jehu cut off the house of Ahab. But to his own family a kind of stability is promised. Is not this, you will ask me, a proof that there must have been something really good about him after all?

Not necessarily so, by any means. He had vindicated God's honour, it was true. He had slain the idolatrous race, and he had crushed Baal-worship. This was the lesson that this stiff-necked people had most need to learn. Elijah had failed to teach it them by *miracles:* it was to be seen whether Jehu would impress it more forcibly upon them *by the sword.*

And so Ahab's house was cut off root and branch;

and Jehu was exalted, to let men see that "those who honoured God He would honour, and they who despised Him should be lightly esteemed." Indeed, we see in the course of daily experience that obedience to God's law, whether of nature or of grace, however incomplete and partial, still, so far as it is obedience, never wholly misses its reward. The man who is sober and temperate, even though he is so on no high and religious grounds, still wins the reward of sobriety and temperance. He prolongs his days, and sees, perhaps, his children's children round about his table. The tradesman who is thrifty and diligent in business reaps the fruit of thriftiness and diligence; sees his till full of money and himself getting on in the world, even though the highest object of his desire is not godliness, but gain.

But in all these cases, as in Jehu's, as it has been a *partial obedience*, so it only wins a partial and imperfect reward. It has the promise, perhaps, of this world, but not of that which is to come. Nay, even the worldly blessing that falls to it may be embittered by a thousand sad accompaniments. The *long* life is not necessarily a *happy* one. The full purse may bring little comfort to the careworn body or the aching heart. The thought of our stored garners, or our richly-furnished houses, or our sumptuous tables, or our fine dresses—though they were what excited the envy and admiration of our neighbours, and perhaps led us to count ourselves happy men—will hardly be that on which we shall care to dwell with satisfaction in the night when our souls shall be required.

They alone are truly blessed of God who serve Him

faithfully with their *whole* heart : who, having ascertained what He would have them to do, do it just as heartily when it *crosses* their inclinations as when it humours them : who feel that Esau's blessing, " to have their dwelling of the fatness of the earth, and to break the yoke of another from off their neck "—as we should say, riches and independence—is, after all, not the blessing God has reserved for His saints, nor that at which the follower of Christ is taught primarily to aim. The children of this world no doubt have their blessings, their advantages, their wisdom, as well as the children of light. But they are carnal, unsatisfying, transitory. While, like Jonah under his gourd, we are basking beneath their shade, God may be preparing a worm to canker them at the root, so that instead of a sweet smell there shall be a stink, and loathsomeness in the place of beauty.

Whatever our natural gifts or tempers, remember, we must all be *created anew;* fashioned into the likeness of Christ; the old leaven purged out, and the whole body and soul and spirit transformed. It is the work of the Holy Ghost, always gradual and often slow. We are to be workers together with Him by prayer, by communion of the body and blood of Christ ; by Bible-reading and holy meditation ; by watchfulness and self-mastery ; by gentleness and love unfeigned ; by the armour of righteousness on the right hand and on the left; by labouring not for the meat that perisheth, but for that which Christ has to give to us; by checking and conquering all proud and self-willed tempers ; by looking not only on our own things but also every man on the things of others. Thus, and thus only, is the snare of such dispositions as Jehu's to be escaped. Thus, and thus only, shall we prove what is " that good and acceptable and perfect will of God." Thus, and thus only, will our *present* issue in a *future* regeneration. Thus, and thus only, shall we show ourselves " blameless and harmless, the sons of God, without rebuke, in the midst of a crooked and perverse nation. among whom it is our Christian calling to shine as lights in the world."

Preached — Cholderton, Eleventh Sunday after Trinity, August 7, 1853.

XVII.

OUR SUFFICIENCY OF GOD.

"Our sufficiency is of God."—2 Cor. iii. 5.

WHAT St. Paul here asserts of himself, and his fellow-labourers in the Gospel, is equally true of every Christian man. The Scriptures teach us this, under a great variety of figures and expressions. St. Paul says of himself, "By the grace of God I am what I am": and again, "I can do all things through Christ which strengtheneth me": and again, when he besought the Lord thrice that the thorn in his flesh might depart from him, the answer he got was not, "Thy prayer is heard, and I will ease thee of thy pain," but "My grace is sufficient for thee, for my strength is made perfect in weakness."

The fact of man's natural helplessness, of his inability in and by himself to do any good thing, or to lay hold on eternal life, is the very foundation stone of the whole Gospel scheme. It is attested alike by history and personal experience. The universal cry of nature is "O wretched man that I am, who shall deliver me from the body of this death?" The very root of all Christian joy and thankfulness is the revelation of that "new and living way, consecrated for us through Christ's flesh," by which "we come boldly to the throne of grace, and obtain mercy, and find grace to help us in time of need."

And yet this doctrine, though so generally acknowledged with the lips, and often so flippantly uttered with the tongue, is received with two great practical denials and perversions by the world. The very people who talk most about it are often the least under the influence of its power. If you will observe attentively the language of the text you will see that it is hardly possible to find five words with a more pregnant meaning. It is *our* sufficiency, and therefore there is, as our Lord tells us, "nothing impossible to him that believeth"; but it is a sufficiency not inherent, but imparted. "Our sufficiency is of God." It is precisely the same truth that is implied in the passage, "work out *your own salvation* with fear and trembling." It is expressly called, you see, *our own salvation*, and yet any false inference that might have followed from such language is immediately corrected by the sequel, "It is *God* that worketh in us, both to will and to do."

The two perversions of this doctrine have a common origin, though a different tendency. They spring from that faulty—and in a matter of such practical concern dangerous—habit of mind, which is ever putting asunder what God has joined. It separates grace from the Sacraments, and faith from works; and the heart from the lips, and the lips from the heart, in congregational worship; and God's justice from His mercy; and repentance from its fruits; and Christ's Atonement from Christ's Example; and religion from the bearing of the Cross; and charity from self-denial; and obedience from love; and the profession of the Gospel from the government of the temper or the bridling of the tongue.

And as it thus divorces what Almighty God, in His revelation, has knit together with an indissoluble bond, so, on the other hand, it is ever contriving the strangest alliances and fellowships of its own. Thus the profession of religion is supposed to agree very well with a full measure and unlimited enjoyment of the pleasures and attractions of the world. Men say they can at once live to Christ and to themselves: they can be absorbed in the love of gain, and yet follow after godliness: they can be drunkards or profane swearers, and still reckon themselves within the covenant: they can habitually turn their backs on the Lord's table, and still say they love Christ: they can adorn themselves with good works, they think, while half their time and more than half their thoughts are occupied about "broidered hair, and gold, and pearls, and costly array." They partition out their hearts between the Gospel and the world; and though the latter gets I know not how much the larger share, they can discover no inconsistencies; they feel no conflicting claims; inclination and duty, in them, never quarrel, or, if they do, duty always obligingly gives way. They think it a very comfortable arrangement which allows them, with so little discomfort, to make the most of this life without foregoing, or endangering, their expectations and prospects in the life which is to come.

Whether this is indeed the doctrine of Christ Crucified, whether the Eternal Son of God left His Father's bosom and lowered Himself to such a depth of humiliation as to become obedient even unto death, to set up such a standard of religion, and to purchase unto Himself such a "peculiar people" as this, you can judge as well as I.

I proceed to show you how the grand and fundamental doctrine of the text is perverted by the false glosses and lying traditions of men.

It is perverted in two ways: first by those who, fixing their attention wholly on the latter half of the words, cry out, " Oh, then, if our sufficiency *is of God*, we have nothing to do with it ourselves: it does not depend upon us in any way: we must leave God to do His own work in His own measures and His own time!" Secondly, by those who, with a too painful consciousness of their own imperfections, say, " What is the use of talking about *sufficiency* at all to a poor, weak, erring creature like man? If the word means anything it must mean a measure of grace and holiness which is consistent with many shortcomings, with much blindness, with large allowances for human infirmity, with the facts and conditions of human nature." These are the two views—widely spread in a practical shape in the world—acted on unconsciously even where they are not entertained deliberately—and which seem to me to empty not only the text, but the whole doctrine that is according to godliness—the whole Gospel Dispensation—of its meaning, its reasonableness, its power.

It is indeed strange that such erroneous notions of

God's gracious purposes towards fallen man are not corrected by the very experience and phenomena of the physical world. In this aspect, at least, God's providence and God's grace appear to move precisely by the same laws. A farmer will hardly get a crop from his land unless he dresses it, and digs it, and plants it, and keeps it free from weeds. And yet we are told, and we know it by experience to be true, that it is "God that giveth seed to the sower, and bread to the eater": "that sendeth the former and the latter rain in his season": "that maketh His sun to rise": "that reserveth unto us the appointed weeks of the harvest." We are workers together *with* God in *temporal* things: why not then in spiritual things? The labour of our hands is needed in the dressing of the fields: how should our co-operation be useless and superfluous in the training and preparing of our souls?

In spite of the confessed difficulty of some few isolated texts, it is quite marvellous, to my mind, how such a notion as that of God's grace being not the *one* but the *only* thing needful could ever gain possession of the faith of any one of us who reads and meditates on his Bible, as a whole. The history of every one of God's saints recorded there gives the direct lie to such a theory.

St. Paul practised a resolute and watchful and daily self-mastery, lest that good thing which he felt God had *begun* in him should be frustrated by his own abuse or neglect of the gift. He himself describes his whole spiritual history in eight words, "I do not frustrate the grace of God." He *could* frustrate it, and it was the knowledge that he had this power which made him all the more careful of his ways. It is God who *gives* the grace: but we ourselves have the *using* of it.

But while we avoid the first error we must not fall into the second. While asserting the necessity of man's own conscious co-operation in the work of his salvation, we must not measure the degree of perfection to which he may attain by any fancied limit of the extent of his own natural powers. We must not get into the way of excusing sin, or even infirmity, by that easy and perfunctory formula—"Oh! after all we are but men: weak, erring, sinful men!" What we are now is no criterion of what we might be, what we ought to be. God's grace is always forestalling and *preventing* our own endeavours. It is from Him, and not from ourselves, that we get the very rudiments of holiness—the power not only to do, but even to *will*, after His good pleasure. There is not a good desire or a holy habit in our nature that did not originally come from Him, however much it may now seem to be part of ourselves.

Those who have ever fought long and earnestly against any besetting sin—wrestled as it were like Jacob with the angel till they have prevailed—can speak of how grace is won, and how "out of weakness they became strong." As there are no limits to the marvels of divine power, so are there no limits to the height of man's perfection. There is no more dangerous or damnable heresy of these latter days than that which lays down a kind of *average* standard of human goodness, and asserts that all who attain to that are quite safe, and that even great allowances will be made for many shortcomings on the score of man's infirmity. You hear it constantly said, "Oh! we are not expected to be saints." Not expected to be saints! What are you to be then? Do not the opening words of almost every Epistle of St. Paul carry a solemn reminder to his hearers' hearts that they are "called to be saints?" Are we not expressly told that "without holiness"— that is, without the grace of saintliness—" no man shall see the Lord?"

We should be Pauls in saintliness, were we only Pauls in earnestness, in watchfulness, in prayer, in fasting. We might use his words did we only lead his life. We shall sit as near Christ in heaven if we only love and serve him as faithfully on earth. St. Paul had plainly as many natural infirmities to struggle against—as hasty a temper, as proud a spirit, as ungovernable a self-will—as any of us; but, as he tells us, "by the grace of God he became what he was." "The grace which was bestowed on him was not given in vain, but he laboured more abundantly than they all, yet," as he adds with a deep and unfeigned humility, "not I, but the grace of God which was with me."

Thus we come back to the point from which we started, "the sufficiency of the grace of God." For this we have to labour, for this we have to take heed, lest we come short of it. God's work is hindered not more by Satan than by ourselves—by our sloth, our unconcern, our lukewarmness, our compromises, our deadness to spiritual things. We know our natural weakness, and yet we do not seek God's strength.

As one instance of this I refer you to the very solemn and remarkable words recorded by St. John: "Then Jesus said unto them, Verily, verily, I say unto you, except ye eat the flesh of the Son of Man, and drink His blood, ye have no life in you. Whoso eateth My flesh, and drinketh My blood, hath eternal life; and I will raise him up at the last day." Now I ask what meaning you attach to these words? That they mean *something*—something definitely and awfully practical—something bound up with the very life and death of our souls, you will hardly deny. But what is that something? The Church gives you an answer. She tells you that these words enforce the duty and explain the necessity of Sacramental Communion with the Lord's body and blood. St. Paul teaches the same, if I understand the meaning of words, when he says "The cup of blessing which we bless, is it not the communion of the blood of Christ? The bread which we break, is it not the communion of the body of Christ?" If you choose to say the words mean something else, I ask you not to tell me, but to answer satisfactorily to yourselves, what spiritual act in your lives you consider equivalent to this eating the flesh and drinking the blood of your Saviour, without which, He has told you Himself, you have no life in your souls. I think you will agree with me that the words can bear no other sense than that which the Church and St. Paul both put upon them as setting before us the bounden duty and the inestimable advantage of feeding upon Christ, by faith, in the Supper of His own divine institution.

How can we expect God's grace if we do not use an ordinance which He has appointed for one of its chiefest channels? Is there one of our excuses that will stand God's searching eye—nay even satisfy our own? "We are waiting." So some of you have been these forty years, and will these twenty years more, if your life is spared so long. In a case of life and death I never knew any good come of waiting. I never found one more drawn to Christ by the cords of love at sixty than he was at twenty years of age. "We have so many cares and troubles." And so you think under such circumstances you will do better without God and Christ than with them! "We are too young." For what? to die? If not, you are not too young to live for God, which is the only preparation for a safe, a holy, a comfortable death.

But what need to go through all these vain excuses? They all come to this—I have no heart for God's service, I do not like a religious life. Disguise it how you will from your minister—even from yourselves—the truth of it all is in David's words, "Your hearts are not set upon righteousness, O ye congregation: you do not seek after God, O ye sons of men." You will not be Christ's servants, and so you are the world's and Satan's slaves.

Oh, my friends, break these unworthy bonds while the Spirit of the Lord is still offered to enable you. Draw nigh to God, before the time of the great water-floods. Feel that if you are to have either part or lot in this matter your heart must be right in the sight of God. Oh, that my words could make you realize the exceeding perilousness of thus halting between two opinions—or rather it is not halting between; for while you fancy you are still free to choose, you are in reality only becoming more and more estranged from God, more and more in bondage to the world.

It is our life, our youth, our health, our strength that God demands for His service; not our decrepit limbs, or "the days in which we have no pleasure," or the hour when we see gathering round us the fearful shadow of the valley of death. Be assured of this: God sets down against us all those opportunities which we have had within our reach, but have not used. These despised sacraments, and neglected prayers, and unfamiliar Bibles, and untended warnings will all bear their damning witness against us at the last day. We shall be called to account for every talent that we have not improved. Our wealth, our worldly position, our personal influence, our religious knowledge, our intellectual gifts, will all be so many grounds of our condemnation if they have been perverted to selfish purposes, or the Giver has been either forgotten or profaned in the gift.

May God Almighty teach you to do, as well as to know, all the good pleasure of His will, that so, although feeling weak in yourselves yet being sufficient in Him, "you may make your calling and election sure;" and " that an entrance may be ministered unto you abundantly into the everlasting kingdom of our Lord and Saviour, Jesus Christ."

Preached—Cholderton, Fourteenth Sunday after Trinity, August 28, 1853.

XVIII.

GOD A REFUGE IN TEMPTATION.

"There hath no temptation taken you but such as is common to man: but God is faithful, who will not suffer you to be tempted above that ye are able; but will with the temptation also make a way to escape, that ye may be able to bear it."—1 Cor. x.13.

IF these words are true, there can be no such thing as pleading an excuse for any act or habit of sin. There is no use in saying, "I could not help it": "the temptation was so very strong": "human nature is so very weak": "God never stretched out His right hand to help me": "I was left alone to encounter the powers of darkness." There is no use in thinking that thus we make out a good case for ourselves, or flattering ourselves that the memory of abominable sins may thus be lightly cast aside, partly because such a way of talking is not true; and partly because, even if it were true, it would not be to the purpose.

It is not true to say of any sin that we could not help it, or were left to battle with it unassisted and alone. It is not to the purpose to allege, even if truly, that the temptation was strong and human nature weak, because the nature of every regenerate person is not simply *human*. As St. Peter says, "we are made partakers of the *divine* nature," and however strong the temptation, it is after all but "such as is common to man"; and the text assures us that "God is faithful, who will not suffer us to be tempted above that we are able, but will with the temptation also make a way to escape, that we may be able to bear it."

Through all the passages of Scripture illustrative of this principle one common idea runs—that temptation is man's portion, the inheritance he has received from his first parents; but, so far from its being represented as necessary or unavoidable that we should yield to it or be overcome by it, it is here lies the very essence of our discipline, the very function of faith, the very trial of our spiritual strength and courage; *the* point, or article, of difference between the wicked and the profane—"between him that serveth God and him that serveth Him not"; or, to borrow St. Peter's instances, between Noah and the world of the ungodly, between Lot and the sinners of Sodom.

Nay, more: to be overcome by temptation, to yield to unclean lusts or passionate tempers or even unbridled appetites, is attributed not so much to *weakness* as to *faithlessness*: to a faint-hearted, cowardly mistrust of God; to a voluntary acquiescence in, or indifference to, sin; to a lack of patience and watchfulness; to a vain confidence in our own strength and a forgetfulness of the maxim that "all our sufficiency is of God." It is not God's way, we are told, to tempt men, or even to leave them when they are tempted. He is always close at hand, if they had only eyes purged to discern Him, "making a way to escape," "strengthening the weak," "delivering the godly," and ever listening to the prayers of the elect when "they cry day and night unto Him." If they fall, it is not because God is not there, with His hand ready to lift them up; but because, like Peter on the water of Gennesaret, they forget for the moment their heavenly Friend, and then find their own strength utterly unable to bear them up against the waves and storms of this troublesome world.

This is the invariable way in which Scripture speaks to us of the nature and power of temptation; but I think it is hardly the way in which we think or speak of it ourselves. Our own weakness we are ready enough to allow—though even this often merely in set forms of speech, and not in real sincerity of feeling—but we are not equally ready to acknowledge God's strength. We say often enough, "Of mine own self I can do nothing"; but we do not say equally often, "In Christ I can do all things." It is very easy to throw the blame of our sins on "the old man, which is corrupt according to the deceitful lusts"; but we forget that we "have put on the new man, which is renewed in knowledge after the image of Him that created him." We plead the weakness of nature, but we do not remember the efficacy of grace. We speak of our bondage to Satan, but forget that God has delivered us "from the power of darkness, and hath translated us into the kingdom of His dear Son"; and that thus we encounter temptation on an entirely new ground, with every advantage on our side, clothed in bright and invulnerable armour on the right hand and on the left. As St. Paul says, we are "*more than conquerors* through Him that loved us"—angels and principalities and powers are unable to separate us from Him, and there is nothing of which we need be afraid, save our own unloyal hearts and treacherous right hands.

I think that all who have endeavoured, with ever so little earnestness, to lead a watchful and decent life, must be able to confirm, by their own experience, the truth of these statements of the Word of God. We must have felt—if not constantly, yet at least occasionally—how strong we were when we have put ourselves in God's hands and committed our cause wholly to Him. There have been times surely when our Divine Master's words have come home with a living force to our hearts—" I will never leave thee nor forsake thee" —so that we have been enabled boldly to say, "The Lord is my helper, and I will not fear what man shall do unto me." At least if we have not known such moments, moments of such unspeakable strength and comfort, moments when we have indeed felt what faith is, and what mighty deeds, through God, it is capable of accomplishing, it must be because our lives have been nothing but one long course of carnalism—a constant acquiescence in fetters which we have felt, but have not had the spirit to attempt to break—a poor, wretched, Laodicean state of worldly-mindedness, which has alike prevented us from being conscious of our needs, or seeking help from God.

And what some of us perhaps have experienced *sometimes* we should experience *always*, if the thought of the goodness of the Lord were that which always *first* occurred to us in seasons of difficulty and distress.

If, when poverty or misfortune or trials of any kind came upon us, we were in the habit of looking up at once to heaven for succour and relief—not from a mere momentary impulse, but with a patient and trustful steadfastness—we should find a deeper meaning than we have hitherto done in those hard sayings of the Bible which tell us so often that affliction, however grievous for the moment, "nevertheless afterward yieldeth the peaceable fruit of righteousness unto them which are exercised thereby"; and that "whom the Lord loveth He chasteneth, and scourgeth every son whom He receiveth."

It is because, in spite of all our lip-profession, we do not really put our trust in God, that we are so often entangled in temptation and overcome. Instead of trying to find out what God would teach us by the visitation; seeking anxiously to ascertain whether by any past misconduct we have brought it down as a punishment upon ourselves, and if we find it to be so, then humbling ourselves under His mighty hand, thanking Him for thus "bringing our sin to remembrance," instead of suffering us to go down with it unatoned-for to our graves; instead of acting in this, which is the only really Christian and religious way, we grumble, and murmur, and complain, and say we are hardly dealt with, and cannot think how it is we come into trouble so much oftener than other folk, and are sure we have done nothing to deserve it; or at least content ourselves with a few cant phrases, which we keep in stock for such occasions, about "the Lord's will being done," and "the Lord giving and the Lord taking away"; when all the while, in the secret depths of our hearts, we are arraigning God for His severity, and are unable to read one sign of mercy in the visitation, and are almost tempted, like the idle servant in the parable, to call the Master whom we serve "an austere man," whom it is alike unprofitable and wearisome to profess to regard.

I do not think I am uttering any over-statement. Take the case of unruly and disobedient children, which —I will not say *always*, but in nine cases out of ten— is the result either of the ill-advised fondness, or inexcusable neglect, of parents. The same may be said of sickness, or poverty, or any other form of affliction. They are not sent, we may be sure, simply that we may acknowledge that God sent them, but that we may feel that they are sent *for our good;* that there is a lesson in them; that God saw that we needed them; that there is something in us wants correction—some idol that we have set up in our hearts that must be cast down; some hold that carnal things have on us which for our soul's health had best be broken; some careless way into which we have fallen, and from which we need to be awakened; some lesson of patience, or resignation, or faith, or meekness, which we have not yet learnt and which in this way can best be taught us.

I do not say that this is the spirit in which trials are generally borne—far otherwise—but it is the spirit in which they may be emptied of their bitterness and turned, like balm of Gilead, to the healing of our souls. All those circumstances which the world calls "hard" wear a different aspect when viewed by the eye of faith, and in the light reflected on them from the Cross of Christ. He who so uses them can realize what David meant when he said, "Before I was troubled, I went wrong: but now have I kept thy word. I know, Lord, that Thy judgments are right, and that Thou of very faithfulness hast caused me to be troubled."

This then must be our strength and comfort under all circumstances of trial or temptation, to know upon the warrant of God's Holy Word that there is a way open to us to escape, if we only choose to look for it. Of course, if we prefer sitting down and folding our hands, and letting things take their course, as though possessed by a kind of Mahometan spirit of fatalism, we shall never find comfort in our trials, or strength in our temptations. Whether we like it or not, our whole life is a warfare, a fighting not simply against flesh and blood, but, "against principalities and powers, against the rulers of the darkness of this world, against spiritual wickedness in high places."

The only practical question is, Shall we enter the battle naked and unarmed, or with the shield of faith on our arm, "and the sword of the Spirit, which is the Word of God," in our right hand? Shall we despair of victory, or hope on confidently to the end? Shall we make terms and compromises with our foe, or hold fast that we have, that no man take our crown? Shall we rather confess our own weakness, or make our boast of God's strength? Shall we say, as David was once almost tempted to say, "it is my own infirmity," or rather with the same saint, recovering his confidence, "remember the years of the right hand of the Most

Highest"? One or the other we must do, and our fate depends upon our choice.

Theirs is the saddest and most hopeless doom of all whom, like the Jewish people of old, "the Lord hath stricken, but they have not grieved; He has consumed them, but they have refused to receive correction; they have made their faces harder than a rock; they have refused to return."

Be assured of this: not a sparrow falls to the ground without your Father which is in heaven. Nay, "the very hairs of our head are all numbered." We have no need to fear anything that either the devil or man can work against us, if we only "commit our souls unto Him, in *well-doing*, as unto a faithful Creator." We know that He has never failed His people who trusted in Him. If ever we have felt faint and discouraged in the presence of trials or difficulties, it is because our faith has grown dim for a while, like Elijah's when he fled for his life to Horeb; or our hands have grown weary of being lifted up to heaven, like Moses when he stood on the rock while the people fought against Amalek, and have need of fresh supplies of grace to recruit their strength and energy.

Our power to resist evil will only continue, like Samson's supernatural prowess, as long as we acknowledge its dependence upon God. If once we cut ourselves off from the means of grace, if we think we can do without prayer, and sacraments, and the presence of the Spirit, as that Israelitish champion thought his strength might remain, though he suffered the cunning Delilah to rob him of his lock of hair, we shall find to our cost, as he found, when the Philistines are upon us, that the Lord has departed from us, and that we are weak and but as other men.

The Christian's strength lies in his uninterrupted access to, and communion with, God. As St. Paul beautifully expresses it, "the life he now lives in the flesh he lives by the faith of the Son of God, Who loved him, and gave Himself for him." In all his sufferings and trials upon earth he can, like the holy martyr, St. Stephen, "steadfastly look up to heaven," and feel that he is but helping to bear that Master's Cross " Who suffered for us, leaving us an example that we should follow His steps." As He was made perfect by overcoming temptation, and " though a Son, yet learnt obedience by the things which he suffered," so must His disciples too. "If ye be without chastisement," says the Scripture, "of which all are partakers, then are ye bastards and not sons."

Little has he learnt the very first lessons of the Cross of Christ who, though perhaps he receives the Word with joy, is fond of reading his Bible, glad to hear sermons, and has a text always ready at his tongue's end, yet has, after all, "no root in himself, but dureth for a while; for when tribulation or persecution ariseth because of the Word, by and by he is offended." He is one of those who would sit at Christ's right hand, but not drink of His cup, or be baptized with His baptism.

We must take the Gospel, as men do their wives, "for better, for worse, for richer, for poorer, in sickness and in health," or we can have no part or lot in it at all. If it has its comforts and promises, it has also its trials and temptations. "My son" says the wise son of Sirach, "if thou come to serve the Lord, prepare thy soul for temptation." That which in all these things makes us "more than conquerors," that which enables us even to take a pleasure "in infirmities, in reproaches, in distress, in necessities"; that which is the balm under every suffering of this present time, is the undoubting conviction of every truly spiritualized mind, that "all things work together for good to them that love God": that "He in Whom we trust will not suffer us to be tempted above that we are able"; and that "neither death, nor life, nor angels, nor powers, nor things present, nor things to come, can separate us from the love of God, which is in Christ Jesus our Lord."

Preached — Cholderton, Eighteenth Sunday after Trinity, September 25, 1853.

XIX.

THE THREE CHILDREN IN THE FURNACE.

"Shadrach, Meshach, and Abednego answered and said to the king, O Nebuchadnezzar, we are not careful to answer thee in this matter. If it be so, our God whom we serve is able to deliver us from the burning fiery furnace, and He will deliver us out of thine hand, O king. But if not, be it known unto thee, O king, that we will not serve thy gods, nor worship the golden image which thou hast set up."—DANIEL iii. 16-18.

WHAT a living faith in the unseen Providence of Almighty God must men have had who could answer a proud and cruel tyrant—one too who had their lives in his hand —in such words as these! In spite of the dreadful alternative to which their refusal to obey Nebuchadnezzar's idolatrous command exposed them, what a cheerful confidence breathes in every syllable they utter; what a sustaining conviction of rectitude; what an unhesitating discernment of duty; what a bold and unfaltering resolution to do that duty, let the consequences to themselves be what they may!

It is a striking picture. There, in that plain of Dura, stands an image of gold, threescore cubits high, at whose gigantic feet the representatives of every nation that acknowledged the sovereignty of the great Babylonish king are seen to bow. There stood too the king himself; the mightiest monarch who had yet sat upon that throne; the proud conqueror of Egypt, and Tyre, and Jerusalem, "whose greatness reached unto heaven, and his dominion to the end of the earth," watching, in the fulness of kingly pride, the abject creatures that bowed their bodies before the idol he had set up; pluming himself perhaps on their absolute submission to his will, thinking how great a thing it was thus to lord it over the consciences of his fellow-men; but never dreaming of a day when he, as well as the meanest subject he saw before him, would have to give an account to the Judge of all the earth of the use he had made of all these prerogatives and opportunities.

Bred up, as he had been, in all the notions of an Oriental despot, it probably never once occurred to him that there would be found in all that vast assemblage any one rash or bold enough to resist his will. He looked for obedience to his commands, however unreasonable, as a matter of course. He had never known the checks of constitutional law, and he expected that his behest would pass unquestioned now.

He needed to be taught a lesson, and He in whose rule and governance are the hearts of kings saw fit to teach him in a strange way. From three men of that nation over which he had achieved his most signal triumph, from three weak captive Jews, he, learnt for the first time the lesson that there is One above who claims obedience before any earthly king, as whose vice-gerent he himself alone had any power, and the slightest intimations of Whose will have more weight with His faithful servants than all the threats and angry words of those who can indeed kill the body, but after that have no more that they can do. In the words I have borrowed for my text, Shadrach, Meshach, and Abednego refused to acknowledge Nebuchadnezzar's sovereignty of the conscience, or to worship a creature instead of the Creator, " Who is over all, God blessed for evermore."

There is a boldness in their words, but no impertinence. .They do not forget the respect due to the office and person of a king, though they refuse absolutely to obey his command. If they are ready to submit to the doom of martyrdom it is only from the homage and allegiance which they pay to truth, and not from any desire to excite popular sympathy or commotion, at which our would-be modern martyrs aim. They put their cause simply in God's hand, feeling sure that as long as they had Him on their side they need not "fear what man could do unto them." They were not careful, they say, to cast about for an answer. They had no need to premeditate. It was given them from above what they ought to say. Their consciences instantaneously suggested the proper reply, and they declare their unalterable resolution not to comply with this idolatrous worship in so cheerful a tone that one might think they expected their answer to secure their deliverance instead of imperilling their lives.

I do not mean to say that any of us living in England in the nineteenth century are likely to be exposed to such a trial as were these three men. But we should read these ancient histories to little profit if we could not discern the application of which they are capable to our own trials and circumstances. So I think that these Hebrews may still be an example to many a Christian man who may much need their strength of faith, though he may never be called upon to encounter the exact form of their trial.

For though the outward circumstances of our individual probation differ infinitely, the inward principle that is to bear us through them is universally the same. No two men or women perhaps are *tempted* alike, but all are *sustained* alike, by the power of faith and hope " which entereth within the veil." Indeed St. Peter speaks of our discipline of suffering in language that may almost make us think he had this scene in the plain of Dura before his eyes. "Beloved," he says, "think it not strange concerning the *fiery trial* which is to try you, as though some strange thing happened unto you. But rejoice, inasmuch as ye are partakers of Christ's sufferings; that, when His glory shall be revealed, ye may be glad also with exceeding joy."

Let me endeavour to adapt the lessons of this story to our own use, and to show you that this record of faith and constancy was not intended merely to make an interesting narrative, but was indeed written and may be applied "to our admonition, on whom the ends of the world are come."

I think that one of the most obvious and at the same time most useful lessons that we should draw from it is, that we are not to suppose our conduct is right and laudable simply because it happens to have in its favour the maxims and fashions of the world. These may be very good; but they are just as likely to be, and often are, very corrupt and bad. No really religious man takes his neighbour's fashions as his standard, or the current maxims as his guide. He refers them, as he does everything else, to the one unfailing criterion of right and wrong, of false and true—the law and the testimony: if they speak not according to this word, he reckons there is no light in them.

These three Jews, if they had wished to deal deceitfully with their consciences, might easily have stifled all uncomfortable sensations by the ready excuse, that to fall down before this image was a mere compliance with a fashion. Everybody else did it. There was no call on them to be over-scrupulous. It would be folly to run any risk for so trivial a point. Even if it were an offence, with so many to share it its guilt and punishment would be infinitesimally small.

This is the way we are, each individually, in danger of deceiving ourselves every day. If Satan can only persuade us, by any subtlety, to act and think like the careless world around us, he knows we are his both in body and soul. For though there are some classes of sins which the world treats with excessive and indeed *unjust* severity—not allowing even the sincerest repentance to restore the offender to his good name, or replace him in his once-forfeited position—there are others, to which it has more inclination of its own, on which it looks much more indulgently, and calls them by soft names, and says it is uncharitable to speak sternly about them, and would fain persuade us that they are compatible with perfect respectability and with a very sufficient amount of religion.

We Protestants are in the habit of finding fault with Papists for their vain distinction between venial and mortal sins: and yet, in our own practice and language, we are constantly doing exactly the same. We measure sins, not by their inherent sinfulness, not by the extent to which they trample on God's law, not by the abandonment of heart which they evince in the doer; but by an infinitely baser and more selfish standard—by their consequences to ourselves, by their departure from a fanciful, and often false, code which we call honour or fashion; by the discredit which attaches to them; by that shifting, variable rule which takes public opinion, not the Word of God—wretched conventionalities, not an enlightened conscience—for its direction and guidance.

Surely, when we stop for a moment to think what most men and women really are; what a cold, heartless, calculating, self-indulgent world this is; how few of our neighbours seem in earnest to promote the cause of godliness in their families, and households, and parishes; what poor and niggard sacrifices are laid upon the altar of duty; how the idol of Self, in one form or another, is universally worshipped; how little vital, heart-penetrating devotion there is in the fashionable customary religion of the day; when we can scarce at length discern a faithful servant of God here and there; one who by a divine charm that he bears about him seems to have escaped the universal contagion of worldliness: it can be but sorry comfort to us to be able to say, "Well, there are thousands like ourselves: we are just as decent and God-fearing as half the people in the parish: if so and so is safe, I think I may consider myself so too." Ah! if so and so is safe: but is he? Perhaps he is measuring himself exactly in the same way by you. And so you are all encouraging yourselves in a monstrous delusion because you will persist in taking up a false standard—*the average of men instead of the pattern of Christ*—and stunting down all your ideas of faith, and sacrifice, and duty, and worship, and self-control to these miserable worldly dimensions.

We cannot really believe that this world, by whose fashions and maxims we are content to be led, is in the right after all. We cannot deliberately adopt the blasphemous language of those who say "The voice of the people is the voice of God." When has it ever been so since the earth was made? When have the current language of men and the revelation of the Divine Will been in harmony? What great Reformation in fact has there ever been where, I will not say the *devout* but even the *philosophic*, cannot trace the Almighty's sovereign hand controlling the madness of the people, educing good out of evil, moulding men's unruly passions into conformity with His eternal purposes, and, one scarcely knows how, maintaining truth and right at the very crisis when they seemed in utter danger of being overborne?

No: as in the researches of a merely human wisdom its mysteries reveal themselves only to a few, as it is only here and there we meet with a man who has penetrated into the secret causes of things, and lives superior to the errors and prejudices of the day; so infinitely more in spiritual things is the truth of God hidden from the natural man, and he gropes his way in darkness, taking shadows for substances, misreading the signs of the times, tossed about by every blast of vain doctrine—in the emphatic words of St. Paul, " deceiving and being deceived."

And it is by the maxims and opinions of these people that we are to be ruled. We are to act as they act and think as they think. We are to be as careless, as vain, as trivial, as unprofitable, as unprogressive as they are, and reckon ourselves safe, as though we were of God's elect, and " our seed within the covenant." We are to bow with them before the images of gold which are set up in our plains and cities, running as greedily as they do after gain, or pleasure, or vanity, and think we are in good company, and travelling to heaven by a *safe*, as it certainly is an *easy*, road!

So far from this, our very duty, as followers of Christ, is to protest, not simply by our words but by our lives, against those very things that we see going on all around us; against those very sins of surfeiting, and drunkenness, and uncleanness, and swearing, and lying, and covetousness, and selfishness, and indifference, which must effectually quench the smallest spark of true religion in the soul. The Christian's daily prayer is to be, not that he may be taken out of the world, but that he may be " kept from its evil," from its blindness, from its wilfulness, " from its putting sweet for bitter and bitter for sweet," from the worse than Egyptian darkness with which it is covered, so that men cannot see the destruction which is overhanging them, though it is nigh, even at the doors.

Shadrach, Meshach and Abednego were Protestants in the true sense of the word—against all forms of falsehood, and profaneness, and idolatry; vindicating for God a true supremacy, and sustained themselves by the inward power of a living faith. I wish our English Protestantism was of the same kind. I wish it did not all evaporate in intemperate agitations, followed, by the necessary law of reaction, by a period of complacent, undisturbed self-righteousness. When I speak of every follower of Christ being bound to be a Protestant, I do not mean that he must be familiar with the stock arguments against Popery or Dissent. I do not mean that he must condemn the Council of Trent, or be always quoting the Thirty-nine Articles, or think it part of his religious duty to call the Pope "Antichrist," or Rome "the city of harlots." I never knew much good come of calling hard names. I mean that his *life* must be Protestant—a continual contradiction to the vanities and delusions of his age; a visible example of the power and fruits of faith, a standing witness of the truth of God; a living conformity to the law of Christ; a weighing all things in the balances of the sanctuary.

This was the spirit of the Protestantism of Jeremiah and Ezekiel and Daniel. In this temper Shadrach, Meshach, and Abednego were content to yield their bodies to the flames, rather than surrender a truth which was to them the very stay and anchor of their souls. There is nothing noisy, or agitating, or ostentatious in such a spirit. It is calm, because assured; secure from the perils of false doctrine and unsteadfastness, because "fully persuaded in its own mind;" bold to speak the truth, yet withal speaking it in *love*, because experience has proved that persecution and coercion in such cases alike fail of their purpose. He that would win souls to Christ must prove himself *tender* as well as wise.

It is this kind of witness *for* Christ, and *against* the world, that every Christian, by virtue of his regeneration, is called upon to bear. No greater curse can happen to any religious community than the notion that the duty of "correction, reproof, and instruction in righteousness" belongs to the clergyman alone. *Each* in his place it is true, and with some differences perhaps of practical detail, but *all* in principle and spirit, *all* in aim and purpose, *all* by example and prayer, are to be "fellow-labourers with God" in the evangelization of mankind; holding forth in their own conversation the word of life, as a light whose diffusive radiance may at once illuminate and warm the dark, drear places which may easily be found, if we take the trouble to look for them in our neighbourhood, *possibly* even in the narrower circle of our own homes.

That was a noble sentiment of Moses, when some one jealous of his honour told him that there were two men prophesying in the camp, and would have him forbid them. "And Moses said unto him, Enviest thou for my sake? Would God that all the Lord's people were prophets, and that the Lord would put His Spirit upon them!" It may be a glorious distinction to stand alone doing God's work, or, like Daniel and his three companions in Babylon, to be of the elect few who are uncontaminated by the universal unbelief and ungodliness around them : but it is more glorious and more blessed still to be an instrument in God's hand for *propagating* the same spirit. It is to every Christian man and woman that the apostolic exhortation was addressed, " Brethren, if any of you do err from the truth, and one convert him; let him know, that he which converteth the sinner from the error of his way shall save a soul from death, and shall hide a multitude of sins."

Here then let us see the application of this history to ourselves. What are we doing as parishioners, as householders, as parents, as masters, as employers, to bear a faithful witness to the truth of God in the face of an unbelieving and careless world ? Do we look upon our daily words and deeds as important not only to ourselves, in the way of forming habits and developing character, but as constituting, each one of them, more or less preponderance to that aggregate amount of good and evil which, in the most retired country village as truly as in the most thickly-peopled town, are battling together for the mastery ?

Whether we have ever regarded it as such or not, this *is* our *simple, primary* duty. " For no man liveth to himself, and no man dieth to himself." We are as members set in a body. It was God's purpose, we are told, in thus placing us, that " there should be no schism in the body, but that the members should have the same care one for another." I am sure of this, that if we do not care for others, we cannot care, as we ought to do, for *ourselves*. No man need ask for a surer proof of the unsatisfactory state of religion in his own soul than when he finds himself indifferent to the spiritual welfare of his brethren. Not a day of our lives probably passes in which we have not some opportunity of being "fellow-helpers of the truth," of sowing seed that may bring forth fruit to life eternal, if only we had the heart to embrace it.

It is as absurd as it is mischievous to throw the responsibility of all this upon the clergyman. The most zealous minister can do but little towards building up God's spiritual temple, unless he has fellow-labourers among the laity: the help of parents bringing up their children in the nurture and admonition of the Lord; the help of masters ruling well their own households; the help of employers discountenancing what is corrupt and ungodly in their work-people, and encouraging what is seemly and decent, and sober; the help of all striving together in prayer one for another, and for all saints, that having not been ashamed of Christ here, He may not be ashamed of us when He comes " in the glory of the Father with the holy angels."

Preached — Cholderton, Nineteenth Sunday after Trinity, October 2, 1853.

XX.

THE RIGHTEOUSNESS OF THE LORD.

"O my people, remember now what Balak king of Moab consulted, and what Balaam the son of Beor answered him from Shittim unto Gilgal; that ye may know the righteousness of the Lord. Wherewith shall I come before the Lord, and bow myself before the High God? Shall I come before Him with burnt offerings, with calves of a year old? Will the Lord be pleased with thousands of rams, or with ten thousands of rivers of oil? Shall I give my firstborn for my transgression, the fruit of my body for the sin of my soul? He hath shewed thee, O man, what is good; and what doth the Lord require of thee, but to do justly, and to love mercy, and to walk humbly with thy God?"—MICAH vi. 5-8.

WE must all feel that there is something very solemn and awakening in this scripture. It would be hard to find in the whole Bible, in the compass of so few verses, so distinct a declaration of what the prophet emphatically calls "the righteousness of the Lord." They do not seem to be his own words, or the *immediate* inspiration of the Holy Ghost that he is here uttering, but the traditional substance of a conversation held full seven hundred and fifty years before, between Balak king of Moab and Balaam the Mesopotamian diviner, whom that monarch fetched from the East to curse God's people Israel. I call it a *traditional* conversation, because there is no mention of it where the story of Balaam is found. But it appears to have been preserved in the memory or in other records of the Jews, and is here appealed to by Micah as a circumstance familiar to them all.

No doubt much more passed between Balaam and the king of Moab than Moses has in terms related. He only embodied in his history as much as was consistent with his plan. It is to the prophet Micah, confirming an ancient tradition with the stamp of divine authority, that we are indebted for the preservation of this striking illustration of the doubts and difficulties that beset, and of the light and truth that guided, the steps of the men of old time.

The king of Moab is represented as consulting the eastern seer on a point of personal religion. He would fain know how he could make himself acceptable in the sight of God, and secure an "inheritance among them that are sanctified." Though bred up in the habits of a fond and idolatrous superstition, his conscience seems to mistrust the efficacy of the means he had hitherto employed, and makes him anxious to ascertain, from one in whom he believed the Spirit of God to dwell, whether he had been trusting to a religious system that could profit and deliver or no.

The very tone of the questions seems to imply that there were painful doubts working in the mind of the questioner. He appears inwardly dissatisfied with the methods of propitiating the divine displeasure and attracting the divine blessing which he had used *outwardly*. He seems to feel the truth of what St. Paul states so forcibly—that it was not "possible that the blood of bulls and of goats could ever take away sin"; that there was need of some better sacrifices than these; that there must be something more deep, more personal, more heart-searching than this, or any other kind of formal services, to deserve the name of true religion.

And so with this faint glimmering of truth breaking in upon his mind—discontented with what he was, yet unable of himself to solve the problem of his being—the heathen monarch comes to one whom he regarded as a prophet, and in whose mouth, at least for this once, God did put His word, to have his perplexities removed, and the path in which he should walk made clear. And from that prophet he got an answer which, even now, is pregnant with wisdom and instruction to every one that hath ears to hear. Surely it was not uttered for Balak's sake alone, but for ours too, who perhaps need it to the full as much as he. "He hath shewed thee, O man," so spake the prophet with more than royal dignity, as feeling himself charged with a higher than royal office, "he hath shewed thee, O man, what is good." He hath shewed it thee in thy conscience, in thy heart of hearts, in those secret whispers and disquietudes which even now have prompted thee to question me: in thy nobler nature, in thy aspirations, in the very weariness thou seemest to feel at this endless round of carnal unsatisfying ordinances. "He hath shewed thee what is good; and what doth the Lord require of thee, but to do justly, and to love mercy, and to walk humbly with thy God?" Could there be a more high-toned utterance, a loftier morality, a more evangelical counsel? Pity that he who thus could speak spoke of what he never himself either aimed at or realized! a mere talker and theorizer, who, while he could thus "preach to others," himself became, there is every reason to fear, "a castaway."

And this is the weighty lesson that the words of the text teach us : that it is in the ordinary, everyday business of our lives, not in any amount of periodic customary service—in our weekly rather than our Sunday behaviour—that the range of true religion really lies, and that we may discover whether we do, in any practical saving sense, either *know* or *do* "the righteousness of the Lord." "To do justly, to love mercy, and to walk humbly with our God," are duties that cannot be discharged in our seats at church, but in our homes; in the dealings of our trade; among our customers, our workpeople, our servants; in the control we habitually keep over our tongues and tempers; in the spirit of kindliness and charity which we carry into all the relations of life; in the zeal with which we forward good works; in the care we take to conquer all feelings of pride, and vanity, and envy, and fretfulness.

We must not measure the spiritual progress, either of ourselves or others, by the frequency of our communions, or the number of times of our coming to church, or by liking to read now and then a chapter in our Bibles, or by our being able to talk readily about the love of Christ, or by anything that may be, and I fear often is, merely formal and outward, having no root in the heart, and bearing no fruit in the life. Like the corn that grows in our fields, the seed of grace must be first planted inwardly before it can bear fruit outwardly. We must judge of the good we have got from sacraments and church services by the increased power we feel we have gained to stand our ground against our three great spiritual enemies—the devil, the flesh, and the world.

If there is no progress in us, no growth, no daily recognition of the doctrine of the Cross, no more and more earnest endeavour to reach after the work of our high calling in Christ; if we are satisfied in our formalities, boastful of the regularity of our services, consciously accepting a low standard of life and conversation, we may be sure that all our outward worshippings have but little profited us; we have but been feeding ourselves as it were with the husks which the swine eat. Like the Jews in Jeremiah's day we have "trusted in lying words, saying, The temple of the Lord, The temple of the Lord, The temple of the Lord are these;" as though we could be saved by sitting in church for a couple of hours on a Sunday, or by mechanically repeating prayers which awaken no response in our hearts, or by listening to sermons which, however searchingly they may set forth God's counsel, we have made up our minds beforehand to disregard. I would have you judge of your spiritual state in the sight of God, of your love for Christ, and your hopes of heaven, by something more trustworthy, more substantial than this.

The "assembling of ourselves together" for the congregational purpose of prayer and praise is represented in the Epistle to the Hebrews as a token of Christian men, a part of Christian duty. The receiving of Christ's Body and Blood in the Sacrament of His Last Supper is so essential an element in our religion, so indispensable a means of grace, that our Lord Himself has warned us that those who "do it not have no life in them." But these are the *means* of grace, and must not be confounded with its *fruits*. They are the ways and methods in which God bestows His favours upon us rather than the services in which He expects us in turn to manifest our love to Him. We come to church not so much *rendering to* God as *receiving from* Him. Public prayer and sacraments should be regarded rather as *privileges* than as *duties*; except that all privileges become duties, when we recollect in Whose strength alone they can be done and how far exceeding all claim will be the amount and overflowing richness of their reward.

Further, as these services of an outward worship are offerings that can be made at so slight a cost, often in so carnal a spirit, with so much hypocrisy and formalism, and with so little true devotion and sincerity, we must indeed feel that this must not be the standard by which to ascertain whether we have or not "tasted that the Lord is gracious," or to what extent we are growing up to the "measure of the stature of the fulness of Christ."

No; follow yourselves to your own homes and your daily occupations, and see how you behave yourselves there! See whether you do indeed "do justly, love mercy, and walk humbly with your God." These are large words, but they comprehend an immense range of duties, and are susceptible of the minutest personal application. I do not take it that they are arranged casually, but in a natural and necessary order. Justice—mercy—humility: justice before mercy; and the crown of both, humility; as feeling that after all we have been able to do nothing of ourselves, but that all our grace and "sufficiency is of God."

We cannot suppose that sobriety, and purity, and contentment, and patience, and faith were meant to be disparaged, though they do not happen to be expressly named. Balaam is here giving to Balak rather a *sample* of the spirit in which God was to be served than enumerating all the excellences that go to make up the ideal of a religious man. He who is just will hardly think he may safely be intemperate or impure; he who has learnt the lesson of genuine humility will also be no stranger to the influences of patience and contentment.

See then how you spend your daily lives. See what fruit Christ's Gospel is bringing forth in your own homes. "Examine yourselves, whether ye be in the faith," by marking the company you keep, the language you utter, the indulgences you allow yourselves, the faithfulness with which you discharge your daily employment, the spirit you carry into your dealings with your fellow-men, the principles upon which you govern your own households, the care with which you train your children, the forwardness with which you are ready to engage in every good word and work.

These are signs and tokens which any of us may ascertain; and in which it is next to impossible to be mistaken. No man can think that oaths, or drunkenness, or impurity, or selfishness, or peevish tempers, or envy, or slandering, or falsehood, or dishonesty are things compatible, I will not say with a *high* standard of religion, but with any amount of it that can minister hope or assurance to its professors at all. "The god of this world" must have effectually "blinded the eyes" of that man from whom the true power and influence of the Gospel is thus entirely hid. It is a mere mockery to bow ourselves before the High God with ever so much outward semblance of adoration while we neglect such elementary duties of circumspection and watchfulness.

But, remember, there is no use in feeling convinced of this, as you can hardly help being if you think seriously on the subject, without also *acting* on the feeling. Balaam felt it all. He knew the hollowness of these outward services standing alone. He could pray that the blessed end of the righteous might be his too. But he never strove to live the life of the righteous. While he talked of doing justice he was seeking "the wages of unrighteousness," and his heart was exercised with covetous practices. While he spoke of loving mercy, he had come from his home for the express purpose of cursing a people who had never done him any harm. While he preached to Balak about walking humbly with God, he himself was in open rebellion against his Maker, Whose Spirit he had tempted and Whose warnings he had despised.

Nothing is so easy as to *talk* about these things: the difficulty is to *do* them. Balaam's is perhaps the most melancholy instance of self-deceit that the Bible or the history of the world contains. A man pre-eminently enlightened to discern the truth, but with no heart to love the truth! Better had it been for him "not to have known the way of righteousness" than, after he had known it, to "turn from the holy commandment delivered to him"! Better shall it be for *us* too. Beware of the crying heresy of these latter days— *hearing* but not *doing* the Word. We live in an age of high profession, and there is all the greater need of self-mistrust and watchfulness. We find so many people thinking and speaking well of themselves, of whose ways the Bible does not speak well, that there may be some danger to ourselves too, as to St. Peter at Antioch, of being "carried away with the like dissimulation."

We can have no doubt of the *general spirit* in which God is to be served, and if we once fully and fairly comprehend that, we shall have no difficulty in accommodating it as a rule to our individual case and circumstances. It is far better, because it is far more practical, that we should form our own principles of action than take them up second-hand at the mouth of another. Each case requires special consideration, and perhaps somewhat different treatment. The Gospel is a law of liberty, and so long as we set about the work in an honest and good heart, not trusting to ourselves, but looking for light and guidance from God, we are not likely to miss the road.

I have done little more than offer suggestions, which I wish you to follow up each for yourselves. Remember that it is a weighty matter: one that will not brook delay: one that cannot be attended to on a sick-bed: one that is even now settling itself for eternal good or evil in our souls. The hardening of the heart is a sure, though subtle, process. It is brought about, St. Paul tells us, by the deceitfulness of sin, by its putting on false appearances, and persuading us that we have plenty of time and it will be all right in the end; and that as we are plainly in the company of so many decent, respectable people we cannot be altogether wrong.

I have warned you of this snare of "respectability." Balaam was a most respectable man, and highly thought of in his neighbourhood. The Bible tells us what God thought of him. Whether we think it worth while to mark the fact or not, our feet are silently and daily advancing either heavenwards or hellwards. We cannot stand still in a kind of neutral ground of "decency." It is worth while to ascertain in which direction we are moving. The Bible will give us a thousand tests for doing so. There is the light if you choose to go to it. " He hath shewed thee, O man, what is good: and what doth the Lord require of thee but to do justly, and to love mercy, and to walk humbly with thy God?" Do this first and then thou wilt find that a principle has taken root in thy heart, which will prevent thy leaving anything else undone.

Preached — Cholderton, Twentieth Sunday after Trinity, October 9, 1853.

XXI.

STANDING ON OUR WATCH.

"I will stand upon my watch."—HABAKKUK ii. 1.

THE prophet's language is probably figurative, but it describes the attitude of a man expecting a message from God, and, with no more than a becoming concern, preparing himself to receive it. It was the attitude of Elijah when he was bid "go forth" out of the cave in which he had sought refuge at Horeb, and stand upon the mount before the Lord: or of Moses when, with the two tables of stone in his hand, he stood in the cleft of the rock of Sinai, and saw the glory of the Lord "pass by" before him in a cloud.

Whether any such revelation of the divine presence was vouchsafed or not to the prophet Habakkuk we cannot pretend to say; but we know that he received a supernatural communication, addressed either to his outward ear or to his inner heart, of the approach of which he was previously aware, and which awakened in his breast deep thoughts of anxiety—I had almost said of *fear*. He felt no doubt, as Jacob and Gideon had felt before, that it was an awful thing for one so frail and imperfect as even the best of men to be brought into such close communion with the "High and Holy One Who inhabiteth eternity." He knew not what the meeting portended, or what the issue of it might be, but one thing he *did* know: that he who is summoned to meet his God has indeed too much need to question himself anxiously and seriously; to "search and try the ground of his heart," to sanctify himself and make himself clean: and he was thankful that *any* time of preparation was allowed, and that he was not hurried off as by a whirlwind into the immediate presence of the Great Father, in Whom he professed to believe, though as yet he had never seen Him.

You must, I think, have anticipated the application of all this to ourselves. You must have recalled to your memories the thousand passages in the New Testament where watchfulness, sobriety, circumspection, carefulness, are insisted upon again and again as the normal condition of a Christian; as the very posture and state indicated by the laws of our being; as the merest, commonest, earthliest prudence; as "the *one thing* needful," without which the day of the Lord is sure to come on us unawares.

It is not only clergymen that are bidden to watch. If any of you have been entertaining the notion that a clergyman, by virtue of his office, is bound to be a more watchful, circumspect person than any other Christian man or woman: if you fancy that a less degree of personal holiness will do for his parishioners than for him; you are encouraging a delusion extremely perilous and utterly unscriptural. The law by which we shall

all be judged is the same. You have exactly the same means of attaining personal inwrought graces as I. The one unvarying note of the Scriptures is that we shall one and all "stand before the throne," to receive, according as our works have been, our eternal portion of weal or woe.

The example of Habakkuk, though a prophet, ought to be of universal influence, as it is of universal application. It is not so much our *duty* as our *interest*—though all duties involve our highest, truest interests—to "stand upon our watch," and as it were "set us upon a tower, and watch to see what He will say unto us, and what we shall answer when we are reproved."

And the reason and wisdom of such a posture is obvious. We may see in a thousand instances every day of our lives the verification of our Saviour's words that "He cometh as a thief," unexpectedly, and when men are not looking for Him; and that when people are speaking of "peace, and taking their ease" for many years, in a single night perhaps "their soul is required" of them. I do not mean that what are called "sudden deaths" are common, though even they are frequent enough to act as a warning and indication of the general law that I have stated. But I call a notice of a few weeks' or even a few months' illness a very sudden one when the whole previous life has been spent in carelessness; when we have left everything to do to these last fleeting restless hours; when the whole work of repentance and conversion has to be not completed only, but begun from the very beginning; when we have all along been quieting our consciences with the thought that we had plenty of time before us; when the time which promised to be so suitable for our preparation for eternity is now arrived, and we find, not only that it is reduced to a few weeks or days, but that it is of all others the most unfitted for the work we had designed to accomplish in it. Habits are not formed in a moment; still less can they be formed in an hour of weakness and failing powers, when they need all a strong man's force and energy for their development. *Every death is sudden which is not the crown of a well-spent life.* Every man goes to his grave unprepared who has not realised and acted on the Apostle's warning of "walking circumspectly, redeeming the time, because the days are evil."

If we did habitually place ourselves in this post and attitude of watchfulness we should often discern the tokens of our Lord's nearness to us, and catch the notes of His voice in utterances as distinct as ever were those which filled the heart of the rapt Jewish prophet with fear and awe. The religiously trained mind looks upon every circumstance of life as a divine encouragement or a divine warning. To such a man there is no such thing—and there ought to be no such word—as "chance," or "luck," or "accident." Everything is foreordained and forewoven into the eternal chain of things by a mightier hand than Fortune's, by a greater power than Nature's; by the unchangeable counsel and over-ruling Providence of an Almighty God.

And so not only the inner whispers of conscience, such as spoke to Elijah, but the outward utterances of nature—the earthquake, the whirlwind, the fire, the famine, the pestilence, nay, the very counsels and handiwork of men, " wars and rumours of wars, nation rising against nation, and troubles in divers places"—we are bidden to regard not as so many casual accidents, but as exhibitions of one eternal, irresistible law, the law of divine righteousness; taking indeed one and leaving another, but in so many cases making it plain, even to the most unobservant eye, *why* one is taken and the other left, that we cannot doubt that one principle lies at the root of all the dispensations ; and that they are all the calls, the plain, outspoken witness, of a Righteous and Merciful God, seeking to win men's hearts to Him either by motives of love or fear.

I am aware that this is not the way in which they are usually regarded, simply because men in general are too blinded by recklessness, too deeply possessed with the evil heart of unbelief, to mark the circumstances that befall them every day of their lives, and to try to read them in the light shed upon them by the revealed records of God's dealings with His creatures. It requires a high degree of faith, a heart kept continually loving and tender, to recognise a " call" from God, as Abraham did, or to believe that He does indeed govern and give laws to this lower world. Yet we should be utterly misreading the Scriptures if we thought that all we read there about God's dealings with Abraham, or Jacob, or Moses, or the Israelites, or Saul or David, was exceptional; was not to be taken literally; was not exactly the same course of discipline that He is taking with us now.

We are told again and again that all these persons who are brought before us in the pages of the Bible were " men of like passions with ourselves," and they were enlightened, assisted, guided, rewarded, punished, taught, exactly in the same way as we are. The miraculous features that occasionally appear in the story in no wise affect its fundamental lesson.

Take the life of Jacob for instance. The dream at Bethel, or the wrestling with the angel at Peniel, are but as it were collateral and secondary points in it. In all essential particulars it might be retold of any one of us. His supplanting his brother in his birthright; his emigration to a foreign country; the riches and substance he amassed there; his return home; his reconciliation with his brother; his re-settlement in the scenes of his youth; his domestic troubles; his foolish partiality for Joseph, so strikingly reproved; his disquietude, so evidently the consequence of early errors; the recovery of his long-lost son; the peaceful death-bed after so stormy a life; his wayward and selfish heart at length disciplined into a humble and trustful submission to the Divine Will—if we can read all this and still think there is no practical lesson in it for ourselves, still say " Oh, God *did* speak to men face to face then, but He has ceased to do so now;" still refuse to recognize His hand in our sickness, in our escapes from danger, our prosperity, our trials, our misfortunes, in a word, "the circumstances" of our daily lives; why, then, when the Scriptures are read, there must be a veil upon our hearts; God's warnings are thrown away upon us; and whatever we may boast of our faith, it really is not of so high an order as that of the very devils, who, the Apostle tells us, *do* believe *and tremble.*

We do indeed drown God's voice by our careless unbelieving ways. We refuse to own Him even when He seems, as at Belshazzar's feast, to awaken us from our slumber of security by writing upon our walls the solemn sentence of our doom, as in characters of living fire. God's neglected laws always avenge themselves. "The sword, the famine, the noisome beast, and the pestilence, pass through a land" now, as truly the instruments of Divine wrath as ever they were in the days of Jeremiah or Ezekiel.

In the manifold diversity of circumstances that happen to ourselves in our individual experience of Providence, if our minds were habitually trained to the task, we should hardly find a single fact of our being, a single incident of our lives that was not distinctly traceable to some cause at once within and without ourselves—some law of God making itself felt and visible in consequence of some *behaviour of ours*. They are all needed either as warnings or chastisements. They are to us as yet— for our lives are still spared—tokens of mercy, and pledges of love. All the circumstances of life are "calls." They are motives to obedience and repentance, and perseverance, and watchfulness. That alone is worthy of the name of "true religion" which so regards them. To be able to trace the finger of God, like the magicians of Egypt, only in what are called miraculous visitations, is indeed blindness and ignorance. To look for His manifestations of Himself only in the earthquake or the whirlwind, is to pass more than half our lives without any living faith or apprehension of Him at all. He made Himself known to Elijah in a still, small voice:

the same that we may hear any day if only, like David, we will "commune with our own hearts, in our chambers, and be still."

Though we live a hundred years, it is a thousand chances to one if ever He speak to us in any other way. He will not show "signs in heaven" to pleasure those who will not mark the signs beneath their feet. He will not shake the strong foundations of the earth to make us feel that "the fashion of the world passeth away." There is no need of miracles where the ordinary facts of life throw sufficient light on the path of faith. "They that hear not Moses and the prophets would not be persuaded even though one rose from the dead."

Do not, then, go through this life—which is the school and discipline for life eternal—in the same thoughtless, unreflecting spirit as nine-tenths of the world around you. Every day you live *ought* to teach you—*will* teach you, if you have only hearts to learn—something new, something hitherto unnoticed, of God and of yourselves. "No man liveth to himself," saith the Scripture, "and no man dieth to himself: but whether we live or die we are the Lord's." Blessed is he who can indeed realize and make his own this most comfortable assurance. Tracing God's ways in what others call "the chances and accidents" of life, he finds to his great support that "all things work together for good to them that love God, and are called according to His purpose." ",Sanctifying the Lord God in his heart, he is ready always to give an answer to every man that asketh him a reason of the hope that is in him with meekness and fear." "Having no fellowship with the unfruitful works of darkness," he is not afraid of their condemnation, nor easily troubled. Committing the keeping of his soul to God in well-doing as unto a faithful Creator, he is persuaded that " neither death, nor life, nor angels, nor principalities, nor things present, nor things to come, nor height, nor depth, nor any other creature, shall be able to separate him from the love of God, which is in Christ Jesus our Lord."

Preached—Cholderton, Twenty-first Sunday after Trinity, October 16, 1853.

XXII.

THE NEED OF CIRCUMSPECTION.

"He that keepeth his way preserveth his soul."—PROV. xvi. 17.

I SUPPOSE that none of us can either hear or read those solemn words of our Blessed Lord, "Strait is the gate, and narrow is the way, and *few* there be that find it," without experiencing some qualms of conscience, some personal apprehension, some fears about his own soul. We can hardly help stopping and asking ourselves the question, in which of these two companies, on which of these two ways *we* are travelling. For the moment perhaps, till some other thought takes its place, we are made a little uncomfortable by the answer.

There are other scriptures hardly less searching, equally productive of disquieting impressions on the mind. When we read of "denying ourselves," " hating our father and mother and brothers and sisters, yea, and our own life also"—the very things on which we are naturally inclined to set most store—of "taking up our Cross daily" (not now and then, but *daily*), and following Christ," and that unless we do so in some true and real sense we cannot be His disciples, a similar train of apprehensive disturbing thoughts must be awakened in most minds. Those who have a real faith in the Bible as the Word of God, and who make it a rule of life at all, cannot fail to see that it must be taken as a whole, and its *warnings* received as implicitly as its promises.

The same kind of thoughts—though it is a less profitable train of reflection to pursue—naturally arise in the mind when friends, or neighbours, or relatives are taken away from us. We are led to indulge in speculations whether they are at rest or in torment; with Lazarus in Abraham's bosom, or with the rich man " where the worm dieth not and the fire is not quenched." In more careless moods we are far too ready to speak of all the departed in whom we have known ever so small a trait of goodness, as " fallen asleep in Christ," as though we had hope in their end ; as though there could be no doubt that they were removed to a higher and happier sphere. But this is merely the language of charitable hope, more often perhaps of random thoughtlessness, of a low and unworthy estimate of what God and Heaven are, and of what sort of men and women those must be " which are written in the Lamb's Book of Life," and may claim admission into that city into which " in no wise entereth anything that defileth, neither whatsoever worketh abomination, nor whosoever loveth and maketh a lie."

If we ever think seriously upon such subjects, if we take the actual word of God, and not popular notions about it, for our guide, we can hardly help feeling that the lives of those about us, those whom we have known best and seen most of, have not been so spiritual and heavenly-minded, so far risen above the world, "so hidden with Christ in God," so marked by evangelical tempers, so fruitful in good works, so consistent in all their parts, as to justify us in speaking confidently about them after death, as though they were undoubtedly reckoned among the children of God and their lot among the saints. I do not say it is wise, or profitable, or becoming, to sit, as it were, in judgment upon the dead in this way. It is neither the one nor the other. It is a matter about which we had better not speculate at all, for we cannot have data to enable us to speculate to any purpose. We cannot know *half* the spiritual history of the person whose portion we are attempting to determine. I am only speaking of what is the fact, of what we actually do, of the correction which such texts as I have quoted cannot otherwise than make in the off-hand assumption that we are so ready to form about the state of the friends and acquaintances who have exchanged the present for the unseen world. The whole question, whether as regards others or ourselves, at last resolves itself into this: are the lives of average men such that we have any just and Scriptural grounds for believing that they are acceptable to God; such as He would have them to be; adequate samples of obedience to the divine law; sufficient to satisfy "the righteousness of the Lord"? And then the next question is a personal one: are *we* individually living *above* or below this average? are we better or worse than others? do we stand upright where they fall? do we act from higher motives, with more direct reference

THE NEED OF CIRCUMSPECTION.

in all we do to God? is the "love of Christ more shed abroad in our hearts"? can we point to more "fruits of the Spirit"? And, if we think we can, are we sure after all that we are measuring ourselves truly? May we not be deceiving ourselves, like the Pharisee in the parable, who "thanked God that he was not as other men were," but went down to his house with but little of the assurance of justification in his soul?

I fear that most of us would have but two answers to give to all these questions. (1) We *are not* better than other men—not so abandoned perhaps, and reckless, as a neighbour here and there, but still not better than the hundreds of decent people about us; and (2) these decent people, as well as ourselves, we can plainly see, in a thousand ways fall below the standard of God's requirements; do not even seem to be trying to live up to them; are going on in a sort of self-satisfied blindness, with little thought, save worldly thought, for the present, and no fear for the future. But this, after all, cannot make either them or ourselves *safe*; cannot lower the standard of Christian holiness; cannot empty religion of its power, or death of its terrors; cannot alter the eternal sentence that has gone forth, that *unprofitableness* in God's service will as certainly exclude from heaven as the most open defiance of the divine law, and that they who have never truly "confessed Christ" in the face of their generation will never be owned as His in the day when "He shall be revealed from heaven taking vengeance" on them that have not known God nor obeyed the Gospel.

We must see that the average standard of religion

which is recognised and adopted around us is but a stunted and most inadequate one. When we have put it side by side with our Blessed Lord's Sermon on the Mount, or with the three last chapters of St. Paul's Epistle to the Ephesians, we discern at once its utter disproportion, its wretched mimicry, of the " measure of the stature of the fulness of Christ." Where is the " saintliness," where the " purity," where the " temperance," where the " meekness," where the sacrifice of self, where " the counting all things but loss that we may win Christ," where " the pressing toward the mark," where " the perseverance," where " the spiritual discernment," that are the marks on the forehead of him " who has set to his seal that God is true," and, believing that all visible things shall be dissolved, is only careful to approve himself to Him that seeth in secret, and judgeth not as man judgeth?

These are the very tokens and characters by which the Bible teaches us to recognise a disciple of the Cross; but we shall look in vain for them generally in the world. Here and there we may be permitted to see a blessed instance of the Spirit's power, but upon the mass of hearts He seems to exercise no influence. They are living pretty much probably as they would have lived if Christ had never come down from heaven to reveal His Father's will, and to point their hopes and desires to " a house not made with hands, eternal in the heavens," and to bid them " seek *first* the kingdom of God and His righteousness," instead of being wholly absorbed and engrossed by temporal things.

I cannot impress it upon you too earnestly that *this*

average religion of the world is a dangerous thing to trust to, a fatal measure to set up for our own. A religion that does not suppress anger, and pride, and impatience, and selfishness, and the spirit of money-making, and rebellious appetites, and inordinate affection—which does not, to use St. Paul's word, check *concupiscence*—is a heartless religion, a dead faith, a thing that will "neither profit nor deliver"; an idol which we may dress out with ever so decent an exterior, before which we may prostrate ourselves with ever so much dissembled fervour, but which can really kindle in the heart no generous feeling, is lifeless and unmeaning, no strength in the time of trial, no comfort in the hour of trouble.

We have most of us, here in England, got into a way of fancying that a certain amount of outward decency is godliness; a certain compliance with prescribed external forms, religion. We have dethroned her from her lawful and only true seat—our own hearts—and set her up instead in the pulpit, or the material fabric of a church; and think that by coming there once a week to offer her, in many cases, a poor, cold, lifeless worship, we have satisfied her claims and cannot be expected to do more. Now I will ask this simple question : do you really think you can be religious in such a way as to offer an acceptable service to Almighty God without daily, hourly, watchfulness? without battling against what experience shows you to be corrupt in your own hearts and practices? without keeping out of the reach of temptation? without removing yourselves from the seat of the scornful? without the consciousness of a struggle with yourselves? Does it come to you as a matter of course "to think and do always" that which is right? "to refrain your feet from evil and your lips that they speak no guile"? "to be kind, and gentle, easy to be entreated and pitiful"? to deny yourselves things for which you have an inclination, but which your conscience secretly tells you you had better be without? to "confess" Christ? to be "patient" in time of affliction? to be cheerful and contented, and thankful for the blessings you enjoy?

Oh! you will say, all this is the work of grace. It is, as St. Paul has it, "the gift of God." True; but will grace come without seeking? will it abide without cherishing? Does the Bible teach us that we may fold our hands, or follow our own ways safely, for God's grace will do everything for us, and we need be careful for nothing ourselves? No man insists so strongly on the doctrine of the freedom and fulness of Divine grace as St. Paul: but no one at the same time impresses so earnestly the necessity of prayer and sacraments and circumspection. What he calls "the whole armour of God" has to be put on, piece by piece, by ourselves. Gospel grace is no mere charm, to work, as by a miracle, the healing of our souls.

The text carries us back to the right principle—that which must underlie all religion, and is the secret of all progress, "He that would preserve his soul must *keep his way*." The reason why we must do so is because there are pitfalls on every side of us; because it is a narrow way and one not easy to recover if once we stray from it; because there are enemies lying in wait for us at every turn; because with most of us the day is far spent and the night is at hand. A heedless life is sure practically to be an ungodly one. A single day spent without watchfulness is certain to have been spent without improvement. One of the best of the Roman emperors—a mere heathen too, but wiser than many a professing Christian—is said to have counted every day as lost in which he had not performed some good action. This man must have been in a constant watchfulness; nay, and in a constant progress!

If we only examine ourselves with punctuality every night we should find, I think, that every day, even if spent in a way that ought fairly to be called *well*, might still have been spent *better*. If we are walking before God in any sincerity, with anything better than lip-service, we shall be dissatisfied with ourselves till we have made a more vigorous and sustained effort to attain a standard which by our own confession is within our reach, and which we feel that we might have *already* attained if we had taken a little more pains. The notion of standing still in religion, of "being good enough," is a simple absurdity, and carries with it its own refutation. The man who can think in this way has not yet the smallest conception of what true religion is. He can attach simply no meaning at all to half the New Testament.

Does St. Paul ever give a hint to the Thessalonians of a time when they may relax their exertions, and remit their watchfulness, and bid their souls take their ease, when he exhorts them "as they had received of him how to walk and to please God, so they would abound *more and more*"? Does St. Peter seem to lay a light burden upon Christians when, having congratulated them on being made "partakers of the divine nature," by virtue of their baptismal incorporation into Christ, he exhorts them "to give all diligence that they may add to their faith, virtue; and to virtue, knowledge; and to knowledge, temperance; and to temperance, patience; and to patience, godliness; and to godliness, brotherly kindness; and to brotherly kindness, charity;" adding that "if these things be in us and *abound*," but not else, "they make us to be neither *barren nor unfruitful*—in the knowledge of our Lord Jesus Christ."

In the old Grecian mythology there is a story of their great hero—Hercules—having to encounter a hundred-headed dragon, and that as soon as he had cut off one of its heads with his sword another immediately sprang up in its place, nor could the weary combatant achieve a victory till he had destroyed the reproductive energy of the monster by searing the headless neck with fire. In this legend these Grecian poets meant to teach their hearers—though of course in a far more imperfect way—the same lesson that the inspired writers of both Testaments teach us—the multiplying aggressive force of sin; the prolonged character of the contest with it; the need, not only of watchfulness, but of forethought, and courage, and unweariedness too. St. Paul expresses the same truth in two of his short, pregnant sentences: "and be ye not weary in well-doing; for God shall bruise Satan under your feet shortly."

If we wish to rid our fields of a noxious weed, we burn it. If we would prevent a deadly poison from spreading through our blood, we burn it. The last remedy tried to stop an effusion of blood in some cases is to sear the place with a hot iron. They are violent, unsparing remedies, but they are necessary. They are not things a person would do for pleasure, but we submit to them cheerfully to save life. So, too, in the eradication of sin: so, too, to prevent Satan's deadly influence from infusing itself through our whole moral system, we must be content to use, if need be, no gentle, half-and-half remedies. Our Lord tells us of His true followers, "Every one shall be salted *with fire.*" St. Paul further adds, even of those who are saved, that it shall be "*yet so as by fire.*"

While we dally with sin, and shrink from ascertaining the real state of our spiritual diseases; and mistake for symptoms of health what are only the signs of that unnatural stillness which often foreruns death; while we talk of its being time to alter our ways by and by, or perhaps flatter ourselves that there is nothing needs altering; while we all have a thousand things within us and about us that ought to call for all our circumspection and vigilance, we are but practising on ourselves a horrible self-delusion, and "healing the stroke of our wounds lightly," and seeing visions of health and peace when destruction and death are all but at our doors.

Are these the warnings of the Gospel, or am I only seeking to frighten you? Does not Christ frighten you —gentle and tender-spoken as His words generally are— when He concludes His denunciations of the whole spirit of Pharisaism and Sadduceeism with the appalling utterance, "Ye serpents, ye generation of vipers, how can ye escape the damnation of hell?"

"Oh, but," you will say, "we are not Pharisees or Sadducees." Do not be too sure of that. The essence of Pharisaism was formalism and self-righteousness: of Sadducceism, practical unbelief and worldliness. And are worldliness, and formalism, and infidelity, and self-righteousness extinct, dead forms of sin—things that have ceased to be, and about which we need not concern ourselves? Be sure when our Lord spoke thus to the Pharisees and Sadducees of Jerusalem He meant His words to reach the ears of Pharisees and Sadducees in England. He meant to warn men everywhere who "for a pretence make long prayers"; or "who do alms to be seen of men"; or who explain away the essential distinctions of right and wrong; or who are occupied with petty ceremonies while they neglect the weightier matters of the law; or who are careful to clean only the outside of the cup and platter; or who talk of themselves as better or wiser than their fathers; or who justify themselves before men; or who seek comfort and ease before everything; or who empty the doctrines of the Gospel of all their power; or who lead self-indulgent, unbelieving lives.

These are the men, whether in the first or nineteenth century, whether in Jerusalem or here, whether Jews or Christians, whom our Lord reminded of there being such a thing to overtake them as "the damnation of hell." They live in contempt, or unbelief, or indifference to it now; but the Day will reveal it. They take no pains to "keep their way"; and they will find too late that they have destroyed their souls. They are confident in their numbers: but they shall at length discover that "though hand join in hand, they shall not be unpunished."

It will be our better wisdom to lay such warnings seriously to heart; to believe that we cannot serve God acceptably without walking circumspectly: cannot escape the evil of the days without redeeming the time: cannot preserve our souls without keeping our way. A wholesome fear is much wiser than a presumptuous confidence.. We have no right to use the language of assurance unless our consciences tell us that we are leading lives of holiness. " *Without holiness* no man shall see the Lord." Into His presence there shall in no wise enter anything that is unclean. Our work in this life is "to purify ourselves even as He is pure": "to look for Him in righteousness": "to set Him always before our face": "to cleanse ourselves from all filthiness of the flesh and spirit": "to have nothing to do with the unfruitful works of darkness": "to be fully persuaded in our own minds," and so secured from the waverings and unsettlements of these latter times; that so keeping our ways we may preserve our souls, and "when He shall appear may have confidence, and not be ashamed before Him at His coming."

Preached—Cholderton, Twenty-fifth Sunday after Trinity, November 13, 1853.

XXIII.

THE WARNING OF DINAH.

"And Dinah, the daughter of Leah, which she bare unto Jacob, went out to see the daughters of the land."—GEN. xxxiv. 1.

THERE are two eminent individuals among the historical personages of the Old Testament who exhibit several striking correspondences in the circumstances of their lives—whose career is a kind of living commentary on God's method of morally governing the world—yet whose characters and example are often strangely misunderstood and misapplied—I mean King David and the patriarch Jacob.

They were both men of singular gifts and many privileges: both inheritors of a promise not simply personal to themselves but descending to their seed: both disciplined by a very similar course of hardships and trials: both finding much of their anxiety and unhappiness in their own families: and—which is the most important point of all to remember—both tracing all the sorrow and trouble of their after years to their own earlier grievous—and with men of less thoughtful mind it would have been *scarce-remembered*—sin.

THE WARNING OF DINAH. 221

There are no two characters in the Scripture that more require and will more fully reward careful study than Jacob's and David's. As we read their doings and their sufferings, their temptations and their troubles, they seem to be men of such exceeding like passions with ourselves, to be placed in almost precisely the same kinds of circumstances that make up *our* experience, that the record of their lives can hardly fail to be most instructive for the better ordering and government of our own. I wish to draw your attention to the *general* lesson they combine to teach us, and to warn you against the *perversion* of their examples, which has so often proved a snare to loose thinkers and hasty readers.

The great mistake that people commonly make in reading these histories of God's ancient servants is to suppose that because Jacob and David, for example, were heirs of very blessed promises, and are spoken of in the Scriptures as persons who, *on the whole*, we have reason to believe, in spite of many infirmities were accepted of God, therefore *every* action of theirs was right and laudable : that we have no right to sit in judgment on them as on common men : that they are exceptional cases not to be measured by the ordinary standards of truth, and justice, and morality.

I cannot conceive any notion more destructive of the first principles of truth and righteousness. If we are to excuse actions in Jacob or David that we should condemn, and most justly condemn, in another individual, I know not what idea we are to form of God as a Moral Governor of the world, or as a righteous Judge of men. So far from the Bible excusing their sins, hiding them, making apologies for them, or leading us to think that they were lightly regarded by God, it does exactly the reverse. It lays them bare in every detail; it follows them out into every consequence; it makes us so feel their enormity by the terrible severity of their chastisement, that even the simplest mind, when free from the trammels of an erroneous theology, can scarcely miss the true interpretation of the history.

If I were asked for an actual illustration of the truth of Moses' homely maxim, " Be sure your sin will find you out," I could not point to a more significant example than these stories of Jacob and David. This is indeed, as it seems to me, *the* lesson we are to draw from them : that God cannot pass over sin, even in His most favoured servants ; that watchfulness and self-control are as necessary for the greatest saint as for the meanest ; that temptation is the common lot of all ; and that when a man feels himself most secure of God's promises, and consequently is least inclined himself to practise circumspection in his ways, then Satan is nearest his elbow—then he is most in danger of a fall.

A selfish desire of self-aggrandisement, coupled with an inadequate sense of the obligations of common truth and honesty, led Jacob, as it were, to forestall the Divine purposes towards him, and to grasp prerogatives (that were already assured to him by promise) by the unworthy artifices of deception and a lie. This was the source of all his subsequent troubles and unhappiness.

Jeroboam's is another exactly parallel case ; while in *this* point David, by the patient forbearance with which in his earlier years he endured Saul's relentless hatred, and waited till God Himself made good His word by putting the crown upon his head, presents a remarkable contrast. In the case before us both Jacob and Rebekah —who perhaps was more to blame in the matter than her son, as she certainly put the notion into his head— as cunning people generally do, overreached themselves. They got the blessing: but it proved, as Jacob apprehended it would, in its immediate consequences, a curse indeed. The mark of the Divine displeasure was set from the very first upon the transaction. The *issue* might accord with His Predestination; the *method* contradicted His Righteousness. He whose chiefest attribute is Truth is not One likely to look indulgently on a lie.

And so Jacob, the heir of his father's blessing, is driven as an outcast from that father's home. He has to seek refuge among kinsmen indeed, but who to him behaved less considerately than strangers—"a little more than kin, a little less than kind." At the end of twenty years' bondage to Laban—and it was a *hard* bondage—the reason he gives to his wives for wishing to return to his own land is this: "I see," he says, "your father's countenance that it is not turned towards me as before; and your father hath *deceived me*, and changed my wages ten times, yet ye know how that I have served your father with all my power." It was the deceiver's turn to be himself deceived. He who had behaved so ungenerously to his brother Esau was now treated after the like fashion by his father-in-law Laban. If we cannot trace a Just God's handiwork in this, where can we read His tokens?

I spoke at the outset of *domestic* unhappiness. This was poor Jacob's *great* trial. His marriage was a source of discomfort and jealousy from the first. He was, as he tells us, " beguiled " here again, and his numerous family of children proved oftener the disturbers than the comforters of his declining years. Reuben, Judah, Simeon, Levi, Joseph, Benjamin, all, at different times and in different ways, contributed to sadden their father's heart, and made his latter days scarcely more free from trouble than his earlier had been.

Plainly there were faults in Jacob's management of his children. The partiality he showed to Joseph, and the want of proper watchfulness over his daughter Dinah, are sufficient instances. I believe it may be laid down as a universal rule that parents may take to themselves the blame of the disobedience and irregularities of their daughters and their sons. Where children are trained, as they ought to be from their earliest years, in the principles of dutifulness and the fear of God; where vicious tendencies are corrected betimes, and they have in their father and mother the pattern of a Christian conversation continually before their eyes, there you find well-ordered households, and happy, cheerful homes; there you hear no complaints of stubbornness, or rebellion, or unmanageableness, because all the members are knit together in one fellowship by the constraining influence of religious motive. Precious experience has proved that the Fifth Commandment holds as good under the Gospel as it ever did under the Law, and that parents who watch over their children and children who obey their parents—the duties being reciprocal—

realize the promise not only that their days are lengthened but their comforts multiplied in the land.

Narratives such as that from which my text is taken are not pleasant to read. Some people think that the Bible would be a much more edifying book without them. Yet I am sure they were written "for our learning." I am sure we could not afford to dispense with the warning for the sake of avoiding the disclosure. With Dinah and Shechem's sin rife on every side of us—one of the most crying provocations of our land—we should be even less able to cope with it than we are if the Holy Ghost had left us without Dinah and Shechem's warning.

St. Paul speaks of the danger of that bad habit into which he says young women are apt to fall, of "being idle, wandering from house to house." Now this was a kind of watchfulness that neither Jacob nor Leah appear to have exercised over their daughter Dinah. She was allowed, it seems, to choose her own company; to keep her own hours; to walk where she pleased, with little questioning and with no control.

She had evidently a good deal of curiosity, a love of gossiping, probably not a little vanity. Her father and her family had just pitched their tents in the outskirts of a new town, and she must needs "go out to see the daughters of the land." I need not dwell on what followed. They are but the oft-repeated circumstances of many a giddy young woman's fall. Parental neglect, love of smart dress and worthless companions, an outward appearance and demeanour such as Isaiah reproved in the daughters of Zion in his day, "walking with

15

stretched forth necks and wanton eyes, walking and mincing as they go"—such are the beginning and forewarning signs; and the end is wretchedness, and sin, and shame.

When I see a number of young people of both sexes gathered together, some of whom are rude and ill-behaved, with no "aged women" near them—as St. Paul advises—no parent either, to teach them to be " sober, discreet, chaste, keepers at home," I cannot help fearing lest in a moment of strong temptation the destroyer of souls may be plotting ruin for some of them as he did by the hand of Shechem for Jacob's unhappy daughter. I warn such parents as think lightly of the need of keeping a watchful eye on their children of such an age —who are too indolent or too careless to keep them from the contamination of evil company, and to train them to modest thoughts and ways—that on your heads will return much, as of the responsibility, so of the unhappiness of their undoing. If they fall, remember, it will be mainly owing to your having neglected the duty that God imposed upon you, of holding them up. The obligation as plainly rests upon you to train their souls as to feed and clothe their bodies. You must teach them—by example still more than by precept— to walk in the ways of "temperance, soberness, and chastity." You must not think that any clergyman or school-teacher, however earnest, can do this in your place. In the order of God's Providence it is the parents' work, and at the parents' hands it will be required.

Let the story of Dinah and of Shechem operate as a

warning not only to fathers and mothers but to young men and young women too. Let it teach them to take heed of their ways betimes ; to avoid the first approaches of temptation—the very "*appearance of evil.*" " Idle, tattling," habits ; love of gay or noisy company ; fondness for seeing and being seen ; a preference for scenes and places of general resort to the quieter but more genuine enjoyments of home—are, we see by this example, the infirmities of a vain and silly mind which Satan makes his easiest prey. Every young woman has, up to a certain point, her honour in her own keeping ; but not if she deliberately or weakly puts herself in the way of temptation. In almost all sins we are led on step by step to their brink, and then some unseen hand pushes us down headlong.

And more perhaps than any other, *this* is one of which at least the temporal consequences can never be repaired. We know that the tears of true repentance can wash out any depth of guilt in the blood of the Lamb ; we know that publicans and harlots shall enter into the Kingdom of Heaven before many a self-righteous Pharisee ; we know that it was for such as these more than " for just persons who need no repentance " that Christ " poured out his soul unto death ": but still the world, singularly lenient as it is in its construction on many sins, is invariably harsh and unforgiving in its judgment on this one. The deed may have been done years ago, but the stain of it still remains. Even the marriage bond cannot blot it out. It is still remembered in too faithful memories and noised abroad by unkind tongues.

We see what Simeon and Levi, who plainly looked at

the matter only in a worldly point of view—flushing for the shame more than sorrowing for the sin—thought of their sister's dishonour. Shechem's offer to atone for his infamy by an honourable marriage was accepted with a treacherous acquiescence, and only for the purpose of facilitating their revenge. I do not mean to say that they looked at the matter in the right light, or acted in it in the right way. Quite the reverse. Years after this bloody deed of theirs was remembered; and the two brothers scarcely escaped their dying father's curse for their fierce and cruel anger. But their conduct shows us how the world, though indifferent to *sin*, cherishes *honour*. It shows us the stigma that a character for immodesty is considered to bring upon a decent family and a creditable name. It shows us how in the rudest natures God has providentially implanted an instinctive abomination of this most corrupting sin.

Let *us*, as many of us as care to be followers of Christ, take our stand upon higher ground. Let us remember that it is only the " pure in heart " who shall see God. Let us remember that " the fearful and unbelieving, and the abominable, and murderers, and whoremongers, and all liars shall have their part in the lake which burneth with fire and brimstone, which is the second death." Let us see who they were who are said " to follow the Lamb whithersoever He goeth, and to be without fault before the throne, being the firstfruits unto God and to the Lamb" (Revelation xiv. 4). Be assured that the spirit of uncleanness and the spirit of grace cannot cohabit in the same soul. The Holy Ghost will not dwell in a defiled temple. " Wherefore come out from among them, and be ye separate, saith the Lord, and touch not the unclean thing; and I will receive you, and will be a Father unto you, and ye shall be my sons and daughters, saith the Lord Almighty."

Preached—Cholderton, Second Sunday in Lent, March 12, 1854.

XXIV.

CLEANSING THE TEMPLE.

"And He went into the temple, and began to cast out them that sold therein, and them that bought; saying unto them, It is written, My house is the house of prayer; but ye have made it a den of thieves."—ST. LUKE xix. 45, 46.

WE should hardly expect to find our Lord exerting His authority *twice* in the course of little more than three years to put down a practice which, one would have thought, could hardly ever have become a *practice*; or at least which all right-minded persons must have been the first to disapprove of and condemn. Yet so it is. At His *first* visit to Jerusalem, three passovers before this, He had done exactly the same thing. "The Jews' passover was at hand, and Jesus went up to Jerusalem, and found in the temple those that sold oxen and sheep and doves, and the changers of money sitting: and when he had made a scourge of small cords, he drove them all out of the temple, and the sheep, and the oxen; and poured out the changers' money, and overthrew the tables; and said unto them that sold doves, Take these things hence; make not my Father's house an house of merchandise. And his disciples remembered that it was written, The zeal of thine house hath eaten me up."

And now three years afterwards, we have a repetition of the same scene. There were again gathered together at the same solemn festival, within the precincts of the same holy house, the same money-making company, glossing over indeed their profaneness with soft titles and specious excuses, but as intent upon gain and merchandise as though they had been sitting in their shop or market instead of in the house that was to be called of all nations God's " House of Prayer."

What too must we think of those who had the care and oversight of this magnificent temple, those chief priests and elders who always professed to be so jealous for God's honour, yet could suffer such practices to grow up under their eyes unreproved ? Nay, what must we think of the state of religious feeling and piety in the whole nation when such scenes, as far as we know, created no surprise ; and indeed, as St. John tells us, some of the spectators even took Our Lord to task for what I suppose they considered *a stretch of authority*, or at any rate regarded as unnecessary scrupulousness.

The profane practice seems to have grown up in this way. By an express article of his law, every Jew was bound to present himself three times a year at the great national festivals at Jerusalem. Each would have some sacrifice or some offering to present in the temple. They were bidden not "to appear before the Lord empty." Since the Babylonish captivity many Jews had become naturalised in foreign countries—in Greece, in Cyrene, in Alexandria, and so forth.

The more pious of these however still thought it part of their religious duty to claim their share in the covenant made with Abraham, by appearing at these national feasts. You will remember the "Jews, devout men, out of every nation under heaven," who were sojourning at Jerusalem (having come thither to keep the Feast of Pentecost) when the Holy Ghost was poured on the Apostles, and "who heard them speak every man in their own tongue wherein they were born." These foreign Jews would bring Grecian or Roman money with them and would want it changed. So far from their homes, they would not be provided with oxen, or lambs, or pigeons, or anything else they required for sacrifice. They must buy them on the spot. There must be tradesmen then to supply them with these necessaries. I dare say, at first, they were content to go into the market or the shops in the street for what they wanted, but in course of time some men of business—those wise children of the world—suggested that it would be much more convenient to remove their stalls and tables closer to the temple. Everything then would be at hand, it would save a great deal of trouble. And so, by degrees, this traffic was carried on in the very House of God—just as one has heard of revels and fairs occurring in churchyards in this country—and it would seem with so small a shock of the religious feelings or prejudices of the people that it created no little surprise, perhaps even some dissatisfaction, when our Blessed Lord—the Lord Himself of that temple—put it down in His summary and authoritative way.

There are two or three things of considerable importance that we may learn from this story. I shall try and set them before you in as plain and practical a point of view as possible.

1. See what I may call the *encroaching* spirit of worldliness: how it spreads itself over and infects times and places and persons which one would have expected to find freest from its influence; and at length cannot be shut out even from the sanctuary of God. There can be no doubt that the more a man lives for the world, the more his thoughts will be occupied and his character moulded by the world. It will at length become quite the uppermost subject in his mind. Other things may interest him transiently, but this is the one paramount, absorbing, all-controlling concern of his soul. God is practically dethroned, and a golden or painted idol set up and worshipped in His room. Whatever the original motive that had turned the temple at Jerusalem into something more like a market or exchange, there cannot be a doubt that those who used it as such entirely forgot its higher, holier purposes; never thought of the Divine Presence vouchsafed to those who worshipped there, cared in fact for nothing but pushing their trade and counting up their gains. By whatever name they might choose to sanctify their traffic, they carried it on with no more reverence than commonly accompanies business transactions: and that we know is not much.

Do not let us flatter ourselves that nothing of the sort is done now. Is there no Sunday-trading, Sunday-farming, Sunday-travelling, Sunday-excursioning? And that not merely of the kind that might perhaps lawfully be done on the Sabbath day; as coming under one or other of the two permitted classes of works of necessity or works of charity, *but in simple disregard of the day;* not reckoning it as a day "to be kept holy" to the Lord; thinking it as much our own for the purposes of business or pleasure as any other of the seven. And what is worse—*for it is always worse when evil acts get fair names* —do we not put a gloss upon such conduct, and instead of acknowledging it to be wrong, try to make out that it is justifiable and even right?

2. It is the growth of ungodliness and irreligion that gives birth to all new forms of self-indulgence, whether among rich or poor. It is the spirit of the world, "the prince who ruleth in the children of disobedience," trampling under foot the Spirit of Christ. It is "the law of the members warring against the law of the mind." It is self exalting itself against God. It is the manifestation of Antichrist. This is its true character, and it is betraying truth for those whom God has sent to declare His will, to speak otherwise. It is the world's wisdom, and is, as St. James says, "earthly, sensual, devilish."

We shall do well to mark the first symptoms of irreverent habits, and of careless, God-forgetting ways. You little think how insidious, how fatal they are: how, laying their seed in little things they grow up into great things: how, beginning in trifles, they end in the utter sensualisation of the soul. I dare say some of you have felt if you stay away from church for three or four Sundays, how you become less sensible of the duty of public worship: how the sin of Sabbath-breaking sits lighter on your conscience : how you might even get to such a reprobate state that you could stay away altogether without any scruple or compunction at all.

Or again, you must all have felt how easy it is to come regularly and yet be none the better for coming; how many words of prayer have passed your lips without one feeling of prayer having warmed your hearts; how you may bring here your pride, your vanity, your selfishness, your very plans of merchandise and money-making.

A single smile, a single whisper to your neighbour, a single irreverent gesture, is quite enough to show, not only the clergyman but yourselves, that though you may be in a church you have no sense of its being God's House, and consequently might as well be anywhere else for all the good to your souls that you get by coming.

And this is the use of all those decent forms and ceremonies, such as making the responses, kneeling, "lifting up holy hands," which either piety suggests or the Church herself prescribes. They help us to shut out the world; they fix our thoughts more on the work in which we profess to be engaged; they make worship easier by rendering it more earnest; they contribute not only to decency, but also to spiritual-mindedness. St. Paul tells the Corinthians that their very manners in church, and the arrangements of their services ought to be such that if any came in that believed not or was unlearned, "he should be convinced of all and judged of all; and himself be led, by a kind of devotional contagion, "to fall down on his face and worship God, and report that God was in them of a truth."

Of course this ought to be the outward appearance of every Christian congregation. It is sheer cant and nonsense to talk about worshipping God in spirit and in truth, when our unbended knees, and wandering eyes, and drowsy postures, show that God is not in our thoughts at all. We are thinking of ourselves or our neighbours, not of Him. With all our efforts we shall find it hard enough to "worship the Lord in the beauty of holiness": but these irreverent habits simply show that it is a matter of pure indifference to us whether we offer Him an acceptable sacrifice or no.

My reason for saying so much about irreverent behaviour in church is that I cannot help regarding it as a kind of sample or token of the general character. Follow that careless worshipper out into his daily life, observe his company at his trade, or when engaged in his ordinary occupation, and in ninety-nine cases out of a hundred you will find him to be an utterly profane and godless man; you will find that you get nothing but harm by associating with him. There is a phrase current which I believe does a great deal of mischief. You often hear it said, "He is very good company." Now my conviction is that the persons who are so described are in all cases the very worst company a religious person can fall into. They may be fond of good cheer and jovial fellowship; they may be amusing and lively; they may have pleasant stories to tell and a manner that is very entertaining; but do they improve us or do they corrupt us? Do they strengthen or weaken our good resolutions? Do they help us to think more of Christ or less of Him? Of which do they themselves savour most, things temporal or things eternal?

Few of us, I fear, are sufficiently alive to the importance of that maxim—which was originally the sentiment of a heathen poet, but is incorporated by St. Paul into his own divine teaching—that "evil communications corrupt good manners." There is no maxim the truth of which every one may more surely measure by his own experience. Half a dozen ill-conditioned men or women are enough to deprave a whole street or a whole village. If the power of grace is contagious, the influence of evil is still more so, because it is more natural to us. No doubt those buyers or sellers in the temple had mutually encouraged and hardened each other. Some of them probably had scruples at first, thought it could not be right; felt uncomfortable at what they were doing; but they had long been persuaded or laughed out of this over-nicety. Money was to be made, why be so scrupulous as to *how?* Gain is godliness, whispered the tempter; and as long as thou doest well in the world men will speak good of thee.

3. Lastly, observe that, even among these unholy buyers and sellers, the voice of conscience was but stifled; it was not destroyed—Jesus put forth no supernatural power. He was but a single man against a multitude, yet they offered no show of resistance. They might vow vengeance on their reprover, but they dared not speak out openly against Him: they shrank away ashamed and self-condemned. It was a moment in which was displayed the majesty of holiness, the sovereignty of truth. If it were not for this, their

inherent superiority, both truth and holiness would soon be over-ridden and perish from the world. Men *love* them not, but they *fear* them. They cannot gainsay them: they are not bold enough to resist them.

Thus God leaves not Himself without witness, even in the most reprobate heart. Thus, without miracles, does he still uphold His cause. Thus is the Church still enabled to bear her testimony to what is right and true, even though the latter days seem drawing on apace, and evil men and seducers wax worse and worse, deceiving and being deceived. Whatever may be said by men of fashion, or men of business to the contrary, the voice of God still makes itself heard above and against the voice of the people, proclaiming with as distinct an emphasis as ever it did of old that "all that is in the world, the lust of the flesh, the lust of the eye, and the pride of life, is not of the Father, but is of the world," and reminding us, lest in a moment of weakness we should hesitate which to choose, that "the world passeth away and the lust thereof, but he that doeth the will of God abideth for ever."

Preached—Cholderton, Tenth Sunday after Trinity, August 20, 1854.

XXV.

SPEAKING PARABLES.

"Then said I : Ah, Lord God ! They say of me, Doth he not speak parables?"—EZEK. xx. 49.

OF course there could be little profit or edification in listening to a preacher of whom such words were said in truth. But then it becomes a question on whose side the fault lay; on the preacher's or the hearer's ; on him that taught or them that refused to receive instruction ; on the unskilful tongue, or on the unwilling ear ; on the messenger who knew not how to deliver his message, or on the people whose dulness of understanding was but one of the many results of their stubbornness of heart ? It may be worth while to try to arrive at a right comprehension of this point.

To "speak parables" no doubt means to utter words the meaning and scope of which people of ordinary education fail to apprehend. Whether the language employed be figurative or not, if it is not intelligible, if it is not grasped by the understanding of the hearer, to all practical purposes it is a "speaking in parables." For it seems to be a mistake to suppose that our Blessed Lord adopted so generally the parabolic method of instruction because it was the *plainest;* that is, because it enabled His hearers to catch His drift with the least trouble and the smallest amount of reflection. We are expressly told by more than one Evangelist that the very contrary was the case. Thus in answer to His disciples' question "why He taught the people in parables"? His explanation of His method is, "Because it is given to you to know the mysteries of the kingdom of God." St. Mark tells us, "when they were alone He expounded all things to His disciples"—"to you, therefore, it is given to know the mysteries of the kingdom of God, but to them it is not given. Therefore speak I to them in parables: because they seeing, see not: and hearing, they hear not, neither do they understand. And in them is fulfilled this prophecy of Esaias" —a prophecy that will explain the phenomenon of unbelief in every age of man's spiritual history—"which saith, By hearing ye shall hear, and shall not understand; and seeing ye shall see, and shall not perceive; *for this people's heart is waxed gross,* and their ears are dull of hearing, and their eyes have they closed, lest at any time they should see with their eyes, and hear with their ears, and understand with their hearts, and should be converted, and I should heal them."

When David again says, "I will open my mouth in parables; I will declare hard sentences of old," he plainly does not mean that he was going to utter truisms which might be caught up, and understood, and practically applied by any careless listener that chose to pay a moment's attention to his words; for in the verse before he exhorts people to be more than usually attentive;

and as he was about "to open his mouth in a *parable*," so his hearers are bidden "incline their ear" if they hoped to profit by "the words of his mouth."

It is not then because the parabolic method of instruction is the *easiest*, that it was so often employed by the prophets, and especially by the Lord Jesus, in the communication of God's will to man; but rather because it was the most *edifying*. To those that not only *had* eyes, but knew how to use them—those that cultivate the gift of spiritual discernment—it opened up wonderful analogies between the Almighty's different ways of dealing with His creatures; between the laws of His Providence and the methods of His grace; between things spiritual and things natural; heaven and earth, time and eternity. It taught men to regard all that they saw and felt—what was going on around them as well as what they were conscious of within them—as parts of one great whole, constituted and governed by one Supreme Mind, each bearing its own separate yet not independent testimony to Him, and all working together not only for the manifestation of His glory, but for the extension of His kingdom—the good of His Elect.

The parabolic method of teaching, established a system of relations between things visible and invisible. It made the creature speak to us of its Creator. It drew out voices from the dumb elements of nature. It made the wheat-grain explain to us the law of its fruitfulness; the mustard seed tell us what meaneth its wonderful expansion; the leaven wherein consists the secret of its subtle, penetrating influence. Simple truths, which have instructed children, while they have perplexed philosophers; for in this as in other parts of His dispensation, it hath pleased our heavenly Father to "hide things from the wise and prudent which He has revealed unto babes!"

There is an old and common English proverb which is substantially the same in sense as the words of Isaiah, and which shows that common sense, our own natural reason, takes exactly the same view of this matter as revelation. It is said, and with great truth, that "None are so blind as those who will not see." It is not that God's message is dark, even when uttered by the stammering lips of an uninspired preacher, but that our hearts are hard. It is not that our faculties are unable to *understand*, but that our wills are loth to *do*. "He that will *do* the saying shall know of the doctrine." This is Christ's own condition laid down for the comprehension of evangelical mysteries. "Why do ye not understand my speech?" This is His question to the Jews; and the reply is, "even because ye cannot hear my word." Their hearts were preoccupied. They had "*no mind*" for the doctrines of the Cross; and so, as St. Paul testifies, they called them "foolishness." Yet, adds the Apostle, "by this same foolishness of preaching it pleased God to save them which believed." "Christ Crucified," who was to the Jews "a stumbling-block," and to the Greeks "foolishness," to them that were called was a manifestation both of the *power* and *wisdom* of God. As none could come to Christ except His Father which was in Heaven "drew" them; so God would seem to have drawn none but those who *accepted*

Him as a guide, and followed the promptings of His Spirit, *unquestioning*, or at least *undoubting*, in the way.

We cannot doubt, I think, how it was that Ezekiel seemed to "speak parables" to his countrymen. Certainly his prophecies in many places are dark, and not always easy to be explained. We seem to fail to follow him in some of his flights of inspired fancy. There are many things for which we must even now wait patiently till the advancing history of the world or the Church, or at any rate the consummating seal of the last day makes them more fully known. But still the simplest, most unlettered Christian may take up the volume of his prophecy and gather wisdom from it. Certain chapters need no expounder to set forth their meaning. "The wayfaring man, though a fool," can hardly "err therein." They all harmonise to one key. They all combine in teaching the same lesson—the long-suffering, the forbearance, but at the same time the fearful vengeance on obstinate, hardened sinners, of Almighty God.

How is it then that not only in the prophet's own day, but *now*, when they are read in the Christian Church, and illustrated by the parallel pages of the Gospel Covenant, so many seem to miss their meaning; and those, generally, the very persons by whom their lesson is most needed, yet, unhappily, who do not feel their need? This is indeed the saddest among the many sad pictures that human nature exhibits to the philosophic eye: that those whom the spiritual judge, comparing the tenor of their daily lives with the letter of God's requirements, must pronounce to be in the greatest danger, are themselves insensible of it; often speaking of their condition in God's sight and with another world in prospect, with the supremest self-complacency—regarding the world without, perhaps, as lying in wickedness, but themselves as sure of their election and acceptance at the last day.

It is no new phenomenon. It has been always so. It is a kind of moral law of the natural man. Thus the Pharisees, hearing our Lord's striking declaration, that "For judgment He was come into the world, that they which saw not might see; and that they which saw might be made blind," asked Him, in a derisive tone of self-satisfaction, "Are we blind also?" and received for an answer words that would have opened the eyes of men less bigoted and less puffed-up, "If ye *were* blind, ye should have no sin: but now ye say, We see: therefore your sin remaineth."

Such men will always receive God's message to them, by whom or howsoever delivered, as "parables." All the preaching in the world will not lead them to look upon themselves as sinners who have provoked the anger, and unless they repent, will one day taste the righteous vengeance of Almighty God. "Oh," they say, if they make any remark upon such doctrines at all, "this is not meant for us: for us decent, respectable people: for us who come to church and know how to behave; for us who have been educated, and form the upper classes of society. It is all very proper for clergymen sometimes to touch upon such points; but, you know, we do not recognise them: we have nothing to disturb ourselves about of that kind. It was a great weakness for a man in a position like Felix to 'tremble' when Paul reasoned with him about temperance, righteousness, and judgment to come. I can hear such subjects handled in a sermon without trembling at all."

And thus it is, by such self-deceiving thoughts and language, that all those awakening motives of the Gospel by which God would draw our hearts to Him, if not by love, yet at least by fear, are ignored and put aside, as suitable perhaps "for lewd fellows of the baser sort," but not for such respectable people as we; and our Blessed Lord's solemn warning to the Pharisees seems to have lost its application now—" Verily, verily, I say unto you, the publicans and harlots go into the Kingdom of God before you."

I am sure that this is the evil against which all of us, who flatter ourselves that we are respectable, have most especial need to guard—the spirit of Pharisaism. There was no *formal* sect of Pharisees in Ezekiel's time, but it was against the *Pharisaical spirit* that he preached. And so, though the *name* be gone now, the *thing* remains. There may be no Pharisees in England, but there is "the leaven of the Pharisees." There is the spirit of self-righteousness, and pride, and carnal security, and formalism, and externalism, and hypocrisy. There are men in England, as there were men in Laodicea, who say they are "rich, and increased with goods, and have need of nothing, and know not that they are wretched and miserable, and poor, and blind, and naked." There are church-goers who, as it were, throng and press the Blessed Jesus, like the careless crowds that ran gaping after Him when He went about Galilee, yet have all their life long, though within reach of Him, never so much as touched in truth the hem of His garment.

And they stumble where every unrenewed heart has stumbled since the dispensation of grace was first preached to the world—"going about to establish *their own* righteousness, they will not submit themselves to the righteousness of God." Satisfied with what they are, they cannot bend their proud and stubborn wills to acknowledge really that they have need of Christ. They think they can get to heaven without Him—without His mediation, without His example, without His Cross, without His Sacraments. And when a preacher would fain awaken them from this pleasant but fatal dream; when they hear anything said about repentance, conversion, renewal, sanctification, they escape the application of all such doctrine to themselves by disposing of it by the help of the simple formula, "Ah, Lord God, doth he not speak parables"?

The words may seem "parables" to us now—prettily told stories, but with which we have no practical concern; but the day will surely come when we shall wish, perhaps too late, that we had given closer heed to them. Oh! that God's merciful dealing with us, both as a nation and as individuals, may open our eyes to this better wisdom in time! God would draw us to Him first by acts of love, and not till those have failed, by chastisements and judgments. Surely He is dealing with us now, *not* according to our wicked ways or our corrupt doings, that we may learn to hate our sins, and to cleave to Him with a more perfect heart. Surely St. Paul's advice to the Romans is the truest wisdom for every man : " Be not high-minded, *but fear.*" Confidence, boasting, presumption, self-justification, are the qualities most out of place in such wayward, unstable creatures as—if we know ourselves—we must feel ourselves to be. Surely it will be the saddest of portions to have lived in pleasure and comfort upon the earth, and to die, as we may persuade ourselves in security; and then to awaken up with the rich man in the parable, and find ourselves tormented in the unquenchable flame of hell

And now, will any of you say of *me*, as his hearers said of Ezekiel, "Ah, Lord God, doth not he speak parables?"

Preached—Cholderton, Tenth Sunday after Trinity, October 15, 1854.

XXVI.

STANDING ON HOLY GROUND.

"And He said, Draw not nigh hither: put off thy shoes from off thy feet, for the place whereon thou standest is holy ground."
—Exodus iii. 5.

THERE are few scenes in the Bible that possess a deeper and more awful interest than this recorded interview between Moses and the Lord Who spake to him out of the bush—between the creature and the Creator—the Arabian Shepherd and the Eternal "I AM."

Let me first briefly group together the circumstances of the place and time.

Moses was now eighty years of age. Exiled from Egypt, whose tyrant he had defied, for forty years he had passed a shepherd's life in the wilderness of Arabia. "He kept the flock of Jethro," priest or prince of Midian, whose daughter he had married. The manner of feeding flocks of sheep then was very different from the method we see employed around us now. An Eastern shepherd in the wilderness led a solitary and adventurous existence. In the absence of regular and systematic cultivation, with no conveniences of permanent farm-buildings and homesteads, he had often to roam far in search of water or of pasturage. Accordingly, Moses, whose home was far to the east of Midian, "led his flock to the backside of the desert, and came to the mountain of God, even to Horeb." It is a range of mountains which occupies the cleft which nature's hand has formed in the northern extremity of the Red Sea. Sinai, from whose summit a few months afterwards was heard the Almighty's awful voice, proclaiming the ten articles of the Moral Law, was one of the principal peaks. It was hither that Elijah fled from Jezebel's murderous rage; and here too, after a wind, an earthquake, and a fire, he heard the still small voice of God speaking to his inmost ear. Nor, as we know from his own lips that after his conversion he went back into Arabia and there heard "unspeakable words," would it be an improbable supposition that it was on Mount Horeb—" the mountain of God," as it was from the very first prophetically called—that it pleased the Almighty Father to reveal the Gospel of His Son to the humbled and teachable spirit of the Apostle Paul.

Hitherward then as he drove his flock in meditative mood perhaps—as can hardly be otherwise when we are conversing with Nature in her grandest scenes—but little dreaming of so high a mystery as an immediate revelation of the Most High, the simple shepherd's eye is arrested by a wondrous sight: a tall thorn bush in a flame; and lo! though the bush "burned with fire, it was not consumed."

His curiosity was naturally awakened; and still as it seems unsuspecting aught but natural agencies, though it was a phenomenon that he never could have beheld before, " I will turn aside," he said, "and see this great sight, *why* the bush is not burnt." So has many a man been drawn to God by motives of which he little knew whither they were leading him at the time. The peculiarity in Moses' case is that a man who began in the spirit of philosophy, which is too often sceptical, should have left off in the temper of *faith:* that the very fact of a mystery seems to have prepared *his* heart for the readier acknowledgment of God, instead of—as it too often does now—making him stumble at the very outset, and call in question the existence of a Divine force or of a Divine Providence at all. An inquiry commenced in such a spirit was not likely to be disappointed of its aim. And so, when the Lord saw that he turned aside to see, God called unto him out of the midst of the bush and said, "Moses, Moses." And he said, "Here am I." And He said, "Draw not nigh hither: put off thy shoes from off thy feet, for the place whereon thou standest is holy ground."

Now plainly the fundamental principle of this Divine command to Moses is grounded on the obvious fitness of reverence, seriousness, humility, as conditions of worship. These are the very first elements of any act of spiritual intercourse between a child of earth and the God of Heaven. What was it which made that spot "holy"? It had not been solemnly consecrated for Divine worship. There was no special space marked off for sacred purposes as there was years afterwards upon Mount Zion in Jerusalem. No wandering Arab, or holy patriarch had raised an altar there and "called upon the name of the Lord." It was nothing of this kind that made it "holy." It was "holy" because it was the place to which a man was "drawing nigh" to hold converse with His God. So it vindicates a like sanctity and an equal reverence, not merely for consecrated houses, for churches and cathedrals, but for our chamber floors, our bedsides—for "every place where men pray, lifting up holy hands, and making their requests known unto God."

No matter what the special form of access, whether in public prayer or private prayer, in reading our Bibles or approaching the Lord's Table, in religious conversation with a neighbour, or in inward musings with ourselves, the first thing required is the "preparation of the heart"; the recollection that it is *God* to Whom we are "drawing nigh," or about Whom we are reading or talking. This recollection should at once drive out of our hearts everything that is unbeseeming so high a Presence, and bend our outward form and posture into harmony with the spirit that should be reigning within. Of course this story teaches us how we ought to behave in God's house, but it teaches us much more. It teaches us how, in every act and thought and place where the reality of the Divine Presence is forced upon us, and we venture to speak either of or to Him, the very sense of that Presence should constrain our whole being, and check all levity and unseemliness, whether outward or inward, before Him.

I think it is one of the saddest thoughts that can occur to a mind that has even the most imperfect apprehension of what a solemn thing Divine Worship is, to reflect upon the vast amount of time that has been ostensibly spent in acts of religion in vain and worse than vain—absolutely wasted and thrown away; and that not only in the case of the wicked, whose very prayers, we are told, are "an abomination," but with the best and purest of us all. How often have we risen up from our knees without the least comfort from our prayers! How often have we closed our Bibles without a ray more of Divine light having been shed across our daily paths! How often have we left God's house without the least assurance that we have been admitted to His presence, or been within feeling distance of that Spirit Who alone sanctifies the soul! When we read of those persons who had eaten and drunk in Christ's presence and in whose streets He had taught, and yet whom He says He "never knew," who wait in vain for Him to open the door to them, how must the anxious thought come home to us—if we have any true concern for our souls at all—that our case is only too much like theirs: that we too, like Jacob at Bethel, only without his excuse, have but too often been where the Lord was and, for any sanctifying influence on our spirits, "have known it not"!

A familiarity with the ceremonial of religion—with its outward things, such as churches, sacraments, forms of prayer, Bibles—unaccompanied with an inwardly devout and reverential feeling—what St. Paul calls the "form of godliness without its power"—is one of the very surest ways to harden and unspiritualise the soul. I do not believe there can be any man so utterly irreligious as he who is continually performing what he calls his "religious duties" out of routine, or in compliance with established custom, in a merely mechanical and formal way. It is a law of our moral being that passive impressions, however vivid and penetrating at first, soon die out and lose their power unless they are quickened into active habits. It is impossible for any man to come to church with any profit who simply comes to say that he has been there; nor can the heart be lifted up heartily in prayer unless there is the daily endeavour to bring our lives into closer conformity to that Spirit which can alone inspire the lips with effectual utterances.

It was this spiritual danger that our Lord had directly in view when He addressed those solemn words to the Scribes and Pharisees, whose profuse lip-service was utterly corrupted by the entire absence of devotion from their hearts—" Verily I say unto you, that the publicans and harlots go into the kingdom of heaven before you."

The Scriptures abound with illustrations of this most important truth. There is the case of Uzzah smitten in a moment for his irreverent handling of the Ark of God, with which it seems he had grown too familiar by having had the charge of it for twenty years. There is the story of the buyers and sellers in the Temple, so little mindful of the sanctity of the place as to think it might be used for the purposes of merchandise without being profaned. There is the example of those members of the Corinthian Church " who came together " as St. Paul says " not for the better but for the worse," " one being hungry and another drunken," even at the very Supper of the Lord. What are all these but cases of men who handled holy things without personal holiness;

who had never felt with Jacob "how dreadful is the place" where the Lord makes His Presence known; who came into a church as unconcernedly as they would into a shop or a tavern, and when there plainly showed by their outward demeanour that they had not the remotest conception of the feeling that was in David's heart when he sang, "We will go into God's Tabernacle, and fall low on our knees before His footstool"?

I say "*outward* demeanour": for though "God is a Spirit, and they that worship Him must worship Him in spirit and in truth," yet it is a mere playing with words to argue from such a text that the body has no part in such worship, which ascends from the heart and the heart alone. My text, which is not the mere notion of a religious man—though even that would have had great weight—but the direct command of God, proves the contrary. By "putting his shoes from off his feet" Moses showed that he did feel that the ground was "holy." Inward reverence was expressed by an outward act. His body and his spirit worshipped God, as it were, hand in hand.

Though it is true that such outward ceremonies are to a great extent symbolical, yet are they influential also. Kneeling, for instance, may be a token of humility. I am sure it is easier for a man to humble his heart, and to realise his position as a sinner at the footstool of Almighty God when his knees are bent and his countenance hidden in his hands, than when his glance wanders restlessly about a church, and he himself is sitting in his seat, only thinking about how he may make himself most comfortable. It was not without a meaning, be sure, that those scriptures were written, "Make a covenant with thine eyes, and keep thy foot when thou goest into the house of God:" or that David sings, "O magnify the Lord our God and fall down before His footstool, for the Lord our God is holy." As St. James says that a man's "inward religion" may be known by the simple outward test of the government of his tongue, so I think it may be safely affirmed that *heart-worship* is evidenced by *body-worship*. ' I do not, of course, mean that every bended knee is the token of a contrite heart, but be sure that every contrite heart will perforce bend a stubborn knee. There may be the form without the power—hypocrisy and Pharisaism can enter here as everywhere; but there will not be the power without the form.

Search your Bibles from one end to the other and see if you can find an instance of a godly man—one whose life and conversation you would take as an example for your own—who thought it mattered not in what posture, or with what outward reverence, he worshipped the Lord His God. Jacob at Bethel, Moses at Horeb, Solomon at the dedication of the Temple, Daniel in his chamber at Babylon, St. Stephen in his hour of martyrdom, St. Peter by the bedside of Dorcas, St. Paul and his sorrowing friends on the sea-shore at Tyre—nay, highest and purest, and most wonderful example of all, the Blessed Jesus, "while his soul was sorrowful unto death" in the agony of Gethsemane, all point our thoughts directly the opposite way; all are to be seen *kneeling;* all show that outward reverence was, with them at least, a part of inward devotion.

I have no doubt that many of you will be able to confirm by your own experience what I am sure I can state from my own, that the more one can shut out the outer world from our thoughts; the more vividly we can realise the fact that we are seeking God; the more strongly we are impressed with the conviction that Christ is very nigh to us, and that to be nigh to Christ is a very awful thing: not only the more naturally do we fall into a reverent and seemly posture of prayer, but the more fully also do we taste that strength and comfort of prayer which at other times, when our hearts are colder and thoughts less fixed, we are only too painfully sensible has been denied. We may always know whether we have prayed aright by the very feeling that still abides with us when we have got up from our knees. If, like the two disciples at Emmaus, our hearts still "burn within us," then may we confidently believe that we have been with Christ, or, as St. Paul says, "through Him have had access by one Spirit unto the Father."

But to experience any of this comfort, which perhaps forms the richest portion of that "joy and peace in believing" of which the Apostle speaks, we must, in every supplication we address to the throne of grace, make our approaches reverently: feel, like Moses, that we are treading on "holy ground:" "put our shoes from off our feet;" get rid, as far as possible, of everything that is earthly, and sensual, and selfish. Too many a man's prayer returns unto him "void" because it never sprang from faith, or love, or earnestness. It was a *mere form*, stunted down, probably, to the shortest compass and hurried over in the briefest time. Or they were *unmeaning* words; words that we did not really wish fulfilled at the very time we uttered them.

How many men, for instance, using the Lord's prayer, give expression to the wish that God's name may be "hallowed," which they themselves, perhaps, take in vain twenty times a day; or that "His kingdom may come," while they are actually hindering His kingdom; or that He would "forgive" them their sins, while they are unforgiving; or that He would "deliver them from temptation," when they often go out of their way to meet temptation?

Oh! what a mockery is all such waiting upon God! What an insult "to honour Him with our lips while our hearts are far away"! What a delusion to fancy we are worshipping, when we only sit through a prescribed form! What irreverence to think that the fact of their being consecrated to God's service does not convey a kind of sanctity to the places where we assemble together in His name, and claim for them an honourable treatment at our hands!

Be sure that prayer, to be heard, must come from the heart, and that heart a contrite and broken one. A broken heart will be sure to be accompanied by a bended knee. The thought of the presence of God will itself be sufficient to check reckless postures, irreverent manners, wandering eyes. We shall feel that we are come here to *worship:* that our presence for any other purpose is simply worthless—nay, is a positive profaneness. "In God's *fear* shall we worship towards His holy temple." *"O worship the Lord in the beauty of holiness: let the whole earth stand in awe of Him. Glory and worship are before Him: power and honour are in His sanctuary. Ascribe unto the Lord the honour due unto His name. Ascribe unto the Lord worship and power. O go your way into His gates with thanksgiving, and into His courts with praise: be thankful unto Him and speak good of His name. O praise the Lord of heaven; praise Him in the height. Praise Him, all ye angels of His: praise Him, all His host. Kings of the earth and all people: princes and all judges of the world: young men and maidens, old men and children, praise the name of the Lord: for His name only is excellent, and His praise above heaven and earth."*

Preached—Cholderton, Fifth Sunday in Lent, April 2, 1854; Kingswinford, Fifteenth Sunday after Trinity, September 16, 1855; Cholderton, Fifth Sunday in Lent, April 10, 1859.

XXVII.

THE POWER OF CHRIST IN HIS MINISTERS.

"Other foundation can no man lay than that is laid, which is Jesus Christ. But let every man take heed how he buildeth thereupon."—I. COR. iii. 11-10.

EVERY one, even moderately acquainted with the life and writings of St. Paul, must be aware that the language of the text, often repeated with perhaps a slight variety of outward form, but with the same inner sentiment, is a kind of axiom or first principle with him; not a conventional phrase or badge of party; not even the utterance of his soul in moments of highly excited feeling and ecstatic rapture, when caught up into the third heaven; but the result of an unbroken spiritual experience; the central truth of his moral and intellectual being; once perhaps a deduction of his reason, but now developed into an instinct or supernatural intuition; the very deepest and most realized conviction of the regenerate man. It was not only that he *preached* Christ, but that to him to *live was* Christ. The sole end of his being, that for which he gave up all besides, was to be "found in Him" : and "the life which he lived in the flesh he lived by the faith of the Son of God, who loved him and gave Himself for him."

The pastor's work is then emphatically wrought *in* Christ. Except as part of His work for carrying out, and proclaiming, and applying the great scheme of redemption, his commission has no meaning, his words no savour, his acts no power. After He had made perfect our redemption by His death, and was ascended into heaven, He sent abroad into the world His apostles, prophets, evangelists, doctors, pastors, by whose labour and ministry He gathered together a great flock in all parts of the world to set forth the eternal praise of His Father's Holy Name.

And therefore St. Paul, than whom personally no man was less given to boasting, yet who never seems to miss an opportunity of magnifying his office, does not hesitate to claim for himself the honour of being "a fellow-labourer with God, a worker together with Christ": "and thanks Christ Jesus the Lord, who had enabled him, for that He counted him faithful, and had put him into the ministry." And so to his every ministerial act he ascribes a divine efficacy. He speaks of the "*power which the Lord had given him* for edification, and not for destruction." His absolution of the penitent Corinthian he pronounces "*in the person of Christ.*" To those who sought "*a proof of Christ speaking in him,*" he threatens that "if he came again he would not spare." And in one very solemn passage, when he would put forth the plenitude of his apostolical authority, and where every word is marked with the deep consciousness both of his own responsibility in the possession, and of the consequences of the exercise, of such power, he says that he judged the offender "*in the name and with the power of the Lord Jesus Christ.*"

Nor can it be replied that these gifts, which St. Paul asserts rather than claims, were peculiar to an Apostle, and cannot without presumption be arrogated to Christian ministers now. For besides the ground of abstract reasoning, on which it may be urged that, though it has pleased the wisdom of God to suspend the miraculous agencies that were once exerted so powerfully for the propagation of the Gospel, the ordinary gifts which Apostles possessed, and by which they at once governed and fed the Churches, are needed now as much as ever "for the perfecting of the saints, for the work of the ministry, for the edifying of the body of Christ"—besides, I say, this unanswerable argument of abstract reasoning, every one who is familiar with the Epistles to the Corinthians (which in an indirect way throw most light on the constitution of a primitive Church and on the ministerial life of an Apostle) must be perfectly cognizant that what the writer in one place claims to himself, in others he transfers to those who are associated with him—to Apollos, Sosthenes, Titus, Timothy —of the last of whom indeed he expressly says, "He works the *work of the Lord*, as I also do."

Remember that I am not attempting to *define* this power. All I wish to press upon you is, that *whatever* our powers are they are divine; they do not come from ourselves, nor from an Act of Parliament: they come, mediately it is true, as every other gift of grace, but still originally and essentially from Christ, as everything now comes from Christ, by the operation of His Spirit.

I know not what other theory—though one hardly likes to call a doctrine so plainly announced in Holy Scripture "a theory"—I know not, I mean, what other view of our commission can justify us in acting as ministers of the Gospel at all. For we do not profess to be mere philanthropists, mere instructors, mere social reformers, mere preachers even of a superhuman wisdom. We use words and we do deeds, and in neither case, I trust, presumptuously or unwarrantably, which far transcend the range of these functions, high and ennobling though they be. We are, or at least St. Paul says that we are, "stewards *of the mysteries of* God." We intercede, we bless, we pronounce forgiveness, we receive into the Church, we wash in the laver of regeneration, we give the body of Christ. And do we these things in our own name, or by a self-inherent power? The Apostle thanks God that at Corinth he had baptized none save Crispus and Gaius, and the household of Stephanas, lest it should be said that he had baptized in his own name. And woe to us if we seek for ourselves the honour that is due to Christ alone. This indeed were priestcraft. This indeed were seeking to have dominion over the faith of our brethren, instead of being helpers of their joy. This were indeed to set up an unscriptural system, for which no true parallel can be found even under the different circumstances of the Mosaic dispensation, and from which our forefathers hoped they had delivered their Church by the Reformation for ever.

But, because we would not stretch ourselves beyond our measure, are we to waive our just pretensions, and suffer the world, unrebuked, to make sport of our claims? No, brethren! we ask for respect, for love, for reverend estimation, not for ourselves, " but for our work's sake." We ask our people to receive the Word which they hear from us; we must handle it so that they shall feel that it *is*—" not the word of men, but in truth the Word of God," " which alone worketh effectually in them that believe." We shrink from, for we know the danger of, personal compliments: but we glory in the honour that is shown us as ambassadors for Christ. It is Christ's work, not our own, that we desire to see magnified. It is thus that St. Paul apologises, as it were, for seeming so to glory. " Would to God ye could bear with me a little in my folly; and indeed bear with me." If in aught he appeared to obtrude *himself* on the notice of the world, it should only be on the side of his infirmities, that so *the power of Christ might be seen resting on him.* For, indeed, it could be by nothing short of the " power of the Spirit of God" that he, " whose bodily presence was weak and speech contemptible," could have made the Gentiles obedient by word and deed, and from Jerusalem round about unto Illyricum, with mighty signs and wonders, have fully preached the Gospel of Christ.

Regard then, brethren, the work to which you have this day been called as a work *in* and *with* Christ; as a work which can only be wrought of the ability which He giveth; a work on which you must daily seek His blessing; in which, when you feel yourselves most weak, you shall find yourselves most strong; in which, finally, you cannot but succeed, if you only persevere, " because mightier is He that is with you than he that is against you." It is a glorious work, and has a great recompense of reward. Its glory is that it is not only a reflection, but, as it were, a supplemental portion, filling up that which is behindhand, of the work of Christ: its reward (ofttimes foretasted by the faithful minister even now, and the consciousness of which is his great sustainer under inevitable disappointments) shall be fully known in that day when "they that be wise shall shine as the brightness of the firmament, and they that turn many to righteousness as the stars for ever and ever."

Nor is the fundamental truth we have been considering less potent in its influences upon the *theology* than upon the *work* of the minister. Making the great objective doctrine, or fact, of the Son of God sent forth in the fulness of time, born of a woman, made under the law, crucified, risen, ascended, glorified, the centre of all his teaching, he will find all other revealed truths group themselves in wondrous harmony round this one, and each derive from it its proper emphasis and illustration. When Christ is set upon His throne in our system of dogmatic teaching; when we preach nothing that is not marked with the stamp and impress of His Cross; when we would not use a single ceremony that does not lead men's thoughts at once unto the Crucified, we need be under small apprehension about our doctrine, lest it should be wanting either in systematic completeness or in applied power. In every age of the Church it has been when men have been least under the constraining influence of the resolve "to bring every thought into captivity unto the obedience of Christ" that they have been most forward to battle for opinions. As St. Paul explains the phenomenon, "not holding the Head," they have been "subject to ordinances, after the commandments and doctrines of men."

But in the Christian's creed and the Church's ritual there are—at least there ought to be—no dumb elements, or enigmatic symbols. "We all with open face behold as in a glass the glory of the Lord." The very purpose of the dispensation of the Spirit is "to change us into His image." We recognise nothing as having a place in a scheme of Christian faith, or practice, or worship, which does not draw not only its power, but its very shape and significance from Him who is at once "the way, the truth, and the life." What becomes of Baptism, unless we see in the dew glistening on the infant's forehead "the blood of sprinkling which speaketh better things than that of Abel"? What of the Holy Eucharist, unless therein we partake of "the Bread of life," and "do show forth the Lord's death till He come"? What of our assemblings together for public worship, unless we are persuaded "that *He* is in the midst of us"?

This, indeed, I take to be the true purpose of sacraments, and, if I may so call them, of sacramentals. They give an objective, definite reality to Christ's work. They remove it from the domain of feeling and imagination. They make us feel that we are dealing with a living *Person* acting upon us; not with an allegory, or a myth, or a sentiment, which we create for ourselves. Jehovah localizes Himself among His people, as in the days of old. There are places and things upon which the Shekinah of the Divine Presence still rests, not indeed as visibly, but as *really*, as when It guided the chosen people through the waste howling wilderness to their promised land.

And if we deny this: if we say, for instance, that Baptism and the Eucharist speak to the Christian only of his profession, but not of Christ, what becomes of them? What place have they in a system, now no longer of shadows, but which is "the very image of the things"? In what do they deserve to be ranked above the "weak and beggarly elements" of the law? Unless they make us partakers of Christ *really*, and not in a mere figure or forensically, as it is called, they are simply incongruous, and out of keeping, with a dispensation in which a ceremony becomes a thing utterly indifferent, and indeed worthless, unless animated by the life that springs from Him.

Do not think, brethren, that you are honouring Christ by degrading His Sacraments, or by reducing His Ministry to a mere convenient human arrangement, or by stripping His Church of prerogatives which she has not thought it robbery to claim. Depend upon it, if you once grasp that central truth "of Jesus Christ, and Him crucified," you will find plenty of room for these as well as for other truths, equally fundamental though less objective; *e.g.* justification by faith, or the necessity of repentance and conversion after post-baptismal sin. As has been often said, no one truth, whether in science or revelation, can ever contradict or quench any other truth. It may not always be easy to adjust them, but we often make it harder by our artificial systems, by the false position from which we attempt to contemplate them. We must ascend the mountain-top if we would behold the landscape in all its varied beauty of hill and plain, river and valley, forest and pasture. And so we must stand on Calvary, and from that elevation trace the spring of life, welling forth from the Saviour's pierced side, parted, like the river of Eden, into many heads, yet each contributing its element of richness and fertility to the garden of the Lord, none without its use in the one great work of all—the healing and cleansing of the nations.

We must place ourselves by the Cross of Christ, if we would have our doctrine possess not only earnestness, but unity. The grand mystery of the Atonement, springing out of the sublime doctrine of the Incarnation, as it is the heart or organic centre of the Church's life, so is it the fundamental article of her theology. It is the *fact* that we have to lay hold of and set forth ; not a theory or explanation of the fact. Beware, I beseech you, of attempting to explain, or even of professing to understand—to bring within the compass of your own reason and the laws of human logic—truths that the Holy Ghost has seen fit to leave wrapped in mystery. I believe that Socinianism is simply a reaction of the mind against these human, and, as they are called, rational theories. I have seen many theories of the Atonement, many elaborate attempts to show how therein God's justice was satisfied while mercy rejoiced ; but I confess that I turn away from them all but little the wiser ; and, with a sense of relief, throw myself back on that single text, which supersedes the necessity of any theory, by giving me the assurance of which I would fain have a deeper sense day by day, that "God so loved the world that He gave His only-begotten Son, that whosoever believeth on Him should not perish, but have everlasting life."

This is the great truth which you must try to make simple souls feel. It must lie at the root of all your teaching: at the root, and therefore not necessarily always on the surface. Simple as it seems, you will be surprised perhaps to find the infinite variety of which it is susceptible. It is not like narrower truths, which at times, in the unhappy heat of controversy, have been lifted out of their proper sphere and forced to occupy a space which they could not fill. It will not oblige you, like these, to be ever repeating the same conventional formulæ; ever harping on the same monotonous string; ever travelling, at length how wearied! over the same ground.

No, there is a freshness and an overflowing fulness in these living waters, which refuse to be confined in the broken cisterns which partisans and controversialists hew out for themselves. No theological axiom, however true in its limits, can ever take the place of the fundamental fact—"Jesus Christ, and Him crucified." There is a spiritual solar system, and this is the centre of it. All other spiritual facts revolve round this, and derive from it, in proportion to their proximity, the light and warmth and energy which constitute their power. There is as much harmony in the revealed truths of the spiritual as in the observed phenomena of the physical world. They all gravitate to Christ. They are His satellites. Each holds its appointed course round the Sun of Righteousness without jealousy, without collision, without encroachment. You will find no difficulty in reconciling dogmas that are commonly supposed to mark the most opposite schools of thought—sacramental grace, for instance, and Luther's article of a standing or a falling Church; baptismal regeneration and post-baptismal conversion; salvation through faith, yet not without works; St. Paul's doctrine and St. James's —if only you can bring them separately under the subordinating influence of the work of Christ.

In no other way, indeed, will you ever make them intelligible to, and, what is of still higher importance, effectual with the mass of your people. The experience of every minister testifies to the wondrous power of the Cross to touch the soul. Our Lord's words have indeed had a rich fulfilment: " I, if I be lifted up, will draw all men unto Me." If you desire a magnet to attract your people's hearts, lift up their Saviour before them in such simple, touching strains as St. Paul uses, " to wit, that God was in Christ, reconciling the world unto Himself, not imputing their trespasses unto them; and that He hath committed unto you the word of reconciliation."

And if it is the *word* of reconciliation, preach it in the *spirit* of reconciliation. Remember, souls are won, not compelled; drawn, not driven; by gentleness and patience, not by sternness and anathemas. The Apostle indeed had his anathema in reserve; but it is only for those " who love not the Lord Jesus Christ." See that you so preach Him that men may perforce love Him.

Make them feel what they would be without Him; what they are with Him. Help them to realize the gift they have received, the grace of which they are partakers, the glory of which they are heirs.

In the glorious message of redemption there is enough to warm the coldest heart, to render eloquent the slowest tongue. He always speaks with power who speaks, however simply, to the living wants and sympathies of men. Let optimists say what they will, human nature, ever since it first felt the burden and the gnawing worm of sin, has been "groaning and travailing in pain together, waiting to be delivered from the bondage of corruption," which it felt, but could not cast off, "into the glorious liberty of the children of God." We have to tell them of this liberty: to preach this deliverance: to cheer them with the tidings that "all things are theirs—the world, life, death, things present, things to come—all are theirs, *because they are Christ's*, and Christ is God's."

Dare, brethren, to be faithful, and leave your reputation, whether for talents or influence, in God's hands. We have been warned, by One who knew what was in man, that there is a danger "when all men speak well of us": and no man has more reason to be apprehensive of this danger than the minister of Christ. For it comes to him as a direct temptation to spiritual pride, that subtlest form of evil which cast the angels from their thrones. The Apostle bids us remember that it is the peculiar peril of "novices." Be it your better wisdom so "to stir up the gift of God," which has this day been "given you by the laying on of hands," that when the last word of your testimony has been delivered, and your fight fought, and your race run, the flock whom you have fed, as they follow your body to the grave, may thus pronounce their pastor's eulogy: "He preached not himself, but Christ Jesus the Lord, and himself our servant for Jesus' sake."

Sermon (abridged) preached—in the Chapel of Bishop's Palace, Salisbury, on the evening of Sunday, December 22, 1855, after the Ordination.

XXVIII.

THE PEACE OF CHRIST.

"These things I have spoken unto you, that in Me ye might have peace. In the world ye shall have tribulation: but be of good cheer; I have overcome the world."—St. John xvi. 33.

This was strange and unwelcome news to the disciples. Their minds were full of a very different picture. They had followed Christ in very different hope. There was no concealing it: they were disappointed and dejected. "Because He said these things unto them, sorrow filled their hearts." He had said other things to them before, things which they did not understand, which they took in a wrong sense, that were much pleasanter to them to hear. They liked to hear of the "twelve thrones on which they were to sit, judging the twelve tribes of Israel." They liked to hear of "a seat on the right hand and on the left prepared for them that loved Christ." Their thoughts revelled in the hundredfold reward for them who had forsaken brethren, father, mother, wife, children, lands, for His Name's sake.

For was not He the Mighty One who should restore the kingdom to Israel? Would not He make Jerusalem again "the city of the Great King"? When He had delivered His people from their oppressors, should not they stand nearest to His throne? When He wore the crown of His father David, should not they share His glory? When all nations bowed down before Him, should not they too be ennobled, and exalted, and magnified? Their faith as yet was earthly; their affections set on things below. All the other words that He so often had spoken, so impossible to be reconciled with their carnal notions, were unable to elevate into its true region of spirituality this preoccupying idea. No, on earth they looked for their reward; on earth they expected compensation for all they had forsaken, all they had foregone. As high officers of the household of a great earthly monarch— as the princes of a kingdom extending from the flood to the world's end—they expected their names to be transmitted and enrolled in the page of fame.

It was time to undeceive them. It was time to tell them that this was not to be their portion. It was time to prepare them for tribulation, hatred, scorn, persecution, death itself, in the fulfilment of the work to which they were called. It was time to dissipate dangerous, because unreal, expectations; to paint the future in its true colours, telling them at once where their danger and where their safety and strength lay.

Their dangers lay in the world, their safety in Him. The world would hate, ay, even kill them; but He and the Father would love them and make themselves known to them. If the external unbelieving world scorned them, they should draw nearer, one to the other, in mutual sympathy and love. "In the world they should have tribulation, but in Him, PEACE"; "His own peace"; "the peace which passeth understanding"; communicable only to holy, loving, obedient souls; the Saviour's special legacy to those that abide in Him.

Our Christian hopes and fears are sadly carnalised. We too ask with Simon Peter, almost in the self-same meaning, "Behold, we have forsaken all, and followed Thee; what shall we have therefore?" Even now we are most times persuaded to be Christians, not from pure love, but from interest—because we find it pay. Even now we calculate that our religion is to bring us more happiness, more prosperity, more good fortune of the temporal kind. Even now we want a Gospel without the Cross, to sit, like Salome's sons, at Christ's right hand, without being baptised with the baptism or drinking the cup. We desire a religion that shall make us popular, not hated, and conduct us to heaven by the pleasant road of earthly advancement and success, not by the thorny path of disaster and disappointment.

I am afraid that we must not dream these dreams. I am afraid this pretty picture of prosperous godliness —as the world estimates prosperity—is not very helpful to form a state of heart that is really Christian. I do not undervalue earthly prosperity. I do not mean to say that if God gives it any man as his portion he is thanklessly to cast it away. I can quite see how it may be a great help to any man on his way to the kingdom of God. It may enable him to forward large schemes of usefulness. It may privilege him to be a benefactor of his kind. It may allow of his doing great things for God, which others, with equal readiness of will, but less favourably circumstanced, dare not attempt. It may cast blessings innumerable round his neighbourhood, and make him a centre from which noble enterprises for Christ may flow.

This is the sanctified use of riches, of temporal prosperity, when a man feels himself but a steward, not an owner; and like David, when he made his rich offerings for the temple, says unto the Lord, "All things come of Thee, and of Thine own have we given Thee."

It would be mere fanaticism to deny that such were a blessed portion. It were folly to attempt to prove that pain, and sorrow, and a low estate, and poverty, were in themselves desirable. Human instinct at once rebels against such doctrine. No one *chooses* such things. It is well if, when they are forced upon him, he can take them patiently. It is well if, when he meets tribulation in the world, he can find peace in Christ; if, even in his darkest hour, the Spirit, who is the Comforter, can enable him to say with St. Paul, "Even in these things I am more than conqueror through Him who loved me."

While we freely admit the dangers of temporal prosperity—while the plain-spoken Word of God forbids us to forget them—do not let us deny or attempt to depreciate its blessings. Rather let us try to persuade those who enjoy it so to use it that they may avoid the danger and realise the blessedness. It will be at once a truer and more effective argument. After all, this blessedness can but be the blessedness of the few. If there are ten thousand rich men there must be ten million poor men in this kingdom of England. Such is the manifest law of God's Providence, which revolutions have not been able to overturn, and theories of communism cannot rectify. There is a time coming, we know, when the distinction of rich and poor shall make no difference in a man's state before God; but it is not come yet. As we see and measure things before us now, it does make a great and very palpable difference.

What consolation then has Christ's Gospel for the poor, the sorrowful, the afflicted, the lonely? What has God to offer those in the kingdom of His grace on whom He can scarcely be said to look with favour in the dispensations of His providence? What has the beggar, the slave, the hard-tasked labourer, the servant subjected to every caprice of his master, the toil-worn artisan, to thank his Maker for? Perhaps, for nothing; but *if he has sought it*, then for *peace;* for a heart at rest; for an assured hope; for the power to endure; for cheerfulness; for household gladness; for the wife that he hath on his bosom, and the children smiling at his knee; for health; for strength equal to his day; for freedom from fretting, and from anxious cares; for that blessed simple faith which trusts God for all, and never yet found itself deceived. All this, and much more than this, much that is secret and incommunicable, much that is precious above rubies, is comprehended in that one word "peace," which Christ, the tender Saviour, offers to those who find tribulation in the world.

Is it not just what we are all striving after, though some of us in strange unlikely ways? Is it not just what we all hope will hover over our death-beds? Is it not the prayer that friends will put up for us when our bodies are lowered into the grave—" *Requiescat in pace* "? Was it not what the angel host foresaw and foresang as the greatest result of the Incarnation of the Son of God, " Glory to God in the highest, and on earth *peace* "?

And yet, with a strange meaning, and a sad irony in His words, this Incarnate Son of God came not to send peace on earth, but a sword. He foresaw the divisions, the bitternesses, the hatreds of Christians. He foretold that a man's foes should ofttimes be those of his own household. It must have been a sad vision to Him to behold men, even in their hour of tribulation, seeking peace, not from Him, but from the world, ay, from the devil; from excitement, from frivolity, from drink, from merry-makings, from artificial stimulants or delusive opiates; trying to drown grief or to deaden themselves against it, instead of letting patience have her perfect work, and from the cross reaching forward to the crown.

The world very seldom sends mourners to Christ. It bids them try change of scene; to go out into company; to eat, drink, and be merry; not to dwell morbidly on painful memories. There is certainly nothing to be gained from prolonged, excessive sorrow. It does not make a man a bit the better Christian. It may have no religious element in it at all. There is, we know, "a sorrow of the world that worketh death." But is it quite wise, quite the best thing to do, to get rid of everything that bears the shape of a trial as speedily as possible? Is there nothing to be gained, in the way of spiritual discipline, from the house of mourning? Why then does Solomon say that it is better to go to it than to the house of feasting? Why did our blessed Lord promise His second blessing on "them that mourn; for they shall be comforted"?

In any trial or tribulation you had better go to Christ for comfort than to the devil or the world. You had better sit with your open Bible upon your knees and study it than go to some wise modern prophet and ask him what you should do. You had better throw in your lot with those who "through patience and faith have inherited the promises." By the bedsides of dying men I have heard many say that the world deceived them, but I have never heard one affirm that Christ or their Bible deceived them. I have heard many say that friends or kinsmen would not come to see them, but I never heard any complain that Christ or the Holy Ghost forsook them.

All things stand out in their true porportions and magnitudes then. Men then discover how they have followed shadows for substances, and have been misled by vanities and lies. There is no use in deceiving ourselves any longer. There is nothing to be gained by dying in a delusion. Our poor flimsy excuses, which we once dressed up to look so substantial, we cast from us in utter scorn, sometimes in utter despair.

If you will listen to me, be taught by Christ *now*, rather than on your death-beds. Seek His peace now, while you can get it; not when perhaps your prayers for it may be unavailing, and it may be hidden eternally from your eyes. Think of that poor wretched man who in hell, in his torment, lifts up his eyes to catch the first glimpse of a peace, before unimaginable, and now unattainable. Think of that unhappy self-deceiver who was promising himself many years of ease and happiness the very night that his soul was required of him. Think of that unprofitable servant who passed his time in a delusive and indolent self-complacency, with his Lord's talent buried in the earth, to have his portion at last with the unbelievers.

These things are our examples, written to teach us wisdom, to show us what the Christian life is—its perils, its hindrances, its safeguards, its rewards. It is, we may be sure, the most blessed life, whether for high or low, rich or poor. Its course may be smooth or rough; but it is always peaceful. Prosperity cannot seduce its love, adversity cannot shake its confidence. And so in the Saviour it has peace, deep as the ocean, sure as the mountains, calm as the stars, unchangeable as eternity.

Preached—Cholderton, May 9, 1858; Trowbridge, May 16, 1858; Leominster, February 13, 1859; Cholderton, May 13, 1860.

XXIX.

THE WORK OF THE CHRISTIAN MINISTRY.

"Then said Jesus to them again, Peace be unto you. As My Father hath sent Me, even so send I you. And when He had said this He breathed on them, and saith unto them, Receive ye the Holy Ghost. Whose soever sins ye remit, they are remitted unto them; and whose soever sins ye retain, they are retained."—St. John xx. 21-23.

THE whole work of the ministry is to bring men into such a spiritual and moral state—call it by what name you please, "regeneration," "conversion," or what not—that their sins may drop off them, like the burden did from Christian's back in Bunyan's wonderful parable. Exactly in the same sense as that in which St. Paul speaks of Timothy's " saving those that heard him," by bringing them to the Saviour, does the priest *forgive* those whom his acts draw to the foot of the Cross, by bringing them to the Absolver. The same power that in the case of those whose hearts God has touched remits or looses, in the case of others who close their ears to the voice of the charmer, by a reaction common to all moral and spiritual laws, retains or binds.

Instruments of this order are never neutral. They are either sovereign or deadly: potent for good or for harm. "To the one," says St. Paul, "we are the savour of life unto life, and to the other, the savour of death unto death"; and by the self-same acts too.

No doubt there are special times and seasons at which this power of absolution is put forth and manifested. It has, so to speak, its proper epiphanies. The remission of sins is part of the Church's idea of *baptismal regeneration*. The Nicene Creed teaches us to believe in "one baptism for the remission of sins." "We call upon Thee," says the minister in his prayer to God, "for this infant, that he, coming to Thy Holy Baptism, may receive remission of his sins by spiritual regeneration." It is part also of the Church's idea of Eucharistic Communion, wherein she bids us trust that we "obtain remission of our sins and all other benefits of His Passion." And more solemnly and distinctly still, it is the one message of exceeding comfort that she empowers her priest authoritatively to declare to the anxious soul of the penitent, now trembling on the edge of eternity, burdened with the memory of many sins, but still clinging to the Cross of Christ, and seeing in the priest only what David must have seen in Nathan, the man to whom God has committed the word of reconciliation, now to be applied in this most needing hour: from whose lips fall the gracious words, which the state of his own heart will tell him whether he may appropriate— "The Lord hath put away thy sin; thou shalt not die."

I do not see that our Church has sanctioned any other times or occasions for exercising the absolving power. I cannot extract another from the indefinite language which terminates the first exhortation to the

Holy Communion. I can see nothing in the analogy of any of her other offices to lead me to suppose that anything approaching the idea of the Romish confessional—of which our forefathers surely knew the mischief as well as we—was the design or purpose of those who reformed the Church of England.

Nay, I think the fact that, in the first Prayer Book of King Edward the Sixth, there was a rubric which directed that the same form of absolution which is still used at the visitation of the sick should also be used in *private* confessions, and that this rubric was struck out of the Second Book, published three years later, and never since re-introduced, almost *demonstrates* what the Church's will is in this matter. In cases of positive law, as Aristotle teaches, "what the law does not command it forbids." In these questions, if we would be dutiful, loyal sons of our mother, we have to consider not abstract proprieties, eternal fitnesses, not what is best in *itself*, or in our own nation, but simply how our commission runs, what are the duties we are actually bidden to discharge.

And so our forefathers in the faith, taught by experience of the past, and with a wise forethought for the possibilities of the future, have cut us off from the possible use of that tremendous engine of social demoralisation—a demoralisation of the *highest* part of man's nature, and all the more perilous from its very subtlety—demoralising the priest and the penitent; putting one in the false position of having dominion over his people's faith instead of being a helper of their joy; and, in the other, debilitating the power of conscience, discouraging all self-reliance, and so destroying alike the clearness of the moral perceptions, and the strength and elasticity of the will. "The benefit of absolution" is to be obtained from the priests of the Church of England, *but not through the medium of the confessional.*

Still less provision is made for the power to bind. There is of course a power of excommunication inherent in the very idea of a Christian Church, recognised among ourselves in the initial rubric of the Burial Office, and still residing, though seldom exerted, in the jurisdiction of the ecclesiastical courts. In the Commination Service a wish is expressed that something more like primitive discipline could be restored. But you cannot see in the Church of England the spectacle of an anathematising priest. You cannot hear sinners denounced by name at God's altar, and given over to a curse. You hear, indeed, on Ash Wednesday, God's malediction uttered against *classes* of sinners. But so you hear St. Paul say "If any man love not the Lord Jesus Christ, let him be anathema." It is not the terrible responsibility from which the prophet once did not shrink, when he turned back and cursed the children that had mocked him, in the name of the Lord.

Would we have it otherwise? Do we, priests of the Lord, desire opportunities to assert a power the exercise of which once—but, as far as I know, *only once*—in a case of imperative necessity filled the tender heart of the Apostle Paul with anguish, and his eyes with tears? If to crush at once that shameful and contaminating sin which had defiled a member of the Church of

Corinth, and found connivers, if not applauders, among his fellow citizens, the Apostle had delivered such a one unto Satan "for the destruction of the flesh that the spirit might be saved in the day of the Lord Jesus," it was an unspeakable relief to him when Titus came back and told him that the penance had produced its effect and might be removed.

Now that the complications of modern society, and the very fact of a Church being co-extensive in area with a great nation, would make the exercise of such a discipline, however salutary in itself, a thousand fold more difficult and perilous than it could possibly have been in the apostolic age, I cannot conceive the motives which would lead a priest of the Church to desire that this power of "delivering men over to Satan"—whatever those words may precisely mean—were one that he could exercise, not as St. Paul exercised it, in concurrent jurisdiction with the congregation, but at his own individual discretion and on his own personal responsibility.

Surely it is a more glorious and elevating thought that the power which the Lord has given us is for edification, not for destruction: that our work is to win and soften souls, not to alienate or harden them. Indeed it is a saddening reflection that even as it is men are alienated and hardened from God not only *under* but *by* our ministry. By the same law acting upon different natures, our work is a savour of death, as well as of life. The same law operated even in the ministry of Jesus Himself. "If I had not come and spoken unto them, they had not had sin; but now they have no cloke for their sin." And again, "If I had not done among them the works which none other man did, they had not had sin : but now have they both seen and hated both Me and My Father."

Well might the Apostle ask, when he reflected upon all these momentous consequences of the word of reconciliation being committed to human agency, " Who is sufficient for these things ? " who has wisdom enough, and patience enough, and tenderness enough, and courage enough, " to make full proof of a ministry," on the faithful discharge of which God seems to hang the destinies of unnumbered souls ?

" Who," indeed, asked the great Head of the Church, as to His prescient mind there was presented in all its stern historical reality the future course of the work—the laying of whose foundation-stone should demand so huge a sacrifice, and the building up whereof in its successive stages was to be committed by the Divine Architect to such frail human agencies—" who is that faithful and wise steward, whom his Lord shall make ruler over his household, to give them meat in due season ? "

Mark the words, " faithful and wise." These are the external aspects of the special gift needed ; and therefore, if sought, we do not doubt received, by the priests of the Lord. " For the priest's lips should keep knowledge and men should seek the law at his mouth. For he is the messenger of the Lord of Hosts."

Mark the words, specially, ye who seek to be partakers of this heavenly calling. *Faithful*, trustworthy, upright, sincere. Faithful ; (1) as rightly dividing the word of truth ; not depreciating one holy ordinance, or one holy doctrine, that ye may exalt another which has more fascination for your own mind : (2) not shunning to declare unto your people the *whole* counsel of God—not keeping back anything that is profitable to them—with perfect frankness and absence of reserve : (3) feeding them also with the sincere milk of the Word, "not as many, which corrupt the Word of God," but "as of sincerity, as of God, in the sight of God, so speaking in Christ": (4) faithful also in this, that ye remember that ye are but stewards set over God's household, in a place of high trust; and who for that very reason shall have to render all the more strict account; bound also to purvey wholesome and nourishing food for all that are in the house, learned and unlearned, rich and poor, young and old, so that none go without his portion.

And therefore, in this restless and wayward generation —which would so often provoke us, if we have not learnt the lesson of patience, "to speak unadvisedly with our lips"—needing, oh ! how urgently ! to be *wise*.

Wise, that we may prophesy not only according to the proportion of the faith, but also, and perhaps even more, according to the demands of men's several needs —feeding babes with milk and men with strong meat, and seeing that all tends *directly* to edifying.

Wise! that we may know how to deal with human hearts, their tempers, infirmities, instabilities, capriciousness, prejudices. *Wise!* to discern a sickly sentimentalism and morbid craving after unnutritious food —the symptom of mental "atony," perhaps of coming spiritual death ; and, as good physicians of the soul, to create a healthy appetite, a real hungering and thirsting after righteousness.

Wise ! also, " to understand the time " when our people need leading and guidance, and when it were better and safer to let them stand, and face the difficulties of life alone. It is no sign of strength to see a man leaning upon a staff. The highest and most perfect spiritual state to which any Christian can attain is that which St. John rejoiced to see in those whom he had himself trained in the ways of righteousness. It was a time when there were anti-Christs abroad, and false prophets, and seducers. And yet he dares trust them to their own moral instincts, supported by that guidance from above which, like the cloud by day and the pillar of fire by night, is given to the Christian to indicate his path in the trackless wilderness of the world. That parish is in the healthiest condition where the good work goes on even though the minister be changed, or whose priest, though absent in the body yet present in the spirit, can rejoice over his people, as St. Paul rejoiced over the Corinthians, " that he has confidence in them *in all things.*"

One more element of pastoral wisdom I will mention —the power to take broad and unprejudiced views; to emancipate ourselves from all four of Bacon's " idols " of the intellect; from all cramping both of our intellectual and moral nature, by a simply *professional* cast of mind; by the habit of looking at all questions, whether spiritual, moral, or social, from the purely ecclesiastical, I may almost say, the *sacerdotal* point of view. If we would sympathise with men, and counsel them to their soul's health—give them real help and guidance—we must be able to project ourselves out of ourselves; to place ourselves in *their* position; to appreciate *their* difficulties; to see things with *their* eyes. Therefore was our Blessed Lord "*tempted in all points* like as we are, yet without sin"; that, by an experimental knowledge and actual contact with human trials, He might "*be able* to succour them that are tempted."

There are two remarkable phenomena of the present age of which we ought to take note: (1) the restlessness of the English mind; and (2) its intolerance of dictation. It wants a guide, but it will not bear a yoke. It repudiates utterly those who seek to have "dominion over its faith"; but it submits itself readily, even credulously, to any one who makes the profession, and with the profession manifests the slightest token of the power, of being able to be a "helper of its joy."

These two phenomena are not necessarily evil in themselves, or the signs of evil. For this restlessness is a token of a craving for *progress*, and of a sense that it is not good for men to be standing still. This intolerance of dictation is a rough way of vindicating the supremacy of conscience, and asserting the great principle that every man ought to have moral *strength* enough to be "a law unto himself," and intellectual light enough to guide his own steps by.

No doubt men in their better moments, and more serious moods, "do delight in the law of God after the inward man." And quacks, and fanatics, and enthusiasts, who "make a gain of godliness"; and they who have a "zeal for God, but not according to knowledge," take hold of this desire; but instead of disciplining, sobering, guiding it, develop it into strange extravagances and unhealthy spiritual susceptibilities, which are generally followed by terrible reactions. It seems to me that were St. Paul, that wise master-builder, living now, it would be neither by theatrical services, nor by services in theatres, nor even by forced and stimulated "revivals," that he would try to educate to the discernment of spiritual truth the Anglo-Saxon type of mind. He was no panderer to the morbid craving for novelty, and he mistrusted alike sentimentalism and excitement. He wished to see men "rooted in Christ" by the strong fibres of their *whole* intellectual and moral nature, their conscience and their understanding; not merely attached to Him by the light and superficial tendrils of the imagination which, like the ivy, too often hinders the growth of the tree round which it twines: nor driven to Him by the turbulent gusts of undisciplined passion which, if the wind do but change a point or two, may wreck them, all heedless, upon some sunken reef, far from the haven where they would be.

"We," says that great preacher of the Gospel, "have the mind of Christ." "I think also that I have the Spirit of God"; the mind of Christ that gives the intuition of spiritual *principles;* the Spirit of God that discerns the modes, and discriminates the seasons of their practical application. We ought to know, we must know, if we would have our work prosper in our hands, "what spirit we are of." The spirit of the two sons of thunder, sternly forbidding here, and calling down fire from heaven there, is not, could not be, the spirit of those to whom has been committed the word of *reconciliation*. If it be right to use severity at all, we can hardly stop short of the logical conclusion that justifies *persecution*.

"And the servant of the Lord must not strive: but be gentle unto all men, apt to teach, patient, in meekness instructing even those that oppose themselves; if God peradventure will give them repentance to the acknowledging of the truth." Our task is not to compel, but to *win* souls; to win them to receive and own our ministry, through which we believe God's saving grace, carrying with it the plenary absolution of all penitent sinners, unquestionably flows. We are retaining men's sins—but to our own perilous responsibility—if by any act or word, or course of acts or words of ours, we alienate them from those ordinances of Divine appointment of which we are stewards, and by which this pardoning grace is conveyed.

There are ways by which men may be brought at last "to abhor the offering of the Lord," to despise His house of prayer and to "snuff at" His table, no less surely and fatally to our success as ministers than if our lives were fashioned after the pattern of Eli's two godless sons. And all from want of wisdom; from affecting powers that are not ours, and neglecting to exercise those that are; from keeping back from our own people what they crave, and forcing upon them what they loathe; from want of faithfulness too, faithfulness to God and faithfulness to the Church— God, who enabled us, for that He counted us faithful and put us into the ministry; the Church, who

THE WORK OF THE CHRISTIAN MINISTRY. 291

when she gave us our commission taught us also in what spirit, and within what bounds, we were to exercise it.

Well might the Apostle thank God for having opened to him such a path of usefulness. Ours is the highest, noblest human work, not only in the end it aims at, but in the means which it employs, the materials on which it operates. Eternal life is its end; grace, flowing through its appointed channels, is its means. Its materials are the spirits, intellects, moral natures of men. Granted that its responsibilities are the most solemn: but if wrought wisely, the most diffusive of all works are its blessings; if wrought faithfully, the highest of all works shall be its reward. Is it not written, "they that be wise shall shine as the brightness of the firmament; and they that turn many to righteousness as the stars for ever and ever"?

Ordination Sermon (abridged)—Salisbury Cathedral, March 4, 1860.

XXX.

THE CHRISTIAN CHURCH AND THE CHRISTIAN CREED.

"The hour cometh, and now is, when the true worshippers shall worship the Father in spirit and in truth : for the Father seeketh such to worship Him."—St. John iv. 23.

CHRISTIANITY is a word embracing two ideas : the idea of a visible and (in a certain sense) material organisation for promoting and propagating a system of faith which we believe to be divine; and the idea of that divine system of faith itself, so promoted and propagated. In other language, Christianity embraces the ideas of the *Christian Church* and the *Christian Creed.*

I. To take these ideas in the order in which I have placed them.

To call the Church a visible form, a material organisation, is not to deny to it the endowment of spiritual, supernatural powers. But we have got into a way of using the epithet "supernatural" as if it were identical in meaning with "magical," which the powers of the Church certainly are not : and we sometimes limit the epithet "spiritual" to the assumed prerogatives of a particular class or caste (as when we talk of "spiritual persons," or "spiritual courts," or "the spiritualty"), which as certainly is a limitation for which we shall find no warrant in the Word of God. Christ hath made all His redeemed kings and priests unto His Father. Certain ecclesiastical functions, which may be diversely distributed in different Churches, are confined, and properly confined, in the interests of decency and order, yes, and of edification too, to a particular class, or classes, of men : but ecclesiastical functions are not spiritual powers, and in the minds of clear thinkers will not be confused with spiritual powers. A conduit, through which water flows, is not the stream, nor the source of the stream : is simply an instrument directing its course to a distinct object. Perhaps we have been more occupied about the size or number of our conduit pipes than in securing an even and ample and continuous flow of the life-giving stream.

Further, the organisation with which we have attempted to work is neither so simple nor so uniform as it was in the age of the Church's mightiest and most rapid conquests. It has become complicated by the complications of modern ideas, and modern social and political systems. It was when the Churches had rest in that oneness of faith and practice, and (so far as *principles* are concerned) of discipline and organisation too, which St. Paul emphasises in so marked a way in Ephesians iv. 3-5, that (in the simple language of their historian) many walked in the fear of the Lord and in the comfort of the Holy Ghost, and were both edified and multiplied—built up, that is, and enlarged. Nineteen centuries of history have not been nineteen centuries of progress : and certainly among the retarding influences must be reckoned that rupture of a visible, outward unity, which in bodies spiritual as well as physical is one of the conditions of equable growth and robust development.

In a letter which I received a few weeks back from the Bishop of Calcutta, he spoke of his greatest hindrance —and not his only, but the greatest hindrance in the way of all those who were attempting to propagate the Gospel of Christ in India—as arising from what he called "the interminable divisions" that separate off the Christian bodies one from another. The missionaries, he said, would seldom allow that it was so: but he felt confident of the fact, and that nothing presented Christianity at so much disadvantage to the mind of the subtle, quick-witted Hindu as the spectacle of a faith for which he was asked to exchange his own, whose propagators could not agree either in its inner meaning or in its very outward form. And yet in spite of this, which would have been a reasonable anticipation even if it had rested on no direct evidence, the tendency of modern ecclesiastical thought and conduct appears to be rather in the direction of intensifying and increasing, than of mitigating and diminishing, these elements of disintegration. Dreaming wild dreams of impossible unities—impossible, I mean, to men, for I do not presume to set limits to the power of God—men turn away from, or close their eyes to, unities which are not only possible, but hopeful, and when unity, if it could be achieved, would be a multiplication of spiritual force hardly to be estimated. Unity with the Greek Church or with the Roman Church, even if it were possible—and every day seems to me to make it less possible—would be little more than the gratification of a pious sentiment, the realisation of a beautiful idea, adding nothing, or next to nothing, to our practical power: but the reunion—on the basis, not of a corrupt mediævalism, but of ancient Catholicity, which is the true basis of all Protestant Churches—the reunion, I say, on these terms, of ourselves and the great Nonconformist bodies by whom we are surrounded and who were once parts of our system, once more within the limits of a broader and freer National Church, would be like pouring new blood into veins where the current of life now runs somewhat sluggishly and cold, would enable us with a hundred fold our present power to propagate Christ's Gospel abroad, to promote the true and vital knowledge of it at home.

II. But I must pass on to consider the other class of difficulties, quite as serious as this—and indeed their origin—which spring from what Jeremy Taylor calls the "somewhat too curious articulation;" the over subtle and metaphysical or else polemical development of the Christian Creed, anciently so simple, and which made the road to heaven so plain and well-defined that the wayfaring man, though a fool, could hardly err therein. In vain will you search the pages of the New Testament for any elaborately systematised dogmatic creed, the precise conditions of a sinner's acceptance with God, the exact mode of the Lord's presence in the sacramental meal. You must come down late into the middle ages—the periods of controversy, the ages of

Tridentine Catechisms, and Lambeth Articles, and Westminster or Augsburg confessions for these. And I venture to think that this metaphysical basis of faith, as distinguished from a moral or spiritual one, this planting the truth in the head rather than in the heart, in formulæ uttered by the tongue rather than in principles governing the life—whether the formulæ be true or not, a point with which I am not at the moment concerned—has been and is an element of weakness, not of strength, to Christianity. For when you have multiplied dogmas, let them be never so true, never so logically deducible, yet if all men cannot see their truth, cannot accept or follow your deduction, you have set up stumbling-blocks to faith, rather than made its way smooth. Dogmas,—accepted principles —of course there must be in every science, in every branch of inquiry—in mechanics as well as in theology, in the laws (as we call them) which govern the material, as freely as in the laws which govern the spiritual world. But it is the glory of science to simplify and reduce the number of its dogmas—its laws of motion to three, its law of planetary gravitation to one—not to multiply them; and St. Paul's great fear for his converts was lest the subtlety of knowledge falsely so called— a $\psi\epsilon\upsilon\delta\acute{\omega}\nu\upsilon\mu o\varsigma$ $\gamma\nu\hat{\omega}\sigma\iota\varsigma$—a mystical theologising gnosticism, should corrupt their minds, and lead away their hearts from the simplicity that is in Christ $\tau\hat{\eta}\varsigma$ $\dot{\alpha}\pi\lambda\acute{o}\tau\eta\tau o\varsigma$ $\tau\hat{\eta}\varsigma$ $\epsilon\dot{\iota}\varsigma$ $\tau\grave{o}\nu$ $X\rho\iota\sigma\tau\acute{o}\nu$ (2 Corinthians xi. 3; 1 Timothy vi. 20). They were not the oppositions of physical science that he feared—for his faith was too surely settled to apprehend any contradictions between God's true Word and His really ascertained works—but it was human γνῶσις—the proud, self-confident mind of man exercising itself in speculations too great for it; and above all it was an actual man setting himself up, and claiming divine attributes and almost worship—infallibility and spiritual omnipotence—sitting in the temple of God, and showing himself as God—*this* was the "deceivableness" that he feared would destroy "*the love of the truth,*" and by doing so hinder men from being saved (2 Thessalonians ii. 3-10).

III. It is not easy to know when or where to stop when one has once touched this far-reaching theme. Nor is it easy—so manifold are they, so infinitely various according to the capacity and bias of different intellects and tempers—to enforce upon a mixed congregation the practical lessons that this view of Christ's Gospel, as the power of God unto salvation upon every one that believeth, suggests to one's own mind. But I think that phrase of St. Paul's which I have just quoted, "the love of the truth"—or as in my judgment it might be more accurately rendered, the "love of truth, *i.e.* of truthfulness"—is the real key to them all. The worshippers whom the Father seeks—we have it on the highest authority, the authority of Him who is the Truth itself —are those who approach Him ἐν πνεύματι καὶ ἀληθείᾳ —in a spirit of truthfulness. There is some peril that we may lose this, even while fighting for dogmas, which are too often the symbols of a party, which we hold because we belong to that party, rather than because we have incorporated these dogmas vitally into our faith, and felt their saving or converting power. Hold fast what thou hast: κράτει ὃ ἔχεις. Be *its* master; let not *it* be *thine*. Call no man master upon earth: for thy only true Master is He who by His Spirit writes His law on the fleshy tables of thy heart, and graves His will as with a diamond upon thy soul. One has seen strange spectacles of the most sudden revolutions of belief in these latter days: what a man held yesterday, rejected to-day: what he holds to-day, to be rejected with equal lightness of heart to-morrow. Ah! that lightness of heart with which a frivolous statesman plunged his country into a ruinous war, and in which a frivolous age contracts or breaks the most solemn engagements, is not the temper in which great deeds can be wrought either for God or man. It was not in that temper in which the elders " subdued kingdoms, wrought righteousness, obtained promises, stopped the mouths of lions" (Hebrews xi. 33). Not in this temper did Athanasius deliver his great protest to the world.

"O Athanasius!"—so sings a true poet and a true man—*true*, because *loving* truth—

> " O Athanasius! thy too subtle creed
> Makes my heart tremble when I hear it read,
> And my flesh quivers when the priest proclaims
> God's doom on every unbeliever's head.

> " Yet do I honour thee for those brave words
> Against the heretic so boldly hurled,
> 'Though no one else believes, I'll hold my faith,
> I, Athanasius, against the world.'

> " It was not well to judge thy fellow-men;
> Thou wert a sinful mortal like us all;
> Vengeance is God's: none but Himself doth know
> On whom the terrors of His wrath will fall.

"But it *was* well, believing as thou didst,
  Like standard-bearer with thy flag unfurled,
  To blazon on thy banner those brave words,
  'I, Athanasius, against the world.'

" Thy faith is mine : but that is not my theme :
  'Tis thine *example* I would preach to all.
  Whatever each believes, and counts it true,
  Of things in heaven or earth, or great or small,

" *If he believe it*, let him stand and say,
  Although in scorn a thousand lips are curled,
  'Though no one else believes, I'll hold my faith,
  Like Athanasius, against the world.'"

And you must love truth for its own sake before you can do this. You must not love it with a mere childish passion if you would stand steadfast amid the winds of doctrine, and the sleight of men. With a firm, you must have a large, and open, and candid mind. You must not measure all men's beliefs by the rule that suits yourself: nor, like those fierce Ephraimites at the fords of Jordan, count and be ready to slay every one as an enemy whose pronunciation of what you thrust upon him as a symbol differs ever so slightly from your own. To be broad, and tolerant, and comprehensive does not imply that we retain only a loose and yielding grasp upon our own belief. It is simply giving other men credit for sincerity, and also for intelligence.

I know that I may be driven into a corner, and told that I must draw a line. The old philosopher Aristotle taught me that, in the domain of practical questions, such hard, fast lines could not be drawn. The Gospel is not a system, or a method, or a philosophy; but a working power, a δύναμις, as St. Paul calls it again and again. The thing above all others to fear, in this our day, is any attempt to reduce the Gospel to a mere mechanical organisation. It must have free course, to be glorified. "The phrases men are accustomed to repeat incessantly" (said Goethe, Lewes's *Life*, p. 343) "end by becoming convictions, and ossify the organs of intelligence." The kingdom of God is not in word, but in power. Satisfied with orthodoxy, men, and even Churches, are sometimes too indolent to engage in action: and though thought has played its part, and that a noble one, in the world's history, it has been thought fruitful of, and followed by, action, and not the mere dry light of the speculative reason, playing with truth as it would with counters.

The one great defect in the Church's life in this our day seems to me to be want of depth, of earnestness, of reality. Confining the remark to the so-called religious world, the largest class of hearers are typified by that seed, in the Lord's parable, which fell upon the rock with a thin layer of soil, which sprang up quickly enough, but as quickly withered, because there was no depth of earth to shield it from the sun's scorching rays, or to retain the moisture of the rain and dew. Deepness of earth is what the religion of this nineteenth century lacks and needs. O brethren, we shall not do our work, each in his own sphere, as we *ought* to do it, as we *could* do it, unless we are ourselves baptised into this spirit. We must rid ourselves of our narrowness, our partisanships, if we are to rise to the full height of the opportunity that God's Providence is spreading before us. I know not—nor do I care to know—whether it was a vision of an actuality, or of a possibility only, that for a moment filled the Evangelical Prophet's eye—all knowing God from the least to the greatest—the earth full of the divine glory, as the waters cover the sea— but of this I feel assured, that if *our* faith fail not, God's promises will not fail, and that all things are possible to him that believeth in this day, which is yours and mine, as truly as in the days of old. In fulfilling her mission to "go and teach all nations," the Church may and must still repose upon her Master's word, " Lo, I am with you always"—πάσας τὰς ἡμέρας—*all the days*, whether of cloud or sunshine—" I am with you all the days, even to the end of the world."

Sermon (abridged) preached—Salisbury Cathedral, July 26, 1871.

XXXI.

THE KEYS OF THE KINGDOM.

"And I say also unto thee, That thou art Peter, and upon this rock I will build my Church : and the gates of hell shall not prevail against it. And I will give unto thee the keys of the kingdom of heaven : and whatsoever thou shalt bind on earth shall be bound in heaven : and whatsoever thou shalt loose on earth shall be loosed in heaven."—ST. MATT. xvi. 18, 19.

I DO do not propose to enter into any critical—much less into any controversial—exegesis of this vexed passage of Scripture, which our Church has selected for the Gospel on St. Peter's Day. But I cannot help, before I pass on, calling your attention to the courageous truthfulness of our Church, when in the white heat of its Protestantism against the spiritual thraldom from which she was just breaking free; fearless of consequences; strong in the conviction that no truth can gain by the suppression of evidence; true to her idea of her function as a witness and keeper of Holy Writ; confident in the entire and perfect harmony of God's Word, she dared to retain among her teachings of this day that Scripture upon which the Church of Rome attempts to found her extravagant, irrational, unhistorical pretensions. She felt as the great commentator Bengel felt, when he concluded his interpretation of the passage: "*Tutè hæc dicuntur : nam quid hæc ad Romam?*" "All this may safely be allowed, for how does it support the claims of Rome?" She felt that no words of Christ, and especially no emphatic words like these, could ever have been intended to fetter the liberty wherewith He was about to make His people free, nor to put a yoke upon the neck of His disciples which time, as it ran on, proved that they were unable to bear; and therefore, though she has nowhere attempted to put an authoritative interpretation upon the words, she left them as they stand, in their naked force and simplicity, sure that those who, in the spirit of rational freedom of inquiry, and withal in a sober and reverent frame of mind, seek to find and gather up their meaning, will never be suffered by Him, who now, as ever, guides the Church into truth, to wander very far astray.

Further, she might well conceive that the freedom of God's blessed Word is not to be tied down and limited to any one narrow and peremptory, and it may be temporary, significance. Where the Spirit of the Lord is, there is liberty. The Word of God is fresh and germinant. The mere letter killeth—killeth by a kind of strangling. Isaiah's glorious prophecies (as we justly call them) perhaps were no prophecies, but merely comments on passing events, to him: it is certain that he knew not their ultimate scope, their infinite range. And it is one of the surest proofs of what we mean by the inspiration of the Bible that its spirit meets, with ever fresh supplies of light and truth, the wants of every age; that its resources are inexhaustible; and that the more freely the waters of life are taken and used, the more abundantly they seem to flow. So, avoiding that field of controversy upon which so many fierce battles have been fought, approaching the text neither as controversialists nor as critics, let us try to draw from it some simple lessons of faith and duty, not out of harmony with the circumstances of our assembling here, and which may perhaps help us to confront with calmer spirits the undoubted difficulties of the time.

Nothing is gained, so far as I can see, by denying, or attempting to evade, the apparent and obvious meaning of our Lord's words that Peter was the rock on which the Church should be built; that to Peter the keys of the kingdom of heaven were given; that on Peter the power of binding and loosing (whatever that power may have been) was bestowed. Any other interpretation at once strikes us as forced and unnatural. But, after this admission, two questions at once arise, and have to be answered. Who was this Peter? and what are or were these powers? Was it Simon the fisherman of Bethsaida? Simon, the son of Jonas? Simon, whom Satan desired to have, and for a brief moment did have, and sifted him like wheat? Simon, whose failing faith had nearly sunk beneath Gennesaret's seething waves? Simon, whose boastful tongue refused its utterance to a little maid's simple questioning? Simon, to whom the women's story on the great Easter-morn seemed but as an idle and incredible tale? Nay, not so. It was not Simon, but Peter, who received these glorious promises; the new name, so to speak, the seal and stamp of the new man—the new creation as Paul calls it. It was Peter raised for a moment above his natural self—caught up like Paul into the third heaven—possessed by, though not yet fully able to retain as he afterwards retained, the sublime, soul-elevating conviction that this Jesus of Nazareth, whom he followed sometimes with such doubting heart and faltering steps, was yet the Christ, the Messiah, the desire of all nations, the long-looked-for One, the Son of the living God. It was not a personal promise, in the sense of being exclusive : rather it was personal that it might be normal and typical. It was not to Simon Peter, as the first in a long line of bishops deriving in their succession from him an imaginary title of pre-eminence, but to Peter, in the strength of his new confession, as the founder of every church that has been baptised into the spirit of the same faith, and not only so, but as the representative spiritual man—the first of those living stones, as he himself calls them, who, age after age, are built by many hands under the teaching of one great Architect into that spiritual temple in which God dwells—to this Peter "are the promises made." And so Origen, commenting on the passage, says, " If any one says this same thing to Him [he is speaking of Christ], not flesh and blood having revealed it to him, but the Father which is in heaven, he shall obtain what was promised, as the letter of the Gospel speaks to that Peter, but as its spirit teaches to every one that becometh such as was that Peter."

For part of the promise at least—the power of binding and loosing, if not the power of the keys and the promise of the rock—was afterwards extended to ten of the Apostolic body (to all in fact save Thomas, whose faith it would seem was not then strong enough to receive it), (John xx. 25) and even (Matthew xviii. 18) to every visible organisation incorporated for spiritual purposes, on which the name of a church could truly be bestowed. " Wherever two or three were gathered together in His name, there was He in the midst ; and what they bound or loosed on earth, should be bound or loosed in heaven." It is simply preposterous to make that personal which was plainly normal; to limit to what proudly calls itself the chair of Peter that which is evidently the common heritage of all the churches possessed by like precious faith with him. He who saw in vision the great city, the new Jerusalem, descending out of heaven from God, took special notice of her walls, and marked that they had twelve foundation stones, and on each was written the name of an apostle of the Lamb. That number twelve again is not exclusive, but typical, and does but answer to the completeness of the vision—to the city lying four square, to the twelve gates, each with its guardian angel, each for the entrance of its own chosen tribe, each tribe with its 12,000 sealed ones, gathered out of the lands, from the north and from the south, from the east and from the west. But twelve apostles' names? And was not Paul's there? nor Barnabas's? nor Luke's? nor Mark's? nor Timothy's? nor Athanasius's? nor Augustine's? nor Bernard's? nor Pascal's? nor Francis Xavier's? nor Luther's? nor Hooker's? nor John Wesley's? nor John Keble's? not, it is true, written there, for to him who has told us what he saw they would have been names without meaning; but surely written now, if not upon the foundations, yet conspicuously among the stones, which have been wrought in, age after age, into the walls of that holy city which has come down out of heaven to earth from God. Of course, and it hardly needs to be said, save that one wishes to guard oneself from the possibility of being misunderstood—in one sense, and that the highest and truest, Christ Himself is the sole foundation (1 Corinthians iii. 11); the only rock; the owner and user of the masterkey. I need not quote the familiar Scriptures which declare this. But He is pleased to call men and women into fellowship with Him in His work. He uses instruments and means. In His house are vessels of gold and silver, and wood and earth; some for high purposes, and some for what the world deems mean. But, as a prophet spake, upon every pot and bowl in Jerusalem and in Judah is, or ought to be, inscribed, " Holiness unto the Lord " (Zech. xiv. 21); and when the instrument, be it mighty or feeble, has done its work, that work will be seen to be so disproportionate to the apparent means employed, so infinitely beyond the visible strength wielded, that the soundest philosophy, as well as the truest faith, will simply bow the head in silent awe, or if the thoughts of the heart find vent in words, will find (as the Mesopotamian prophet foretold) the confession wrung from them, " What hath God wrought ! "

And now, if you ask me to tell you in four words what I conceive these promises of Christ to His Church to be, I would answer, the promises of steadfastness, enlargement, of kingly prerogative, of victory: of steadfastness, for she is founded upon a rock; of enlargement, for lo! Christ sets before her an open door, and puts into her hand a key; of kingly prerogative, for it is hers to bind or loose, to hold fast or set free—not arbitrarily, but according to the principles of her great charter; of victory, for it is written that against her the gates of hell—the might of the mysterious power of evil which sometimes looks as though it was almost a co-equal power in the world with God—shall not prevail. The promise may be more, but it certainly is not less than this; and thus much of the promise, thus far at least, has indisputably been fulfilled. The rock still stands—it seems to me to cast the only shadow of true refreshment to those borne down by the burden and heat of the day in a weary land—the rock of a living faith, in the living Son of the living God. The Church is still—slowly it is true, just as Israel lost heart when Joshua was dead, but still—enlarging her borders, and no voice has yet been heard saying, "Thus far shalt thou come, and no further." She binds and looses in the sense that the world still recognises and abides by her standards of right and wrong : her faith, and not a human system of philosophy, is the director of man's conscience: her dogma of a judgment to come, of individual accountability, is the great controlling influence that at once looses and binds, holds fast and sets free, making the good man a law unto himself, and so enabling him to taste the truest freedom, and binding the bad man, in spite of himself, in the fetters of what I may but call the aggregate human conscience, which, when he tries to break them for any evil purpose, he finds to be stronger than bars of iron. For the gates of hell have not prevailed against her.

No doubt she has had her trials, her temporary defeats, her discouragements. No doubt there have been moments in her history when the battle has gone sore against her; when one after another of her positions have been taken; when her batteries have been silenced; when the hearts of her leaders have failed; when the flag round which her soldiers were wont to rally went down rent and trampled in the fray; and rout and discomfiture seemed inevitable. And yet that she has revived, and again filled up the gaps in her ranks, and again and again found leaders, and again and again delivered battle to the enemy, and even in this, one of her darkest days, bates not heart nor hope; like Gideon and his three hundred at the passages of Jordan, "faint yet pursuing"—why this miracle of an undying strength, of an indestructible energy, would seem to prove, as truly as though one standing among us could bid the sun stand still upon Gibeon or the moon in the valley of Ajalon, that the Lord God, as of old, has been fighting for His Israel.

And so, upon this day, the festival of that Apostle to whom His Master made such glorious promises, and to whom He granted so conspicuous a place among the builders of His temple, it is well that we should remind ourselves, as ministers and members of a National Church, what our true position is, and in what spirit and with what aims we should gird ourselves to the work which God, by His providence, is so manifestly setting before us. To no living Church in this day, as it seems to me, is God giving grander opportunities, or a larger capacity, for serving Him. A simple and intelligible creed, a reverent and sober ritual, hierarchical order such as in its main outlines prevailed in the Apostolic age, a discipline sufficient to direct, but not aspiring to enslave, the conscience, a spirit of free inquiry encouraged, an open Bible put fearlessly into her children's hands, a pure and scriptural liturgy of which it is hard to say whether the devotion or the sobriety is most to be admired, a constitutional system of government only requiring to be released from the trammels of a few obsolete laws to be adequate to deal with the spiritual and social phenomena of the age—these are the features which seem to me to constitute, I will not say the glory of the Church of England—because as she has received them, they are not fit subjects for glory—but which do mark her out, in a way and to an extent in which no other existing religious community amongst us is marked out, to be the expression of the nation's spiritual life, and to transmit the faith of our forefathers to the generations of them that are yet for to come.

It is a noble mission this that seems laid upon us, if only we are worthy to discharge it. The course which the order of Providence seems to have marked out for the Church of England has often been called a middle way. It is as truly so now as it was in the Reformation age. She takes it, not, as has been alleged, in the cold and calculating spirit of compromise, but as really believing, as Aristotle thought of virtue, that truth lies

in it. On one side dogmatism, on the other free
thought; here an intolerant bigotry, there an indifferent
pseudo-liberalism; to the right extravagant ecclesiastical claims, to the left an Erastian conception of the
Church as a mere function of the State; on one side a
superstitious and almost materialised ritualism, on the
other a theory of spiritual life divorced from ordinances
and independent of the use of visible means of grace.
Between these opposite oscillations of religious belief,
the Church of England threads her calm and sober way,
holding firm that faith and order once delivered to the
saints, which is at once the check upon, and the
criterion of, all such extravagances and aberrations.

In one sense, of course, the truth is the pillar and
ground of the Church; in another sense, and an equally
true one, as Paul witnesses, the Church is the pillar
and ground of the truth. The body of truth held, and
the body of men holding, act and re-act with a reciprocal
influence one upon another. But the lives of Christians
affect their faith oftener, I fear, and more vitally than
their faith affects their lives. A feeble, inert faith
naturally and proportionately stunts the spirit's growth,
and quite as naturally, and quite as proportionately, a
sordid, or selfish, or false, or impure life taints with the
elements of corruption a faith that in itself may be
sound and true. It was not flesh and blood that
revealed to the Galilean fisherman his great confession.
You may name the name of Jesus as Sceva's sons named
it, but you shall cast out no evil spirit thereby. No
man can say that Jesus is the Lord, cries Paul, but by
the Holy Ghost. Yes, friends, it is the Spirit of the

Father drawing us to Christ that we need to feel. It is the living faith of its members that builds, restores, enlarges a Church. "Ye are straitened," said Paul to the Corinthians, "not in us, but in your own bowels." Their own narrow conceptions of the Divine power and of the Divine work were hindering the manifestation of that power, the completeness of that work amongst them. The eye sees nothing but what it brings with it. It tints the landscape with colours, it endows the portrait with an expression of his own. So, too, faith. We draw from Christ the virtue that we wish to draw. He gives us what we ask for, as we ask for it. Covet, friends, and ask Him for His best gifts. Why ask for silver when you can have gold? why for gold when He has jewels? Ask, at least, for what you most need; and if, with Peter, you own Him as the Christ, the Son of the living God, remember that that confession involves duties, and that unless our lives are the reflex of our faith, that faith, as we profess it, is vain.

Preached—At the Consecration of Bolton Parish Church, St. Peter's Day, June 29, 1871.

XXXII.

REALITY IN RELIGION.

"What doth it profit, my brethren, though a man say he hath faith, and have not works? Can faith save him?"—
ST. JAMES ii. 14.

THERE is a stern, almost pitiless, tone about the teaching of St. James. Some have thought that with him faith has almost relapsed into morality, and the freedom of the Gospel has again been exchanged for the bondage of the law.

And yet the Spirit of God, who inspired the man, and the Providence of God which has preserved for us his words, no doubt foreknew that the time would come— would come possibly again and again — when such teaching would be profitable, even necessary for the Church.

Some have thought that St. James breathes a lower spirit than St. Paul, belongs to an earlier age, before men had quite shaken themselves free of the bonds of Jewish thought; that he makes too much of human merit, of the righteousness of works; and that his teaching needs to be corrected, and, so to speak, evangelised by the teaching of the Epistle to the Galatians or the Romans.

This probably was the view of the great Reformer, Martin Luther, who, because he could not quite make the Epistle fit into his theory of justification, called it an " Epistle of Straw." The fact that the epistle of St. James was addressed to " the twelve tribes which were scattered abroad," that is, that it was primarily intended for Jewish, not for Gentile converts, may account for its not being universally received by the Church as canonical, even at the time of Eusebius, in the fourth century.

No doubt it is well to read the Bible as a whole, remembering only that it is a whole composed of independent parts, the offspring of independent minds, though all guided by one controlling Spirit. It is well to compare things spiritual with spiritual, and in framing a theory of justification—if we must needs frame one—to bear in mind what has been said upon the subject both by St. Paul and St. James.

But it seems to me there can be no possible contradiction between the teacher who tells us that " as the body without the spirit is dead, so faith without works is dead also," who is St. James : and the teacher who tells us that " in Jesus Christ neither circumcision availeth anything nor uncircumcision, but faith which worketh by love," and who tells a young bishop to " affirm constantly that they which have believed in God"—they, that is, which have faith—" should be careful to maintain good works," who is St. Paul.

The two teachers had different aims, were writing for different sets of readers. The difference has thus been well stated : " St. Paul was opposing the Judaising party, which claimed to earn acceptance by good works, whether the works of the Mosaic Law or works of piety done by themselves. In opposition to these St. Paul lays down the great truth that acceptance cannot be *earned* by men at all, but is the free gift of God to the Christian man for the sake of the merits of Jesus Christ, appropriated by each individual and made his own by the instrumentality of faith. St. James, on the other hand, was opposing the old Jewish tenet that to be a child of Abraham was all in all; that godliness was not necessary so that the belief was correct. This presumptuous confidence had transferred itself, perhaps with double force, to the Christianised Jews. They had said " Lord, Lord," and that was enough without doing the Father's will. They had recognised the Messiah; what more was wanted? They had *faith;* what more could be required of them?

And so the object of St. James was to let these men, who were trusting either to a ceremonial or else to a legal righteousness—a righteousness which they supposed to be satisfied either by an external service or by a formal title—to let them now see what the character of " pure and undefiled religion " really was—what it was to *believe* God, and what it was to *serve* God.

I admit that there is a *primâ facie* ground for the charge brought against St. James's Epistle by some commentators, mostly of the German school, that it is deficient in spirituality, and that the writer himself was as yet but half penetrated by the essential principles of Christianity; and it is quite possible that the ruder mind and possibly more phlegmatic feelings of St. James may have been more slowly brought under the influence of the genius of the Gospel than the more enthusiastic temperament and the more disciplined intellect of St. Paul.

In the Epistle of St. James the name of the Lord Jesus Christ only occurs once—a striking contrast to the ten repetitions of the Holy Name in the first ten verses of 1 Corinthians. Its precepts are rather ordinary rules for godly living than counsels of perfection—rules for visiting the sick, for treating "poor men in vile raiment" with proper courtesy, for governing the tongue, for paying fair and prompt wages to those who have reaped down our fields, for restraining lust, and envy, and evil-speaking, and that "wrath of man," the vindictive and implacable spirit of party, which "worketh not the righteousness of God."

But in the history of all churches and in the spiritual life of all congregations there are times when such teaching is profitable; even necessary. We continually need to have our religious profession brought to some touchstone to test its sincerity. We need to be kept from the peril of those comfortable but delusive assurances with which some still the voice of conscience —some who honour God with their lips "while their hearts are far from Him." We need to be reminded that taking part in a gorgeous religious ceremonial is not necessarily a religious act: that the poor have souls to be saved as well as the rich: that the fulfilment of contracts is not only a legal but a moral and religious obligation: that partisanship—fierce, unreasoning partisanship—whether in religion or politics, is a mischievous, baleful thing: and that religion, where it is real, does act as a bridle, restraining those who are under its influence from gratifying themselves in everything which they may imagine to do.

And yet there are thoughts running through this epistle, like a weft of gold in a tissue of silk, which show that while the writer's keen, searching eye was mainly looking at things on earth, his mind rose far above the mists. The springs of his life—to use a phrase of St. Paul—were "hid with Christ in God." And so he speaks of the power of the fervent "prayer of a righteous man": of the spiritual strength by which a man may "resist the devil" and make him flee: of that calmness of temper, as far as possible removed from fanaticism, which feels that life and action—the buying and selling and getting gain—depend solely on the Lord's will: that wisdom descendeth from above, "first pure, then peaceable": that "every good gift cometh down from the Father of lights, who begat us to be a kind of first fruits of His creatures": that there is a "blessedness" and a discipline in temptation: and that he who hath "endured it," borne it without flinching, passed through it without contamination, shall receive the crown of life "which the Lord hath promised to them that love Him."

Surely here are proofs and tokens enough of a spiritual mind.

I think that any one who will take the pains to read over carefully the Epistle of St. James will see that the writer's great aim was to help his readers to apprehend two great truths: (1) the reality of religion; (2) its diffusiveness and penetrating power.

It is the leaven leavening the whole lump, put in

the *three* measures of meal (a man's body, soul, and spirit), till the whole is leavened. To use another of our Lord's figures, "The whole body must be full of light, having no part dark"; or St. James's own words, "Whosoever shall keep the whole law and yet offend in one point, he is guilty of all."

Now I confess that this does seem to me to be a doctrine specially needing to be enforced just now.

(1) Religion is a very real, a very inward thing. It is simply setting God always before us; recognising that bond of obligation—of duty—by which we are tied to Him. It is not an outward, ceremonial service, a θρησκεία—it is not building sumptuous churches for rich folk to worship their Maker in at their ease; it is not the possession of an ancient heritage of formulated truth, or of hierarchical organisation; it is not the mere thinking pious thoughts, or having compunctious feelings from time to time aroused; it is not beholding the natural face in that glass which reveals its ill-favoured features only too truly, and then going our way and straightway forgetting what manner of men we were; this is not religion. It goes below all this, and instead of being a mere passing emotion, or a bright vision of heavenly things such as those saw for a brief moment who were with their Lord on the Holy Mount, it is like the central strain which the ear catches now and again and ever amid the rapid and almost bewildering movements of some varied harmony, giving tone, and unity, and character to the whole.

(2) And not only is religion real—lying at the foundation of what morally and spiritually *makes* the

man—establishing, strengthening, settling him, but it is diffusive, pervading. It covers the whole ground of life. It penetrates the nooks and corners of existence.

It gives not only depth but consistency to our character. It makes a man radically the same in church and out of church, on Sunday and on week-days, in pleasure and in business, with his inferiors and his superiors, at home and from home, where he is under those social restraints with which God's Providence in mercy ordinarily encircles us, and where, for the moment, no eye that he recognises is upon him, but God's alone.

And so you will find that really religious men are something more than churchgoers, something more than communicants, something more than orthodox. There is a power within them conforming them to Christ's likeness, "lifting their affections to things above," "casting down imaginations," "bringing into captivity every thought," "keeping even the body in subjection," "delivering them from the dominion of sin," quickening them with a sense of strength, and life, and freedom.

To win this power, and feel that he has won it, a man must live in close and real neighbourhood to God. St. Paul seemed to feel that Christ had laid His hand upon him, and that he had only to follow the gracious leading. "I do not frustrate the grace of God" he cries in one place; "I follow after, if that I may apprehend that for which I am apprehended of Christ Jesus," in another; and "I can do all things through Christ which strengtheneth me," in a third. And so, "forgetting those things which were behind, and reaching forth unto the things which were yet before, pressing towards the mark for the prize of the high calling of God in Christ Jesus; running not as uncertainly; fighting, not as one that beateth the air," he was enabled, when his great career was drawing to a close, to look back upon noble opportunities nobly used, great gifts put to great purposes; and to feel, with a most real meaning in his words, that he had "fought his fight, finished his course, kept the faith," and that now there was almost within his reach and before his sight the promised crown.

The law of the Christian life is growth, and we all need much and careful practising before we have learnt to take, each one, his allotted part in that new song which is sung in heaven before the throne.

Preached — Doncaster, May 23 (Morning), 1872; Wigan, September 14 (Morning), 1872; Sonning, July 23 (Evening), 1874.

XXXIII.

THE RIGHTEOUSNESS OF A NATION.

"And the work of righteousness shall be peace ; and the effect of righteousness quietness and assurance for ever."— ISAIAH xxxii. 17.

ISAIAH is popularly called "the Evangelical Prophet," the messenger of glad tidings. And this not because his words roll onwards in one swelling tide of triumph or joyful exultation ; not because he sees no visions but those of peace for God's people ; but because far above all the burdens and woes and desolations and destructions which are proclaimed, now against Tyre, now against Damascus, now against Moab, now against Judah, there swells forth from time to time the undying conviction of the advent of what the old heathen dreamt of—though they threw it back into the past, not forward into the future —a Golden Age. He foretold that a kingdom should be set up into which "all nations should flow": whose officers should be "peace and its magistrates righteousness": whose king should be "of quick understanding to maintain the cause of the poor": in which men should not "labour in vain, but enjoy every one the work of his hands": where "the wolf should dwell with the lamb, and the leopard lie down with the kid": for it should be an age of universal peace, and "the earth should be full of the knowledge of the Lord as the waters cover the sea."

We apply, and are right in applying, these and kindred utterances of Isaiah to the Kingdom of Christ. Whether the prophet *meant* them to be so applied is another matter: I mean, whether, when he used them, he had the same clear, distinct perception of the outlines of the Messiah's glory that we who have read them have. It is not very probable, if we judge things on rational grounds—and the truest faith *is* rational—that he had. The God whose words he believed himself to be uttering was, as he almost complained, a God whose far-reaching purposes he could not fathom. The Spirit which was in these Hebrew prophets "who testified beforehand the sufferings of Christ and the glory that should follow," was a Spirit who was revealing things not unto them, but unto us of the latter days.

To us, as we read the eleventh or the sixtieth chapters of Isaiah, nothing can seem plainer than the call of the Gentiles to be fellow-heirs with the Jew, and of the same body, and partakers of God's promise in Christ by the Gospel. Yet St. Paul declares this to be "an exceeding mystery," "hid from all foregoing ages," and only now in *his* day "revealed unto the holy apostles and prophets"—the *New* Testament prophets, not the *Old*—"by the Spirit." Even the passages which our Blessed Lord directly applied to the circumstances of His Passion cannot be supposed to have carried that definite meaning to the prophet's own mind. They probably served, for the comfort of God's people, some local and temporary purpose, before it was fulfilled in its grand and crowning purpose at all.

Many have attempted to give, but no one has yet succeeded in giving, a consistent and satisfactory theory which harmonizes the Divine and human elements in the complex phenomenon, and, while acknowledging that the message came from God, acknowledges also that the words were spoken by man. Perhaps we have, from the necessity of the case, too few ascertained facts on which to found a theory, and the best and wisest course is simply to accept St. Peter's words in their literal significance, and to believe that "prophecy came not in old time by the will of man: but holy men of God spake as they were moved by the Holy Ghost." In the domain of pure science we are often obliged to accept and act upon ultimate facts, which we can neither analyse nor account for. That God the Holy Ghost "spake by the prophets" is one of the ultimate facts of the Christian creed.

The case may thus be simply and rationally stated.

Into the prophet's mind—take Isaiah for instance—there rushed a crowd of grand and noble thoughts. They naturally clothed themselves, when they found vent in words, in imagery borrowed from the events and circumstances of the time. He was a true patriot; he was a man of the purest moral aspirations—of the most absolute faith in God. It broke his heart to see the degradation of his country. He was sure, if there was a God in heaven Who governed the world on principles of justice, that such a social condition of a nation as marked Israel then must draw down what men called a judgment. He saw the ruthless Assyrian massing his troops on the northern border, and from that quarter the desolation threatened to come. It should be a trouble "for many days and many years," till the nation was regenerated by a new and better spirit "poured out from on high": till "righteousness should occupy the throne and equity the seat of judgment": till men were estimated at their true value: till education should reach the ranks of the lowest, the poorest: till villainy and hypocrisy were scouted and frowned down: till the frivolities of fashionable life had given place to earnestness of purpose: and the "work of righteousness brought peace," and its effects proved "quietness and assurance for ever." Then, to a regenerate people should be a restored kingdom, and Israel, when fit to occupy its place among the nations of the world, should once more see "the Lord of Hosts reigning in Mount Zion and in Jerusalem and before His ancients gloriously." It needed little more than profound moral convictions to inspire such readings of the future. History, in its principles, is ever repeating itself; for its phenomena are but the expression of eternal, unchangeable laws. Solomon's homely proverb—"Righteousness exalteth a nation, but sin is a reproach to any people"—is just the philosophy, the solemn undertone, of all Isaiah's saddest as well as of his most ecstatic and rapturous utterances.

We fit these words of the prophet to Christ and His Kingdom simply because He is the only King, and His the only Kingdom since the foundation of the world, in whom they find any adequate realization. I do not say that they have ever been completely fulfilled even *here* in Christ's Kingdom : but in Christ Himself they have had their fulfilment. He is all, and more than all, that Isaiah ever pictured to himself in the "King whom his eyes hoped to see in His beauty."

But then we know what has hindered the development and extension of that Kingdom. "We see not yet all things put under Him." He is, so to speak, a limited monarch because He chooses for His own the noblest type of monarchy—to reign over a free people. But though, so far, the glorious anticipations of the prophet—the vision of "a people all righteousness, of a land in which violence shall be no more heard, wasting and destruction no more seen"; the dream "of swords beaten into plowshares and spears into pruninghooks" —have not been realized: though some think despondingly that the time of its realization is receding rather than drawing nearer, and that the world is getting worse as well as growing older, still in Christ's Kingdom, if only it had free course, are the only *possibilities* of its fulfilment. A kingdom such as Isaiah dreamt of *is* in the world potentially : it might be there *actually*, if the eternal principles on which it rests were believed in and practised as widely as they are professed and nominally avowed.

It is better to look forward than to look back ; to think what Christianity may yet accomplish, rather than to bewail the little it has hitherto done. True enough, the Gospel has not done half its work ; but the last half need not take so long to accomplish as the first has done. In far less than nineteen centuries "the kingdoms of the world might become the kingdoms of the Lord and of His Christ" if they who profess the Gospel were living instances of the *power* of the Gospel, and our preaching were not so often contradicted by our lives.

In England, we have only just recognized it as a national duty that every child shall receive a sufficient and suitable education. The Roman historian spoke of the age in which he lived—it was what we call the Augustan age, and it has imposed upon men ever since with its flimsy and unsubstantial glories—as an age which had reached that pass that "it could neither tolerate its vices nor their remedies." We have waked up, somewhat late, 'tis true; and resolved that we will no longer tolerate our vices—at least the vice of ignorance, with its concomitant vices of poverty, intemperance, degradation, and crime. Will we, I wonder, tolerate the remedies? Will we go to work fearlessly, earnestly, decisively? Will we probe the wound to its depths, or just heal the surface, leaving the canker to spread below the surface as before? Will we purify the homes of the people, as well as enlighten the schools? Will we dare to touch our thousand social sores with a really firm and healing hand?

Time alone will show. This at least is clear. We have a noble opportunity. The mind of the nation is aroused to something like a sense of past shortcomings. Great things may be done if only we have men equal to the work that lies before them. In Isaiah's yearning eye, it was to be a *man* and not a *law*—a living agent, not a piece of parchment—a *man* and not a system, or a Board, or a Department—that should be "a hiding place from the wind and a covert from the tempest, as the shadow of a great rock in a weary land." What England needs, in every department of Church and State, is *men:* men inspired with a high sense of public duty: men above low, selfish, partisan aims: patriotic, experienced, intelligent, able, Christian men.

Let them be patriotic Christian men, and we need not care from which of the many sections which divide the Church and the State they come. A true patriot will look at the interests of his country first of all : a true Christian will look at the interests of righteousness first of all. When these are the interests which a public man puts before him as the lodestars of his course it would be like doubting whether there were a God in heaven to suppose that either State or Church would suffer disaster in his hands.

Every one who has read the utterances of the old Hebrew prophets with any attention can hardly have failed to be struck with what I may call—in the highest and widest sense of the word—their *political* tone and character. What draws from them, now the most passionate and tender appeals, now the most sad and serious rebukes, now the bitterest and most scathing sarcasms, is the national degeneracy which they saw threatening to overwhelm both Church and State, the throne and the cottage, the whole fabric of the commonwealth, in one common ruin. It was not too late, if only men would open their eyes and see—their ears and hear —by timely reforms, possibly to avert, certainly to delay, what else seemed coming on with the irresistible force of fate or destiny. "They cried aloud," therefore, and "spared not," but "lifted up their voice like a trumpet, to show the people their transgression, and the house of Jacob their sins." They desired to purify the nation's moral life at its source. They mourned over the loss of ancient simplicity of manners; over the growth of selfish luxuriousness; over the unequal distribution of wealth, so that the rights of the poor were practically taken away; over the aggregation of property in fewer and fewer hands; over dishonesty of trade and commerce, the inadequate renumeration of labour, the frequency of divorce and the violation of the sanctity of family life; and, by the side of all this, over a hollow ecclesiasticism, with its vested priests and rising clouds of incense, crying out ceaselessly "The Temple of the Lord, the Temple of the Lord," but laying hold on no consciences, and apparently constraining no one to amend his ways.

These were the social phenomena that confronted the prophet's gaze, and, as one of them tells us, made them feel that "the Word of God shut up in their bones was a burning fire, so that they were weary with forbearing and could not stay." They knew the peril, the folly, of building political or ecclesiastical structures upon unsound foundations—"of daubing walls with untempered mortar." "In the day of the great hailstones and of the stormy wind" such walls *must* fall. To see "visions of peace" for a people, when there were no sure grounds for them, was in their eyes the silliest of illusions or the guiltiest of frauds.

They tried to awaken their age from its soothing but

false dream that "to-morrow should be as to-day, and even much more abundant." In vain did the servants of God rise up early and preach, and prophesy, and rebuke, and plead. A spirit of deep sleep was poured out upon the people. They could "discern no tokens of the Lord rising up out of His place to visit them for their iniquity." They thought that they had made a sort of "covenant with death," and that though "the overflowing scourge might pass" through other lands, it would not come nigh them.

And so their politicians trimmed their course, and were occupied with the noble anxiety whether it was, better for them to follow the rising star of Eliakim, or to cling a little longer to the declining fortunes of Shebna; and their statesmen applied feeble, partial remedies to great social wrongs, compelling for a moment the princes to emancipate their serfs, but, as soon as they had passed the law, suffering it to fall into impotence and desuetude: and their foreign ministers relied on the usual tortuous arts of diplomacy, now arranging a conference with Tiglath-Pileser, now buying off Sennacherib, now hiring mercenaries from Egypt, now trusting to a diversion on the side of Ethiopia: and their priests swung their censers, and chanted their ritual, and brought their vain oblations—vain, because offered by impure hands—while the spirit of the people —that which constitutes the strength of a nation—was more and more "failing in the midst thereof"; and when the first snorting of the invaders' war-horses was heard in Dan, " every face gathered blackness and the whole land trembled at the sound."

"The thing that hath been, it is that which shall be: and there is no new thing under the sun." So philosophised on history an ancient sage. The degeneracy of Israel and Judah runs in parallel lines with the degeneracy of Greece, of Rome, of nations nearer our own shores, and nearer our own time. Have we no lesson to learn from it too? Did it not startle you—I hope you did not dismiss the impression with an idle sneer—when a gallant Frenchman, who had stood to the post of duty in his country's darkest hour, attributed that country's ruin to Italian corruption and *English luxury!* Can you be, *ought* you to be, satisfied with life as you see it whirled before you in its gay, thoughtless round, disguising its anxieties, its jealousies, its disappointments, its weariness by that vapid, unmeaning smile, that silly, fashionable air? If our eyes could only penetrate, as perhaps the eyes of angels can, below the surface, and "the thoughts of many hearts could be revealed," and we could trace these selfish ambitions, and these pitiful rivalries, and these wretched dissimulations, and these hollow pleasures, and this laborious idleness to their source and their end, we should stand amazed that men and women could so miss the true and only worthy aims of life, and sacrifice the possibilities of a great or at least a useful career to the fleeting and palling gratifications of an hour.

O that God's blessed Spirit were poured out upon us from on high in some of His enlightening, uplifting, invigorating power! There are three things of which when He comes, He reproves the world—of sin, of righteousness, of judgment. My faith is that national sins bring national judgments, not in the way of miracle, but of natural, necessary sequence : and that national righteousness averts them. May we ever be delivered from that false and most degrading of all heresies, that the State has "no conscience"—no sense of discernment between right and wrong; and a consequent irresponsibility in regard to either. Worse, infinitely worse, than any merely speculative error, even in relation to the sublimest mysteries of the faith— mysteries so far beyond the natural range of our faculties as justly to be called incomprehensible— would be a cynicism which would make public morality impossible, and would hand over society a helpless victim to that most miserable form of godlessness which recognises no motive but self-interest, no law but that of unscrupulous ambition or anarchical desire. The deadliest atheism is that which denies the supremacy of the principle of righteousness in the government of the world.

Preached—All Saints' Church, Manchester, Fourth Sunday in
 Advent, 1870 ; Westminster Abbey, July 9, 1871.

THE END.